Arthur and me

Ann Treherne

Copyright © March2020 Ann Treherne

All rights reserved.

No part of this book may be reproduced, or stored in a retrieval system, or transmitted in any form or by any means, electronic, mechanical, photocopying, recording, or otherwise, without express written permission of the publisher.

ISBN: 978-1-0892-2538-6

Cover design by Shereen Elder. Graphic Upload by Scott Canevy
Cover Image of Arthur Conan Doyle by W. Ransford, 1921

{{PD-US-expired}}

DEDICATION

This book is dedicated to

Jim Cleary

for your friendship, your dedication and your overwhelming trust, I owe you a debt of gratitude. Without your support and belief in me and in Spirit we would not have achieved all that we have. Thank you.

QUOTATION

"When you have eliminated the impossible,
whatever left, however improbable,
must be the truth."

Sherlock Holmes

STATEMENT FROM THE EDITOR

"Many people have claimed to be in communication with Sir Arthur Conan Doyle since his death but few of them have documented their claims as carefully as Ann Treherne, and there are none whose communications have resulted in the establishment of a large Centre in his name (in Edinburgh).
I have personally been able to verify the transcripts of spirit communication recorded in this account with the original taped recordings of the actual events and can vouch for their authenticity and accuracy."

Prof. Lance St John Butler,
formerly of University of Stirling.

ARTHUR AND ME

FOREWORD

As a high achiever in the financial sector, Ann Treherne seems among the least likely to believe in so-called paranormal phenomena. But then, as she describes frankly in this book, she was confronted by a profound personal experience that seemed to be a premonition of a national tragedy. Her struggle to make sense of that experience is very familiar to me as a research psychologist with an interest in parapsychology; her concerns about seeming credulous - or worse, having some psychological abnormality that was the trigger for the experiences - is a very common reaction among members of the general public. Ann describes her relief when she is informed that she's not the only one to have such premonitions. In fact, paranormal experiences are surprisingly common, and can occur spontaneously to people who are otherwise healthy and functional, but they can raise challenging ethical concerns. Ann's experience triggered in her a sense of guilt for not attempting to act on the information she had been given, and she felt a weighty responsibility to trust her intuition should the phenomenon occur again. By the time she did have another premonition she felt better able to attempt to do something about it, illustrating what is known in parapsychology as 'the intervention paradox' – if we have a premonition about the future and intervene so that the future event (an accident, or a disaster) doesn't happen to us, then how could we have had a premonition about it in the first place, since the trigger event never actually happens? It seems as if we can be sensitive to possible (or even probable) futures rather than that future being fixed and inevitable.

Ann had the good fortune to meet an academic with a sympathetic interest in the paranormal and this gave her space to take her experiences seriously but to acquire skills in research methods that could help her take into account conventional explanations such as coincidence or expectancy bias. Part of her education involved trying out investigative methods such as conducting vigils at allegedly haunted locations, evaluating mental mediumship and sitting for physical phenomena. Even under these more controlled conditions she had some remarkable experiences. She also attended development classes to explore how to become sensitive to and trust her own intuition so that the phenomena could be more controllable.

Some of the phenomena Ann describes are truly incredible, such that even direct witnesses may come to doubt their own senses. For those of us who were not there, we may be faced with the dilemma of accepting at face value reports of occurrences that go well beyond our personal boggle threshold (as Mairi says in Chapter 14, "You wouldn't believe it if you hadn't seen it yourself"), or doubting the testimony of someone whose integrity and acumen we trust implicitly. In such cases, the wise claimant would do well to follow Professor Archie Roy's advice to make immediate records and compare accounts from independent witnesses, and then to explore every possible way that the effects might have been produced by normal means. These are exactly the steps followed by Ann in documenting the experiences of members of her circle; some of these checks and balances (such as asking questions and receiving answers in a language not known by the sitters) are ingenious ways to protect against self-fulfilling prophesies. Nevertheless, the reported effects seem comparable to the most striking claims made during the heyday of the Victorian séance era. Ultimately, the reader must make sense of them for themselves, since despite academic interest in Spiritualism for over 150 years, we seem no further forward in constructing a scientific understanding of people's experiences. Ann describes events in such a matter of fact way that they can seem almost mundane, and we may need to remind ourselves that in making sense of them they may be construed as evidence of survival of bodily death. This metaphysical question seems to fall outside of the scope of science, but surely nothing could be more important to science than exploring the full nature of what it is to be a human being and to recognise the fundamental properties of consciousness.

Professor Chris A. Roe
President, Society for Psychical Research, London.

CONTENTS

	Foreword	Pg iii
1	The Massacre	Pg 1
2	Dunoon	Pg 7
3	A Vigil	Pg 18
4	Another Premonition	Pg 25
5	SPR and Scole	Pg 31
6	The Group	Pg 36
7	The Game's Afoot	Pg 44
8	Let's get Physical	Pg 53
9	Recorded Transcripts	Pg 62
10	This place aint big enough for the both of us	Pg 74
11	Blue Goldstone	Pg 84
12	The Caduceus and the Portal	Pg 91
13	Someone's knocking at the door – Someone's ringing the bell	Pg 107
14	Levitation	Pg 114
15	Diagnosis	Pg 122
16	The Glen	Pg 132
17	The Sound of Silence	Pg 139
18	Pennies from Heaven and the Keys to the Castle	Pg 156
19	Hit and Run	Pg 170
20	What happens when we die	Pg 186

21	Spontaneous Phenomena	Pg 193
22	A New Year	Pg 197
23	Creepy Crawley – or Crowley	Pg 207
24	Synchronicity	Pg 217
25	From Wilderness to Wonderland	Pg 229
26	The Sir Arthur Conan Doyle Centre	Pg 242
	Afterword	Pg 244
	Photos	Pg 249
	Testimonials	Pg 255
	With Thanks	Pg 260
	References	Pg 261

1 THE MASSACRE

In 1996 I was a Senior Manager working in the Head Office of a Building Society, in Scotland. I was responsible for the retail network of building society branches and agencies throughout the country and I had two Regional Managers, one covering the East of Scotland, the other the West, who reported to me to assist with this task.

My job involved making monthly Board Reports on the expected profit generation figures and the performance against target for mortgage lending, investment income, amongst other sales and income targets. As head of the branch network this also involved me travelling extensively in order to visit branches to review business figures. It was during one of these visits when I was travelling in my car along the M8 motorway that runs between Edinburgh and Glasgow - and probably driving faster than the speed limit allowed - when suddenly this flash of an image came into my mind. I suppose you would say into my mind's eye, but it was a 'blood and guts' image, with lots of dead bodies strewn around.

What on earth was that? I thought to myself, and where did it come from? I quickly dismissed it out of my mind, not knowing why it had come into my head in the first place. I am not the sort of person who watches horror movies, nor was I aware of having seen anything like it on the TV, so I couldn't understand why images as distressing as these should pop into my mind when I least expected it.

These flashes of images continued over several weeks, nearly every day, usually when I was driving or working alone at my desk, but they never appeared as day-dreams or nightmares. Along with the images I also got the impression that I needed to *'do something'* or *'tell someone'*. These urges kept playing over and over in my head until I could stand it no longer. I began to feel that the images were driving me mad.

On Friday 8th March 1996 I walked into the Head Office Building where

I worked having endured this imagery once again during my drive to work. By now my need to *'do something'* or *'tell someone'* had increased in its intensity so much that it was like a craving that couldn't be satisfied.

I crossed the floor of our large open-plan building. It was early in the morning; most of the workforce had not arrived yet. As I wove my way through the sea of empty desks I passed through the H.R. Department; no-one there. Then I passed the Training Department; no-one there - but wait, sitting at her desk, which was partly screened off by those room-divider panels which are common in open-plan settings, was the Head of Department. Like me, she was probably in early to get ahead of the game.

'What are you doing at lunchtime?' I said to her.

Hesitating and looking slightly quizzical, 'Nothing', she said.

'How about you and I going for a pub lunch?' I asked. Again, looking even more puzzled than before, she rather reluctantly agreed.

Although I knew this colleague from a neighbouring department, we were not friends. I wasn't accustomed to meeting her, or anyone else for that matter, for friendly chats in the pub. I was always much too focused on work for such trivialities and she knew it. So, I'm sure she probably sat there all morning trying to figure out what it was I wanted to say to her. In fact, I half expected her to cancel our proposed meeting by suddenly 'remembering' some prior engagement or other. But no, come 1 o'clock, I met her in her own department and drove her to the local pub.

Having ordered, we sat there making polite conversation whilst I mulled over in my mind whether I really wanted to do this – and tell her or not. After all I hadn't put any pre-determined plans in place in asking her to the pub. It was just a spur of the moment thing when I saw her sitting at her desk when I arrived after having sat through further repeated flashes of now much clearer images and of longer duration, on my way to work.

In fact Heather, the person sitting opposite me, could have been any of my colleagues. I think I just asked her because she was the first person I had encountered on my arrival in the sea of empty desks.

'You're probably wondering why I've asked you here, Heather', I said.

'Well, yes', she said, hesitatingly.

'Well, what I'm about to tell you is going to sound very strange. What I would ask is that you just listen - that's all'.

Because I was quite a dominant character in the Building Society I felt I had to put her at her ease. By reputation I was tough, determined and assertive. I was used to getting results and didn't suffer fools gladly. I was a fair and objective manager but I wasn't slow in getting rid of poor performers – there were no seats on my bus for passengers. Whilst Heather was not under my authority, indeed she headed up a department of her own, I knew she would have been anxious about why I wanted to speak to her.

So, I told her, 'for the past few weeks now, I've been getting these flashes of images in my head'. I told her of the first one that had happened whilst I was driving on the M8. And that these images had grown in intensity and frequency since then and become more detailed, so that now I was telling her 'There's going to be another Hungerford![1] There's a gunman on the loose and he's going about shooting people. I can see him wearing camouflage and khaki. Army-type clothing (although he's not in the army) and he has multiple guns and belts of bullets that criss-crosses his chest like Rambo. He is walking through a building; it has two storeys with lots of windows and a low-rise roof. I can see in the building and there are lots of desks and he's calmly walking through this building shooting people at random. There are lots of bodies and blood'.

There was silence and I saw that she was looking at me wide-eyed and speechless. Strangely enough, in these few moments of stillness I felt decidedly relieved. The urgency and burning desire to tell someone had been satisfied. Eventually, she spoke, 'Where do you think this is?'

'I have no idea', I said, 'but, I do know it's in Scotland. Not England, like the Hungerford case.' At this point I remember being surprised that she had taken me seriously; I felt that I might not have been as patient with someone telling me a story like this.

'Do you think we should go to the police?' she said.

'No, I do not', I said. 'What would I say? – They'd never believe me – and, where is it to happen? – I don't know'.

'Oh my god', she says. 'I know why you've been given this information!'

This response made me even more curious about what she was thinking.

'Why?' I said.

'It's *our* building. We have a two-storey building, with lots of windows, and desks. *And*, that Roy Ingman, he's got guns, and he goes shooting! I've always thought he's a bit odd'

Believe it or not, she was referring to the Head of H.R.

'I think we should tell the Board!'

'You've got to be kidding', I said. 'I'll be sacked on the spot – or burned at the stake for being a witch.' My relief at having unburdened myself was short-lived. For now the seriousness with which my colleague had surprisingly accepted all this meant that her ardour to 'help' might now create a situation in which I risked not only my professional reputation but my whole career as she contemplated reporting my experience to the Board of Directors.

I was 37 years old - young to hold this senior managerial position - but I had worked hard for it. I had gone straight into banking when I left school at 16. I had worked my way up the career ladder working for various banks and building societies and breaking through various 'glass-ceilings' in this traditionally male-dominated environment. I was a highly respected manager. I enjoyed an excellent reputation. I was a high-achiever, focused, results-orientated and well known throughout the financial services industry at that time. Suddenly, through having an off-the-record chat with a colleague about something that had nothing to do with my career or indeed financial services, I realised I was putting it all in jeopardy.

Nowadays this may seem like an over-reaction but I could just see the newspaper headlines, 'Building Society Manager claims to be psychic'. Or worst still, 'Building Society employs a Psychic as a Senior Manager'. If my name were to be published alongside that headline, the newspaper wouldn't even have to name the Building Society for it to reverberate through the industry and upon the organisation where I worked. Given that I was responsible for the Branch Network, how could I manage them if my credibility were to be called into question in this way? My position would have become untenable.

I was also concerned that another colleague – the Head of H.R. - was also suddenly vulnerable. Again, through no fault of his own other than being a bit odd, and strangely enough, owning a gun - something which I had not been aware of. I stressed to her that the reason I had taken her to the pub was so that our conversation would be confidential. I didn't want anyone else to know. And I certainly did not want her to tell the Board. She promised to keep it to herself and I drove her back from the pub with a sense of relief regaining its dominance over all the other emotions of the discussion.

That weekend somehow things were back to normal. Gone was my craving to 'tell someone' or 'do something'. There were no more images and whatever it was, it had gone as quickly as it had arrived. I was pleased. It was almost as if it had never happened. It was forgotten. My relief was to be short-lived, however. The following Wednesday (13th March, 1996), I was again working in Glasgow, visiting one of our city centre branches for the day. My company car was parked in a multi-storey car park in the centre of town and as I walked back to it after work it was just beginning to rain. Although it was March, it was very cold. It had been snowing that morning and now the rain had that sleety feel to it as I walked through the dark, city centre streets.

I climbed the stairs to the fourth floor of the car park and heard the stiletto heels of my black-patent shoes clicking on the cold concrete floor as I walked towards the car. I jumped in, throwing my briefcase and handbag into the back seat, knowing that although it was a long drive home, when I got there, the business suit and these shoes would be thrown off too and I could relax and be myself in my jeans and slippers.

As I turned the key in the ignition, the radio burst into life. That's when I heard it. 'There's been a shooting at a school in Dunblane. Multiple casualties – a number dead!'

I burst into tears – it was a school! How did I not know it was a school? I had all the other information. If I had known it was a school perhaps I could have done something about it. Why had I not been able to see that those 'people' who were being shot were children?

I don't know how long I sat in that car and cried, but it was a long time. I think I was probably in shock. After telling my colleague about my visions the problem seemed to have disappeared as far as I was concerned. I don't even know whether after telling her I even expected anything to happen. It was as if I had had an issue that I needed to do something about, in this case to tell someone. I had done that and it was over. Since speaking to my colleague I had almost forgotten about the whole thing and gone back to focusing on my job and now, suddenly, people (children) were dead – and as illogical as it was – I felt it was my fault.

I was traumatised. I think that's the right word for it, or I had immediate PTSD, post-traumatic stress disorder. I don't know how many hours I sat in that car crying in the multi-storey car park. Apart from anything else I had to wait for my legs to stop shaking long enough for me to attempt to drive the car home.

To this day, I have no knowledge of what happened after that or over the next few days. It's as if that part of my memory has been completely wiped out, or didn't register as I tried to continue to function whilst carrying this overwhelming burden of guilt, grief and responsibility at not having done something to prevent it. What I do remember distinctly however, was returning to my Head Office Building for work the following Monday. Monday was always the day to be in Head Office, it was Meetings day. I tried to cram as many meetings as possible into this one day so that I could spend the rest of my week travelling around the branches.

There was a feeling of déjà vu as I once again arrived early and followed the same path through that sea of desks in our open-plan building, this time without the craving to tell someone. There was a completely different operation going on in my head. I was suffering a kind of depression as I tried to deal with my secret burden of guilt. I walked across the floor and in a repeat of the previous week there was Heather, my colleague, again sitting at her desk. As I walked slowly past, she glanced up at me but I was totally unprepared for the way she looked at me. Not a word was spoken as our eyes met but that look conveyed all that she wanted to, 'You are the devil incarnate'.

It was clear she was blaming me for the incident, or at the very least blaming me for not doing anything to prevent the incident. I think I sensed a little of her own guilt too, guilt at also having been given this information and not doing anything about it. I wondered if she thought I had somehow made her complicit by confiding in her. In any case, when I saw that look, it conveyed another message to me – I would have to leave! It was clear to me at that moment that sooner or later this was going to become an issue, so I'd have to start making plans to leave. It took me another four years during which time I quietly investigated premonitions (precognition' in the language of Psi investigators), and began to realise that my true path was not in financial services - I resigned from the organisation. That was in the Millennium Year, 2000.

What I was later to discover was that Heather *had* actually confided in one of the members of the Board, and this too was prior to the massacre taking place, so there were actually three of us carrying this burden of guilt. And, one was a General Manager (Board Director) but I was only to discover this at the point of leaving. Thankfully.

Over the next few years I engaged in all sorts of investigations into precognition, mediumship and the 'spiritual' in general as well as attending courses and workshops to find out more about what had happened to me and to try to enhance my own development. I was ready for a new life.

2 DUNOON

Now, you're probably asking yourself 'what happened in those four years between the Dunblane Massacre and you eventually leaving work', and, 'how did you continue to function in a senior managerial role with such a burden of guilt hanging over you?' Well, let me tell you.

After encountering Heather and that look of horror and disgust on her face that morning, I resolved to stay away from our head office building as much as possible. Obviously I still had meetings to attend that required me to be there, but these had previously been arranged to take place on a Monday, so that I would have the rest of the week free to visit branches. Being in charge of the Branch Network, I could have worked from any of them – not that they would have welcomed their boss parking herself in their place of work for any length of time.

I did have a great team of Managers working for me and I prided myself on having a good working relationship with them, but none of them would have wanted me sitting in their branch watching their every move. However, I did have another office with its own function room that I used for meetings and for running training courses. It was situated above our main city centre branch in Glasgow, but with its own private entrance, so the branch staff was often unaware of whether I was 'in residence' or not – they didn't feel subjected to my beady eye. I decided this was the best place to 'go into hiding' until I could figure out what had just happened to me; how I was going to cope with it; and what I should be doing about it.

Apart from the crippling guilt that weighed on my shoulders like a millstone every waking minute of the day, there were questions continually circling in my head like marbles rattling round a metal colander, with all the clatter and random crashes that dodgems have in the fair. What was I supposed to do about it? Could I have prevented it? And worse still, what if it happens again – what then?

This last question exercised my brain perhaps more than most. I was, and still am, a very logical, practical person, with my feet firmly planted on the ground. Suddenly this cool, calm logic that I used so readily and easily to make decisions on whether to lend many thousands of pounds of my employer's funds on various projects, mortgages and complex financial transactions was now under attack by this newly found 'ability' to 'see into the future'. It just didn't make sense. What was I to do?

My analytical thinking kicked in almost as an automatic reaction - clearly I had received my Dunblane visions for a reason. It's a small leap of faith from this point to deduce that I was supposed to do something to prevent it. Otherwise, what was the point of sending this information in the first place, as all it had succeeded in doing was making me feel responsible and guilty for something I had no control over? I needed to find some answers. I needed to find someone who could help me – but who?

It had to be someone who would know about such things, and advise me. Someone who could tell me what I was supposed to do. Can you control these things? Could I have found out more about where it was to take place? And ultimately, should I, or could I, have done something to stop it? I didn't know. This was all alien to me. I had heard about Mediums. Indeed I had had a 'sitting' with one many years before, when I was only 18. I had just started working, straight from school and I worked for The Royal Bank of Scotland, in Edinburgh – I was the Office Junior. The other girls in the office had decided we were all going to have a girls' night out, and Pamela, the Senior Cashier, said that we should go and see a Medium. She knew a very good one and wouldn't it be great if we all went together to see her, then we could go to the pub afterwards.

My instinct was screaming 'NO', but politeness and my very junior position prevented me from shouting out that I really did not want to go and see a Medium. My upbringing had been in a Christian family. My Father was a long-standing Church Elder. My Mother was President of the Women's Guild and I had been brought up to go to Sunday School, then Bible Class and we went to Church as a family every Sunday. I certainly did NOT want to see a Medium.

I think if truth be told, I was scared. I had been conditioned by my Christian upbringing to think that these people were 'dabbling with the devil', or 'raising the dead' and at the very least contravening the instructions from the Bible. I certainly did not want to see a Medium; after all these were the people who exploited people's grief and insecurities, the people who ripped off the bereaved and the lonely. They were the people who made up stories – and the gullible bought it. I certainly didn't want to see a Medium.

But who then? I needed to find an authoritative source – who would that be? – and where would you go to find such a person? Remember, this was before Google and Wikipedia. The World Wide Web was in its infancy and not known as the source of information it is now. So, where was I to find such a person?

It is often said in Spiritualist circles that there's no such thing as coincidence – things happen for a reason – there's a higher intelligence using coincidence to draw our attention to things – it's to make us sit up and take notice. Obviously I wasn't aware of such a view then, but I am now and you will find it cropping up again in this book as I take you with me through a whole host of strange experiences. For example: I had driven through from Edinburgh early that morning to my Glasgow office, speeding on the M8 as usual to avoid as much of the traffic as possible; I parked the car in that same multi-storey car park that held such bitter memories for me; and walked the short distance to my office, in Bath Street. As I climbed the stairs to what now had become my sanctuary, I placed my briefcase on the desk. This building had previously been a bank, and somehow I had inherited the Bank Manager's huge desk with its inlaid green leather – scuffed with many years of financial transactions that must have crossed over its surface long before my time. I hung up my coat and walked to the kitchen to click the kettle on. Having made my cup of tea I settled down at my desk and sorted the papers from my briefcase into order as they related to the work that awaited me for that day. I was organised. I was ready.

Still early, I picked up the newspapers. These were delivered daily to my office. It was almost a duty or a chore in my eyes to read and familiarise myself with all the financial news of the day. The Financial Times, the Glasgow Herald and the Telegraph were all 'must reads' for local, national and financial news. With my normal workaholic's attitude I didn't have time to sit and read all these papers. Instead I just skimmed the financial sections and then read anything of interest more carefully. The rest of the paper could wait. I had to get on with the real work.

Now, however, there was something much more urgent exercising my mind – a paranormal dimension I couldn't ignore. For the first time in my life I was out of control faced with a situation that I just didn't know what to do about. So, having read all the boring bits, I tried to distract myself by looking for something more interesting to read as I sipped my morning tea.

And there it was. In the Glasgow Herald, a double-page spread about a Professor Archie Roy, Emeritus Professor of Astronomy at Glasgow University but the article was about what he did in his spare time. He was a Paranormal Investigator – a Ghost Buster, and he had been studying the paranormal for the last 30 years. He had set up an organisation to investigate these things and now he had decided to run classes for those with an interest in studying various types of paranormal phenomena. These classes would take the form of night-classes at the university. This was it. This was the man who would help me. This was the man I had to find. I could not believe my good fortune at the timing of this 'coincidence'.

I immediately sprang into action, picking up the telephone from my desk at the same time and hastily ringing the number of Glasgow University from the small print of the Herald. The receptionist answered the phone, 'Glasgow University, how can I help you?'

'I want to enrol on the evening-class being run by Professor Roy on Psychical Research and Investigation', I said.

'I'm sorry that class is already full, would you like me to try another one for you?'

No, of course not – these were my unsaid thoughts - how could she possibly grasp the urgency of the situation. Didn't she realise this was the man who was going to sort my life out for me, and tell me what's going on, and what to do about it, and I just *have* to see him?

My instant elation at having found *the* answer to my problem had disappeared as quickly as it had appeared. Reluctant to accept her answer, I said, 'but I've only just found out about it and I've phoned straight away, how can it be full so quickly?'

'Well, there's a double-page spread in today's Glasgow Herald so it filled within ten minutes of us opening up this morning.'

'Yes, I'm looking at The Herald, and that's why I've called too. So, because of demand, will he be running a second class?' I suggested, hopefully.

'I really don't know, but I wouldn't think so as the evening classes are all booked and published in advance. It'll probably be next year before there's another intake.'

Oh no! My brain urgently calculated what other options I could put to this woman who couldn't possibly have grasped the urgency of the situation. 'Is there a waiting list and can I put my name on it and I can pay now, and if you should get a cancellation or even if someone doesn't turn up on the night, I'll come! I can be there at short notice, I could even come along on the night just in case someone doesn't turn up – what do you think?' I rapidly fired every possible scenario at her.

'I can't take a payment from you as I don't have a place to offer you. I can put your name on our waiting list, but I should warn you, it's already a very long waiting list, so it's extremely unlikely that you'll get a place from that – we will give priority to the waiting list for next year's intake, though.'

She was trying – very trying - but she had nothing else to offer me that was going to soothe my desire. My name now on the waiting list, I thanked her and reluctantly hung up.

What now? I needed a Plan B. What would that be? I didn't have one at that moment, but I'd think of something. For now I consoled myself at having found someone who seemed to be an authority on the subject – exactly what I was looking for.

I resolved to call this unfortunate receptionist at Glasgow University each day, asking if there had been any cancellations for this course, and each day her answer was the same, 'No'. Plan B seemed to take the form of hassling her into submission, but she wasn't for giving in to my pestering. Then one day, she said, 'Oh, it's you again. I still don't have any cancellations on that course, but... I shouldn't really be telling you this, but....'

'Yes', I said, eagerly awaiting her response.

'Well, he's running a Weekend Workshop. It's in a hotel. It's nothing to do with the University, but since you've been so anxious to get a place, I thought I'd mention it. It hasn't even been published yet.'

'Great', I said, 'Where is it. Which Hotel?'

'The hotel is called, Ardfine and its in Dunoon'.

Quickly obtaining the final crucial piece of information from her – the date when it was to take place – I thanked her for her help and even although this date was nearly 6 months away, Plan B was beginning to take shape.

I called Directory Enquiries and got the number for this hotel. I rang the number and eventually a male voice answered, 'Ardfine Hotel.'

'You are running a Weekend Course with Professor Archie Roy of Glasgow University,' I said.

'Are we?' the voice said quizzically. 'I didn't know that, and I'm the owner.' 'Oh, well I got the dates from Glasgow University', realising at that very moment that I had dropped my confidante in it, but I was desperate.

'Well we have talked to Tricia Robertson, a colleague of Professor Roy about running a Weekend Workshop here, but she was going to come back to me to confirm details, so I can't book you on the Course, I don't know what they're doing or how much it will cost.'

This was all sounding vaguely familiar. I couldn't let this opportunity slip through my fingers again. 'Well I'll just book into the hotel then. Book me a single room for the Friday and Saturday nights, and I'll book onto the course whenever you have the details.'

'That's a strange way of doing things,' he said. 'What if you don't like the course content and decide you don't want to be on it after all?'

'I won't change my mind, and, I do want to be on it. It doesn't matter what the content is, I'll be there.'

'You see we're just a small hotel, we don't have many bedrooms, so I have to take payment for your room booking now, and there's no refund for cancellations?'

'That's fine', I said, paying over the telephone with my credit card. I was in. Plan B now had some substance and although it was still several months away, I had something to focus on. I knew by booking into the hotel I would somehow get the opportunity to speak to the Professor, perhaps over dinner or in the bar in the evening, and could confide in him and get the answers I so desperately required.

Time seemed to slow to a snail's pace after that phone call. I was booked in, Plan B was in place, but it was a long way off. I tried to tell myself just to get on with work as usual, but my focus wasn't on it any more. The days dragged by slowly. I tried to stay away from our Head Office Building, and Heather, as much as possible. I would visit branches without any real purpose, hoping that they wouldn't collaborate on what they must have surely seen as a change in my whole demeanour. You see I ran a tight ship. Not only was I a high-achiever, I wanted all my managers to be high-achievers too. I would encourage them, motivate them, incentivise them. I would take them on nights out and even offered holidays for the best-performing Branch Managers and their partners. On one occasion I sent three Branch Managers and their partners to New York on a city break. I knew how to manage a successful team.

But if they didn't perform then there were consequences – and they knew it. I didn't like it, and I wasn't proud of it, but I had a reputation for sacking people. Apparently the Branch Managers' used to say, 'If Ann turns up at your branch with the Head of HR – just hand over your keys'. There was no point arguing.

Now, however, Ann was going to turn up somewhere not really sure why she had come. I needed to get a grip and pull myself together. At home too, after that fateful night when my car radio had made the announcement that meant that life would never be the same again for the people of Dunblane – nor for me – when I had finally managed to get home I had spoken at length with my husband about what had happened. Now he didn't know what to do, or to say, nor was he able to help me. Life was in slow motion.

As the days slipped into months and they too dropped off the calendar I began to look forward to meeting the man who was going to solve everything for me – I was putting a lot of faith in him – I had big expectations. I wanted my life back. And now I had booked myself on to Professor Roy's Weekend Workshop at the hotel in Dunoon. I hadn't paid much attention to what it was or the content of it, as long as he - my saviour - was going to be there, and I'd get a chance to speak to him, nothing else mattered. I had I suppose envisaged that one evening in the bar after dinner when I'd get him to myself in a quiet corner so I could confide in him my guilty secret; and he would somehow have the answer and make it all go away.

As we got nearer the date I started to think more about what would be happening on this workshop. What would they do and what should I wear? Will it be casual? I thought so. But then again, he is an Emeritus Professor – he's sure to be wearing a suit, collar and tie. Perhaps I should be more formally dressed to meet the Prof?

I reasoned with myself that when I ran workshops and training courses for my managers, I ran them as 'dress down days'. I would organise venues where this was possible - not in our own Head Office building which also had a training suite but where they would have needed to be in their suits. I used to run team-building events in rural venues where the managers could wear casual clothes and I'd have them build rafts and rope bridges to cross streams and other such team-bonding activities.

That thought struck me and an alarm was ringing in my head. The workshop I had just booked myself into was going to be held in a rural location. The Prof, no doubt, would have access to training rooms in the Uni, yet here he was taking a group out of his 'Head Office' and into the wild. Just what would we be doing on this workshop? I was beginning to get worried. Why had he chosen to leave his domain in the university? What would his motive be – he wasn't doing team building. Who were these people who would be attending? And why had they chosen to meet in this far flung hotel?

My mind was racing now. What did they actually do at these workshops? How do people study the paranormal and psychic stuff? Do they sit in the dark? Maybe they hold hands or put their hands on a table under a dim light, like you see in the films? The question kept repeating in my mind, why choose that hotel? A hotel that is so remote and so difficult to get to. Maybe it has a basement or darkened room. The manager did seem to be familiar with Professor Roy when I had spoken to him on the phone. Maybe these are not random people who are attending, but a regular group of people who get together at that hotel – like a coven?

As I imagined naked men and women dancing round a cauldron on a moonlit moor at night chanting spells and hallucinating from the potions they had just concocted, my stomach clenched into a knot. What on earth was I thinking? Why had I not seen this before? Of all the places to hold a 'Weekend Workshop' why would you choose Dunoon? It's almost an island. You have to get a ferry to it – and I had already booked my car on to the ferry, just to be sure that I got there – was I mad?

Maybe I had inadvertently infiltrated a regular meeting of this secret sect who met from time to time in this secluded venue to raise the dead and muster all sorts of spells. After all, I had never actually seen this workshop advertised – then again, I hadn't looked for it. I was just so glad I had managed to get on it. I had been very pushy in persuading the manager to take my booking, when he didn't even know there was a workshop happening – so maybe it's not a workshop but a secret society that's meeting there and 'workshop' is just a code. Dunoon, of all places – there's no escaping that place – not without a ferry, and they don't run in the middle of the night. And whilst we're on the subject, *who pays the ferryman?*[2]

Calm down Ann, don't be so ridiculous, I said to myself. What's the worst that can happen? This was another one of my strategies that I used at work. If I had a difficult situation where I wasn't sure if my proposed actions would be the right thing to do or not, this is what I would say to myself. And after I had evaluated the worst possible scenario, I still wanted to take the risk even although I didn't know what I might face. So, in other words, *What's the worst that could happen?* Hell knows.

Seemingly Plan B had potential disaster written all over it – and I had put it in place – idiot. However, the desire to have answers and be free of this overriding guilt was greater than the fear of being trapped on an island with a bunch of ghouls. But I needed Plan C.

I looked at the map. If I needed to make an escape in the middle of the night when the ferry wasn't running, where would I go? I was thinking of the famous scene from Robert Burns' *Tam o' Shanter*, when Meg the grey mare has to carry its drunken rider across the bridge to escape the devil and his warlocks and witches. The trusty steed loses her tail – I wondered what I'd lose. In the poem the horse has to make a mad dash for the bridge over the river Doon, as it is said that witches cannot cross running water. Great, I'm going to a place surrounded in water but with no bridge and no ferry running when you most needed one. I studied the map with interest. If I was to make an escape, it was going to be quite some 'dash'. It was about 200 miles to get home from here and was across remote country roads, exposed moorland and hillsides. I didn't fancy it, especially not at night, in the dark – but at least it was an escape route – Plan C was born.

Contingencies now in place, the day finally dawned when I'd be undertaking this risky business to be in Dunoon with Professor Archie Roy. It was now September and although summer had nearly ended, it was a bright sunny day with hardy a cloud in the sky. I had arranged to work again in Glasgow; in fact I had chosen to visit one of the branches in the Southside of Glasgow, in Shawlands. I had lunch with the branch manager in a nearby restaurant, and since it was Friday, the chat moved to 'what are you doing for the weekend?' I've no memory of what he was doing, but I know that I made a point of telling him that I was going to Dunoon – I even told him the name of the hotel. Of course I didn't tell him anything about the purpose of my visit and he would naturally have assumed I was going for a weekend with my husband. In fact what I was doing was leaving a trail behind me in case I didn't return – at least that way when they retraced my movements they would know which hotel to start searching for my remains.

I left him and drove to Gourock where I boarded the ferry. I had taken the precaution of filling up with diesel beforehand in case I had to make that mad dash in the middle of the night. When I thought of the 200-mile 'dash' I was thankful that my employer had insisted I have a diesel engine in my company car – something I had objected to at the time but had to accept because of the large distances I was covering. It was much more economical. Previously I had had a rather sporty VW in hi-gloss black with alloy wheels and low-profile tyres – I used to delight in burning people off at the lights. This wasn't possible in my Citroen ZX diesel – but it *would* cover 200miles without the need to stop for fuel.

The ferry only took 25 minutes, which seemed too short. I drove off the boat and made my way to the hotel which I found surprisingly quickly and easily. As I turned into the gravel driveway I saw that the building was an imposing Victorian villa with dormer windows and traditional, Scottish, crow-stepped gables. It seemed to sit in quite extensive grounds. The original render had been whitewashed now. This would have been a grand building in its day and it retained a sense of old-world quality.

I parked the car and took the unusual step of turning it round so it was facing outwards, towards my escape route. There were only two cars in the car park in front of the hotel and I suspected more were to come, so I positioned my trusty diesel to make sure she wouldn't get blocked in when others arrived.

At reception there was no sign of anyone, so I gingerly rang the brass bell that sat on the countertop, silencing it again immediately with my hand as if I didn't really want anyone to hear me. Almost immediately the manager appeared, a man far too loud and talkative for the tension of the situation. He welcomed me and carried my bag up the flight of stairs to my room as I followed sheepishly behind him. After seeing me into my room he said, 'there's another two ladies in the lounge having tea, so you may want to join them', and with that he disappeared.

Did I want to join them? I wasn't sure. But it was now time to face the music, to go downstairs and see what type of people I was going to spend the weekend with. As I entered the lounge there were the two women sitting having tea out of china cups and saucers that matched the red roses of the chintz. I had taken the precaution of bringing my laptop downstairs with me. This was always a standby when staying in hotels on my own. It meant I had something to do, or something to look at when I had no-one to speak to. Or I could use it as an excuse not to speak to anyone when I didn't want to engage in conversation. In this situation it was an essential piece of kit.

As I walked into the small lounge, the women stopped their conversation, looked up at me and said hello. 'Are you here for the workshop', one of them asked.

'Yes. You?'

'Oh Yes, we come here all the time.'

Aha, just as I suspected, here were the first two of the coven. But they looked normal and as our conversation continued they employed the usual West of Scotland technique of drilling down to find out who you are, where you've come from, what your Mother and Father did and, most crucially, which school you went to. In Edinburgh we are always much more discreet, private and circumspect about such matters – especially when I was supposed to be sussing them out. So, in a lull in the conversation I quietly opened up my laptop, pressed the on button and waited for it to spring into life.

'What are you doing?' one of them asked.

'I'm going to do some work.'

'Work. I thought you had come for the workshop?'

That one sentence hit home. What *was* I doing? I *had* come for the workshop. I had come to find Professor Archie Roy and some answers. This was important. I put the laptop away.

That weekend I met some really interesting people, all from different walks of life, mostly professional people including a solicitor, a psychiatrist, a teacher and of course a Professor. Archie Roy was every inch the gentleman. Dressed as I had suspected in a dark suit although it was well worn. He had gold-rimmed glasses and grey hair which was thinning on top. He spoke in a well-educated West of Scotland accent with a dry sense of humour and a laugh that was infectious. He gave lectures throughout the day on children who remembered past lives and of possession cases in India.

His colleague, Tricia Robertson, who was the organiser of the event, conducted a number of psychic experiments and I was fascinated to learn that I could 'see' the Zener Cards whilst blindfolded. This involved others in the room 'transmitting' telepathically the design they were shown on a particular card, and the blind-folded recipient attempting to 'receive' the image. I was surprised to learn that I could 'see' these images as clear as day in my head and correctly identify them. Was I psychic?

Then the opportunity for which I had come arrived, almost as I had predicted. Everyone had drifted off to bed, the place was quiet and there in the lounge bar I got my opportunity to tell the Prof about my experience. As I relayed what I had seen he said, 'You weren't the only one – there were lots of people who received a premonition about Dunblane, but it's no good as evidence to be told after the event that you saw something that has now taken place'. Well, he didn't realise it at the time, but those words, 'you weren't the only one' was as if he had sprinkled fairy dust over my head. I thought I *was* the only one. I felt like the only one. I felt it was all my fault. I was supposed to do something about it. I was the one who should have stopped it - and didn't.

Although he was focused on looking for evidence, he realised by the tears now welling up in my eyes that it meant much much more to me. 'If you did get that premonition, you should also have had the desire to do something or to tell someone?'

'Yes, yes, I did,' I said regaining my composure.

'And did you?' he asked.

'Yes, I did.'

'I suppose it was a friend?' he said.

'No. No, it was a work colleague.'

'And this was before it happened?' he asked.

'Yes, yes it was, but she can't even look me in the eye any more.'

'Excellent, excellent', he exclaimed excitedly, thumping the table with delight at the same time. 'And, would she give a statement do you think?'

'Well, I suppose so, but you'd have to ask her, she's not very happy with me,' I told him.

'Excellent, excellent'. There was more table thumping and I could see the Professor was deep in thought about that last statement, as if he was wondering when he could make the journey to see my colleague. He returned from his imaginary trip as he realised he was off without me, and I was still sitting there looking for answers. 'No-one knows why premonitions happen', he said, 'But, they're always about impending doom and disaster - they're never about happy events. It's as if an early warning signal goes out somehow and those who are especially sensitive to this type of thing, can pick it up. It happened with Aberfan[3] in Wales and it's also happened with various plane crashes.'

'But what was I supposed to do about it? I didn't know where it was,' I pleaded.

'Yes, you'll find that various people would have been able to pick up different bits of information. It's like pieces of a jigsaw and when you put together what everyone has, it makes sense, but by that time, it's usually after the event. You got more than most and your description is very accurate, but there's nothing you could have done. You were not to blame.'

These were the magic words I had so wanted to hear, but didn't dare ask - but he told me nevertheless, as if he was reading my mind. I fired questions at him: 'Well what's the point of it? Are people able to stop the event? And, what if it happens again?'

'It probably will happen again, since you are sensitive enough to pick up these signals, there will be other premonitions. As to, 'can you stop it? Or change it?' No-one knows.'

I went to my bed that night with mixed emotions. He had alleviated the burden of guilt but replaced it with apprehension. 'It probably would happen again,' he had said and the thought filled me with dread. Little did I know that the next time, was closer than I thought.

3 A VIGIL

I did manage to 'escape' Dunoon, but only after enjoying a very interesting weekend, and strangely enough with nice people. Normal people. However, as it turned out the proprietor was a Trance Medium – and an excellent chef. So that explained some of the reasons behind this choice of hotel. But I had been given plenty food for thought and not least that prediction from the Professor that I could expect further premonitions. But I also learned about The Scottish Society for Psychical Research (SSPR), an organisation he had set-up with the aim to study and investigate the paranormal. And what's more he was keen that I should join and come along to their next meeting. The meetings were held in Glasgow University, in one of their lecture theatres, where he worked in his day job. I told him; I'd be there.

Although the Prof had relieved much of the immediate pressure of those feelings of guilt and of being responsible I still needed to know more and especially what the point of all this was. My life was going along pretty much according to plan. I had a husband, a nice house and a good job - my ducks were in a row. But all this had been thrown into disarray by a disturbing premonition that came about in the most traumatic fashion - surely there had to be a meaning to all of this, a purpose - and surely this purpose has to be, to stop it from happening. That was my logic. How that would happen, I did not know. Nor, it seemed did the Professor, but little did I know that my question would be answered by another dramatic premonition.

In the meantime, I attended the SSPR meetings in the Boyd Orr Building of the university which is just off Great Western Road, obviously to the west of the city and the main road out towards Loch Lomond and The Trossachs National Park. The meetings took place in the evenings, and usually involved a speaker on a specialist subject. I found it fascinating, very interesting and intriguing all at the same time. And although I read avidly a number of the books recommended by the speakers and some which were reviewed in the

SSPR's monthly publication, I was clearly out of my depth in this strange paranormal world.

I was also very quickly recruited as a Paranormal Investigator when I joined the SSPR. 'What does that involve?' I enquired of the kindly gentleman whom Archie Roy introduced me to with a suggestion that I'd make a good recruit. The SSPR was based in Glasgow and although at the time I joined, they did have an Edinburgh Branch, which I did attend, it stopped very soon afterwards with the untimely death of Stewart Menzies, the organizer.

So, when Archie - as the Professor was known to everyone - introduced me as coming from Edinburgh, I was aware of the implied suggestion that my recruitment as an investigator would be fortunate for the organisation.

'We conduct investigations where people report problems in their homes or place of work, or wherever' he said nonchalantly.

'Problems?' I enquired.

'Yes, haunted houses and the likes,' he says.

'Really? But what would I do? I wouldn't know what to do about that?'

'Can you write a report?' he enquired.

'Well, yes, of course I can.' He was now becoming slightly condescending.

'We would pair you up with one of our investigators - we always work in pairs - and he would conduct the investigation, and you would take notes and write the report.'

Of course he would. He was not about to send me on my own into some spooky shack to encounter who knows what. He was going to pair me up with an experienced investigator who would know exactly what to do. I just had to take the notes - I could do that.

I complied readily. I was keen to work with these people. They were the only people I now knew who were investigating these strange happenings and what's more, investigating them, scientifically.

They have a protocol:

- They only work in pairs - never alone. This is for the personal security of the investigator, but also for the security and protection of the client, so they don't feel they're inviting a strange person into their home. Wherever possible it would be a male and female combination of investigators.
- They will only accept independently corroborated information as evidence. Whilst anecdotal information can be very interesting, it remains just that, and only falls into the category of 'evidence' when someone else has also witnessed the phenomenon.

I liked this about them. There was a very strict, no nonsense approach to everything - there was no place here for the sensationalism that is seen now in some TV shows.

Meanwhile my would-be recruiter continued, 'Oh, and we also do Vigils.'

'Vigils?' Was he not one of the Thunderbirds – no that was Virgil.

'Yes, we look for reportedly haunted locations and we go as a group and stake them out, basically,' he said, facetiously. In response to my puzzled look, he continued, 'These tend to be public buildings where there's a reported problem that can be corroborated *(there's that word again, and I now knew exactly what it meant with regard to paranormal investigations)* and we are either invited, or we ask permission to sit in the place overnight. We then report on any findings.'

'Oh', I said, trying to take it all in.

'In fact there's a vigil coming up. You should come. You could also meet Archie Lawrie. He's the only investigator we've got in the East of Scotland'.

There it was. Any notion I may have had that they wanted me for my sparkling wit and intelligence disappeared at that moment, when it was confirmed that the reason they wanted me, was because I was from Edinburgh. Little did they know that I would have travelled to Timbuktu to keep involved with this organisation and Archie, who was such an expert on all things paranormal.

And so it was that I was invited along to my first 'vigil'. It was to be held in the Shanter Inn, Kirkoswald, Ayrshire. It had been the old Schoolhouse where Rabbie Burns went to school in 1775. Opposite was a graveyard which housed the graves of Souter Johnnie, Tam O' Shanter, and Kirkton Jean – all characters from his famous poem and based on real people living in the village at that time.

The Schoolhouse was now a pub with letting bedrooms on the first floor. The building was long and narrow with a kitchen to the back in a flat roofed extension entered via a doorway behind the bar. The stairs to the first floor letting bedrooms were at the farthest end of the building and had its own separate entrance from the street with just a small reception table at the foot of the stairs. At the top of the stairs the corridor was to the right and ran along the centre of the building, with bedroom doors to either side, spaced along the long length of this corridor, to a fire exit at the far end.

Our group of Paranormal Investigators rendezvoused in our cars outside the pub and waited until it closed for the night and the last revellers left for home. The Landlord then signaled us to enter. He had made it quite clear that he wanted no-one to know that we were going to be there overnight handling an investigation. He had told us that various guests had left in the middle of the night – some leaving money to pay for their room, others not – but they all had reported something disturbing in one of the bedrooms. He wanted us to investigate.

The protocol for the SSPR in such cases was to pair people up and allocate each pair to a certain location in the premises. Each pair would sit in silence, in the dark for an hour, record anything they had experienced, then someone would ring a bell or blow a whistle to indicate that it was time to change locations, then the whole thing started over. This process would continue throughout the night, until dawn, when everyone would get together and compare notes. As with investigations, evidence is not evidence unless it is corroborated. So, both individuals in the pairings would have to witness the same phenomenon for it to be accepted as evidence; otherwise it could be just one persons' imagination.

I was paired up with another Archie, Archie Lawrie, whom I met for the first time. He was a retired Head Master and the Investigator from Fife, whom Professor Roy had mentioned previously. Each pair was handed a rota of rooms and locations where they were to be stationed throughout the night. Archie and I were to start in the kitchen, which I was quite relieved about since I already knew that the problem was somewhere upstairs in one of the bedrooms, no-one knew which one, but at least it wasn't in the kitchen.

The other protocol when conducting vigils such as this is that each pair will sit diagonally opposite each other in any room. This means sitting in the corner of a room so that each person has as wide a range of vision as possible, rather than sitting straight opposite each other, say with your back to the middle of the wall in a room, as this would mean having to turn your head to see the corners of the room – try it, you'll see what I mean.

So we went into the flat-roofed extension building behind the bar that housed the kitchen. This was a large rectangular room with stainless steel tables in the centre, fridges, freezers, ovens and various other pieces of equipment spaced around the walls. The outside wall had a full line of windows almost the length of the room and below them the sink, dishwasher and other low-level cupboards.

As we looked around, Archie said, I'll sit in this corner, near the end of the line of windows. I looked for a position diagonally opposite him, and sat in the corner next to one of their large free-standing stainless-steel fridges. As we checked that we were in line of sight of one another, the signal that the lights were about to be turned off was given, and then we were in darkness.

I was surprised at how frightened I was. I couldn't see a thing, in the pitch darkness. My heart was pounding, I was hyper-ventilating as here I was in this haunted house, sitting in the dark with a group of strangers – and the one opposite me I had only just met - hoping to find a ghost! What was I thinking of?

However, as I gave myself a talking to, I started to calm down. 'Don't be silly Ann, it's only the dark. This is just a pub kitchen, there's nothing here.' As my eyes started to get used to the dark, I could focus a little more and I could see the outline of Archie, my partner for this exercise, sitting with his silhouette now outlined by the faint moonlight from the window.

Just as I was regaining some composure and beginning to feel calm again, the thermostat from the fridge kicked it into life and as it gave a shudder right next to me - my palpitations began all over again. Fortunately, I manage not to scream, and as I later realized, Archie had a hearing problem, so I got away with it – reputation intact.

Soon the bell sounded and it was time to move on again. After several moves around the ground floor locations in the building, we were then moved upstairs. By that time, it was the early hours of the morning, I had got used to the dark, was beginning to get tired, and had used up my adrenalin in the earlier escapade, so I didn't have the energy to be frightened any more.

Archie and I were assigned one of the bedrooms, the door was open to the corridor and so we settled ourselves opposite one another again. I sat near the door into the room and he sat opposite me, again near the window. The door remained open to the corridor, so I could actually glance outside the room too and see Nick, one of the other investigators at one end of the corridor, nearest us and his wife, Sarah, was at the opposite end, although she was not in my line of sight.

We sat again preparing for another hour with nothing happening again, and as time passed I was getting bored so I glanced out of the room towards Nick at the end of the corridor and I saw what looked like tiny blue lights circling around him, very close to him. As I watched, making sure my eyes were not just too tired or reacting to reflected light, I watched these lights circling quite quickly now so they were leaving a trail of light in their wake. There used to be an advert for a washing powder called 'Ariel', which showed a symbol which looked like atoms in motion, leaving a blue trail which identified it as 'biological'. This is the nearest example of what I was seeing.

Knowing my information was just that, unless I could have it corroborated, I quietly called Archie over and asked if he could see the blue lights circling around Nick.

'Yes', he said, 'I can, but where are they coming from'.

This is typical SSPR thinking – eliminate the possible, and only then, are you left with the probable. As our eyes searched the corridor for possible sources of light or reflection, we realized there were none. Nick was sitting at the darkest end of the corridor with his back against the Fire Exit Door, there were no other doors near him and no windows in this corridor.

As we continued to view this, I had a sudden concern for Nick. 'Are you okay, Nick?' I said.

'I'm not sure,' came the reply. 'I'm feeling kind of strange.'

'How do you feel?' I asked, as his voice was kind of slow and laboured.

'I feel like there's something here, but I don't know what it is and I don't like it very much.'

No sooner had he said that, than the bell rang for the changeover, the lights were switched on and the blue lights disappeared. As he tried to regain his sense of composure he again seemed very slow as if he had been in a sort of trance-like state and he said he didn't know what had happened to him.

Now it was our turn. We swapped over with Nick and Sarah, they went into the bedroom with the door open, and Archie and I were allocated the corridor. Archie immediately seated himself on the chair that had been placed at the far end of the corridor and I took the seat that Nick had been sitting in.

The lights went out and we were again plunged into darkness. I sat alert, looking for the blue lights again, but as time passed and nothing happened, I began to feel sleepy again. Then, suddenly there was a blue light at the top of one of the bedroom doorframes halfway along the corridor. As I watched, again making sure it couldn't be a reflection, there were more blue lights now circling around the doorframe like chaser lights. Then slowly one of the lights moved from the doorframe on to the wall next to it, followed by another and another, so they were now forming a line of trailing lights slowly moving along the wall at about head height, towards me.

I immediately looked to my partner at the opposite end of the corridor, hoping for verification and at least some words of comfort and support. Only to see Archie slumped over the chair sound asleep at the other end. Great, I thought, not only can he not corroborate what's happening, he can't help me either. The thought had just left my mind when Nick's deep voice said, 'Don't worry Ann, I can see them.' Thank the Lord.

As the blue lights neared me, they went out of my vision and I assumed they were doing much of what I had seen them do with Nick, in circling above his head. I could sense a feeling of static energy in the air that seemed to be charged somehow. I then became aware of something rolling towards me at a low level, along the carpet of the corridor. I don't know how I knew it was coming, I just did. And as it approached me I could feel a tremendous coldness first on my toes then on my feet and ankles, then the fronts of my legs as if it was a wall of coldness slowly moving forward and engulfing me. As it started moving up my thighs I didn't like it. I knew that next this coldness would hit my torso and I didn't want that. I stood up out of the chair. By this time, Nick was standing right next to me, as he had witnessed what was happening and he switched on the lights. Almost as soon as he did so there was an almighty bang, which appeared to come from the bottom of the stairs. It was as if someone had hit the front door with a sledge hammer, but there was no-one there.

Another precaution the SSPR take in these situations is to have a couple of investigators stationed outside the building so that no-one can play tricks on us from outside, should they get wind that we are going to be there. But, upon checking with them, all was quiet at the front of the building and in the car park.

One of the most frustrating things I was to learn from SSPR is that although they go through a very professional method of eliminating the possible explanations for the many strange happenings that I've witnessed over time. Once all efforts to explain the phenomenon through 'normal' means have been exhausted, the conclusion that is then appended to it, is 'unexplained'.

I wanted more.

4 ANOTHER PREMONITION

Meanwhile the financial services industry carried on regardless - unaware of all the goings-on. And following my meeting with the Professor I was now feeling a lot more comfortable too with the thought that I wasn't alone with my premonitions so my work ethic was getting back to normal as well. That was until my next premonition – and this time, I knew exactly who was involved.

As well as managing the branch network, I also managed a direct sales team. This was a hand-picked team of individuals whom I had trained and motivated to be top sales people. They reported directly to me rather than to a Branch Manager and I used them to go into various branches around the country where the performance was dropping. By putting one of the sales team members into a branch they would not only boost sales but the branch staff would learn skills and techniques from watching them work. This seemed to be a winning formula.

Each sales team member was strategically placed around the country to respond to local branch needs within their allotted territory and each had a company car to help them cover this territory.

In my next premonition I saw a car crash. A young woman was slumped over the steering wheel with blood streaming from her head. I couldn't tell if the woman was dead or not but I was aware that it was a serious head injury and not one from which you would always recover – at least not without serious brain damage.

Another gruelling scene, but the worst bit about it was I recognised the car and I recognised the woman – she was a member of my own Sales Team. It was Shona.

Now I've learned in the subsequent years that I only need to think a thought e.g. why do these things happen? and, are you able to stop them happening? and I very quickly get my question answered – even when I'm not always aware of having asked it. But at that time, all I was aware of was that Professor Archie Roy's own premonition was coming true – yes, I was receiving another premonition – and this time I knew who it was, so what do I do about it this time?

I realised that I would have to find a way of warning her, without revealing the fact that I was receiving premonitions – mainly because it was highly unlikely that she would believe that her boss was having premonitions, therefore any warning would be disregarded. I had to save her – but how? I was determined, this time it was going to be different – I would make a difference. But how?

Shona covered a territory on the East of Scotland from Dundee northwards to Aberdeen, indeed she was based in Aberdeen. Although she was an excellent sales person, she was a bit 'dippy'. She always appeared a bit disorganised and although Filofaxes were the organiser of choice back then, Shona would have scraps of paper all over the car and several little postit notes some in the car, others in the branch and some in her handbag. Her clients' notes were often mixed up with a hair brush, a CD cover and a lipstick. The car always looked like she lived in it, but despite all this she was a nice person who was good at her job.

I acted quickly; I didn't have a sense of when this calamity was going to unleash itself but I wasn't going to delay. I organised a Sales Team Meeting. I did this from time to time so it wasn't unusual, except that we had just had one a couple of weeks before, so that was going to look odd – I could cover that, I decided to come up with a new sales campaign and I would set up the meeting to present it.

I arranged the meeting and pulled in my team from all corners of their respective territories, into our Head Office building. The meeting went well, as always there was a sense of high energy in keeping the team motivated to perform. At the end of the meeting everyone was leaving, buoyed up with renewed enthusiasm and Shona was chatting excitedly with another sales team member as the two of them headed along the corridor towards the exit door to the car park.

In the strictest voice I could muster I said 'Shona, come back here, I want to have a word with you'. The joy on her face turned to concern as she registered the tone of my voice. She immediately responded and started to walk back towards me with her head bowed a bit like a dog that's just had a scolding.

'What've I done?' she said.

'Nothing yet,' I said, 'but I've had a look at your car and I can see notepads, CD's and other bits and pieces on the passenger seat – that tells me that you're not concentrating when you're driving. You've been given a company car and I do not want to see it damaged; do you hear me? When you're driving the car, you concentrate on driving, not trying to look for notes or the next CD you're about to play. I do not want you to bring that car to the next meeting with a bash in it, do you hear me?' At this point she was standing looking stunned at the reprimand she was receiving even although she hadn't actually done anything – I'm sure she was thinking – why me?

She left and was probably feeling quite aggrieved and hard done by. I was thinking that this was the best that I could do. I didn't want to frighten her, which might actually cause an accident and I couldn't sit in the car with her every day. I was hoping that by being annoyed at me, she might want to prove me wrong and make damn sure that there was no damage to that car.

Like the last time, after I had 'done something' and 'told someone', the urgency of this 'message' ceased and normal life resumed once again. That was until a couple of weeks afterwards. I was again working in Glasgow when I received a message relayed from our Head Office that I was to phone Tayside Police. It wasn't uncommon for me to be in touch with the police, indeed at that time there had been a spate of branch raids by the criminal fraternity robbing our branches by various means. In the aftermath, this often involved me comforting traumatised staff – something that is not generally recognised – or speaking to the press and of course, the police.

When I called the number I had been given, I was wondering if they were going to update me on the latest criminal case they were pursuing or telling me that they've got away with it – again.

But no, after each of us identified ourselves, in his voice of officialdom that can only come from a policeman, he said, 'Do you know a Shona Atkins?'

'Yes', I said, suddenly realising we were on a different subject altogether.

'Her car has been involved in a multiple pile-up on the M90.'

My heart sank – here it was - the news I had tried so hard to avoid- I steeled myself to ask the question: 'How is she?'

'I don't know, the ambulances took all the casualties to Ninewells.' (Ninewells Hospital).

I was stunned into silence my mind racing to figure out whether that meant she was alive or dead. Do they take everyone from multiple pile-ups to a hospital to determine whether they're alive or dead – I didn't know but assumed they did. As my mind tried to work out this scenario, the policeman on the other end said, 'So, you need to go to Tayside Police Compound to collect her belongings.'

Belongings – the term confirmed my worst fears – no one asks you to collect belongs for someone who might still need them. For someone still alive. 'Is she alive?' I tentatively ask.

'I really don't know. It's bad, we're expecting fatalities, I suggest you get yourself to Dundee as soon as possible.'

My long drive from Glasgow to Dundee was worrying. What was I going to find when I got there? I started going through in my mind what I knew about Shona – did she have a husband – no, divorced. What about parents – I didn't know, but we would have those records in HR Dept. I'd have to get their contact details and phone them. That's not a job I've had to do before, I wasn't looking forward to that. Then that sinking feeling and my stomach sank to my knees as I remembered - she did have a son.

As I approached the police compound I offered my identification at the gate and was waved in and directed to park my car in a small area to the right of the large security gate that I had just entered by. I got out the car and began to walk diagonally across the large square compound that seemed to be littered with cars and vans – all of them smashed up in various ways and suddenly, there in front of me was a low-loader lorry and on the back was our company car – Shona's car.

It was concertinaed to about half its usual size and had obviously been hit both back and front. Clearly it had been squashed between what I could only surmise must have been two large vehicles to reduce the car to this wreck that was sitting in front of me on the back of the lorry. And then I saw it, the blood stain. Blood had been running down the driver's door frame from about head height on the door pillar down on to the door panel. I felt sick in the pit of my stomach. The evidence that was being presented to me was corroborating the vision of the accident I had so clearly seen in my premonition. This was awful – all over again.

I swallowed hard and walked over to the office to speak to the officer on duty. Yes, I could confirm it was a company car belonging to my employer – this was how they had tracked me down via the DVLA[4] records. Would I accept belongings, he asked. Then disappeared from the desk into a back office and re-emerged with a large clear plastic bag about the size of a dustbin bag, tied with a pink cable tie. Immediately I could see in the bag, a laptop, Filofax, a hairbrush, a selection of CD's and one shoe, splattered with blood.

'Is she alright?' I asked again.

'She's been taken to Ninewells Hospital.'

'But do you know how she is?'

'No, you'll have to contact accident and emergency – all the casualties were taken there by ambulance.'

That official voice spoke again, 'Please sign here to confirm that you are taking possession of these items which were collected from the car'. I signed and was handed this rather heavy plastic bag. I carried it back across the compound to my car and placed it in the boot. As I did this the contents of the bag spread out across the floor of my boot, still encased in their plastic bag but now I could see more closely some of the personal belongings in this bag. There was her handbag, which had spewed its content out so I could now see a small compact mirror, a tampon and money that must have spilled from her purse. The personal nature of these items served to intensify this feeling of apprehension and nausea I was suffering.

I slammed the boot shut, jumped in the car and headed for Ninewells. The Accident and Emergency Reception Desk asked if I was a relative but resolved to release information to me as I had been the only point of contact they could find following the accident. 'How is she?' I asked this question again knowing that this time, I *would* get an answer.

'She's been transferred to a ward. She's in Ward 11.'

'Can I see her?'

'Yes, it's further up the corridor and through the door to your left.'

I was off and smartly walking up the corridor to find that ward before realising I hadn't asked what type of ward it was. Was it for head injuries, was it a pre-operative ward? Too late now - I was halfway up the rows of beds either side of the central walkway.

As I walked up the centre of this ward, about three quarters of the way up, I saw her. There she was in bed with a large bump with a small cut on her forehead but with both legs in plaster and the bed covers pulled back to expose her legs, which were raised up above the level of the bed on a sort of platform. She recognised me and immediately burst into tears.

'I'm sorry Ann, I've bashed up the car!'

I felt my own tears well up as I said, 'It doesn't matter about the car, as long as you're all right.' The relief I felt at that moment was incalculable. I was so pleased to see that she was alive and her injuries seemed slight.

'How are you and what's happened?'

'Well I've broken both ankles and some bones in my foot,' she says. 'I was driving up the motorway and it was a brilliant day, sunny with hardly a cloud in the sky. I was driving along quite happily in the fast lane when all of a sudden I drove into this cloud of smoke – it was coming off the fields – they were burning off the stubble. I drove into this thick smoke and realised I couldn't see a thing. Then suddenly there was a large lorry that had stopped in the fast lane, in front of me. I slammed on the brakes, I remember thinking I better not bash this car or Ann will go mad. I didn't think I was going to be able to stop in time as I saw the back of the lorry quickly getting closer and closer to me as my car sped towards it, tyres squealing. Eventually the car came to a stop and the tailgate of the lorry was right in front of my windscreen at eyelevel there was only about an inch to spare – the bonnet of the car was actually under the lorry, but I had stopped in time – I was relieved. I was actually thinking that if I hadn't stopped in time, the tailgate of the lorry would have burst through the windscreen and hit my head. But, as I was sitting there thinking, phew, I'd made it and I wasn't going to have to explain to you how I bashed the car, then I realised I could hear traffic coming towards me from the rear. Somehow I knew it was going to hit me and it sounded like it was coming really fast. I unleashed the seatbelt, threw open the driver's door and I dived out my seat towards the central reservation aiming to get over the crash barrier – and I made it, I landed in between the two crash barriers in the middle of the road. But as I dived out of the car, the lorry that was coming towards me fast from the back hit my car as I was in mid-air. The impact shunted the car forward and the door pillar hit my feet as I dived out the car.'

'That's amazing,' I said aghast at her story, 'what happened next?'

'Well I couldn't walk or stand because my legs wouldn't work. I didn't realise at the time that my ankles were broken - I didn't have any pain, but the nurse here said that was probably the adrenalin. So, I decided to crawl like a commando on my elbows and my stomach because I had to get away from there. I didn't know how long the crash barrier would hold because the vehicles kept piling up and the noise of the crashes were really loud because the cars were coming fast and then I could hear people screaming and moaning – I had to get out of there. Eventually I could hear the sirens of the police vehicles and I started screaming myself because I was frightened that they wouldn't find me. I was scared that I was going to be left there lying in the dirt and the gravel between the crash barriers.'

'Oh Shona, I can hardly believe it. Thank God you're alright.'

'Thank *you*, I'm alright' she said, 'It was you that kept going through my head and what you said about not bashing the car. I think that's why I reacted so quickly when I saw the smoke, otherwise I don't think I would've braked so hard, and I would probably have hit the lorry in front of me and then I would probably have been injured by that crash so I wouldn't have been able to jump out the car. If it wasn't for what you said, I probably wouldn't be here – I wouldn't have been paying that much attention.'

Now as you're reading this you are probably thinking this is just coincidence. And you could be right, but to me I had proven to myself that you can change the outcome of these things. And that made sense to me, otherwise what was the point of these premonitions? If they really were 'early warning signals' as Professor Archie Roy had claimed, then surely we were supposed to do something about it – 'do something' or 'tell someone'. And, I had just done that – and Shona was alive. Sure she was injured but not severely – she'd be okay, and so would I.

5 SPR AND SCOLE

The Scottish Society for Psychical Research (SSPR) Meetings took place in Glasgow on the first Tuesday of every month – and I made a point of being there. I used to plan my branch visits so I would be working in Glasgow on these days so it was easier to attend whilst being careful to ensure that no-one in my working environment knew about where I was going.

All of their speakers were either university professors, academics, scientists or other such luminaries like Professor Archie Roy. However, once a year they would have a Demonstration of Mediumship from an invited Medium, conducted for the enjoyment of the society members. I distinctly remember attending my first demonstration as I was utterly amazed by the content of the information given. The Medium was giving names – Christian names and surnames – and at one point told a woman in the audience that she had an appointment card in her bag for the hospital but she had missed the appointment and would have to make another appointment. The woman recipient promptly opened her bag to show the appointment card and said that she had just realised that day that she had forgotten the appointment, which had annoyed her as she had waited for the appointment for some time and now would need to go through the process again. I was utterly amazed by the content of this demonstration. Despite this, a common sceptical public perception – apart from thinking that Mediums are all charlatans – was that any information provided by Mediums was so general that anyone could accept it and that it was not specific enough to undergo scrutiny. The Professor was ready to challenge this thinking. He had decided to conduct an investigation into the quality of the information provided by Mediums.

Initially with colleagues from the Society for Psychical Research (SPR) and representatives from the Spiritualists National Union (SNU) Archie, together with his colleague, Tricia Robertson, both from SSPR, formed a group called, 'PRISM'. The acronym stood for Psychical Research Involving

Selected Mediums. The Study was conducted 'triple blind'. This meant that random members of the public were asked to participate. If they agreed, they were given a card with a number on it. These cards had been randomly shuffled. They were then asked to sit in a room secluded from the Medium, who was in a separate room. When they entered the room, they were asked to sit on the seats with the corresponding number to their card. The seat numbers had previously been set out by Archie and only he had a written plan of the arrangements. Tricia Robertson would hand out the cards and as she had no knowledge of the arrangement of seat numbers, she could not influence the results. Only Archie knew the seat number that he had chosen to receive a message.

In this way, the Medium had absolutely no contact with the recipient whatsoever, nor did the recipient have any knowledge of what was happening so equally could not influence the result, indeed the participants were told that the message could be for them. (A normal session would have somewhere between 25-40 participants).

The information given by the Medium would be written down and issued as a scoring sheet. The second investigators job was to assess the information against the responses from the invited public, in the form of a number of statements that the recipients were asked to mark according to the accuracy and relevance to themselves. This would result in an overall accuracy score.

To test the theory further, the third investigator would give the score sheet to random members of the public to assess whether *they* could accept this information and again to rate the levels of accuracy and relevance to themselves.

This was an extensive piece of research which took place between 1994-1999 and involved some of the biggest names in psychical research in their time: not only Professor Roy of course and Tricia Robertson but also Arthur Ellison, Maurice Grosse, David Fontana, Ralph Noyes and Montague Keen. It resulted in three lengthy papers being published in the well-respected Journal of The Society for Psychical Research in London, in 2001 and 2004. This established conclusively that the information given by Mediums was specific to the recipient and could not be accepted by just anyone.

As well as founder and President of the Scottish SPR, back in 1997 Archie Roy was also President of the SPR in London. This was, and still is one of the most prestigious and recognised organisations internationally for the study of the paranormal. It hosts an annual conference where papers are presented by Scientists, Professors and Lecturers from around the world. In 1998 their annual conference was due to be held in Durham University and since I was thirsty for knowledge, I decided to book my place.

When arriving in Durham for the event and entering the walled grounds of Durham University I was met by the caretaker - the students and tutors all having gone home for the summer – I was shown to my room. This involved climbing a spiral staircase where the steps were all worn down with age and entering a tiny room at the top housing just a single bed, a sink against the wall and a rather dilapidated utilitarian wardrobe which I guessed came from a period sometime just after the war. The bathroom was down the corridor. There was a tiny window in the room, about 18inches square and the walls were about three feet thick. The window had ancient wrought iron bars which criss-crossed this tiny space. At that moment I was thinking that the Society didn't need to go far to find their ghosts.

Upon entering the lecture theatre however, the scene was completely different. Like Glasgow University that I was familiar with, Durham had a tiered theatre with comfortable modern seating, sound and light that would put a commercial theatre to shame and state of the art telecoms and IT equipment – this was going to be good.

I had already met Archie Roy and Tricia Robertson in the car park – I was sure they had better rooms than I did as they headed off in the opposite direction but before doing so they re-introduced me to Nick Kyle also from the Glasgow SSPR and a committee member. I had last seen him in The Shanter Inn with strange lights around his head. We shook hands as he too headed off to find his room. The lectures began on Friday afternoon and continued throughout the day on both Saturday and Sunday. Amongst other lectures we heard from Dr Susan Blackmore on Astral Projection as she talked us through the theory and then regaled us with information on her own attempt to put the theory into practice – but she hadn't been able to achieve astral travel.

By the Sunday morning, my mind was boggled by sitting listening to speaker after speaker extol the virtues of their protocol – which to some of the lecturers was apparently more important than the experiment itself. As I looked around trying to find an alternative focus for my eyes - I had been sitting there for the last day and a half and to be honest a lot of it was very boring – my eyes met those of Nick Kyle, who seemed equally bored. He motioned to me to go to the exit at the back of the theatre, which I did, where we met up.

'I'm going to take a walk down the town,' he said, 'want to join me?'

My first reaction was that I didn't know this man who was offering to go for a walk with me, but as my Edinburgh reservedness softened to the Glasgow friendliness I decided it would be safe to go with him – he was after all a fellow member and indeed committee member of the organisation I had just joined. We walked out of the hallowed walls of Durham University and over the ancient stone bridge over the river into the town centre. As we walked we talked. I asked Nick about himself – he was a Depute Headteacher in a Scottish School. His partner Sarah was also a Depute Headteacher in another School. When I asked him how and why he had become involved with the SSPR he said that following psychic experiences in childhood he developed an interest in Spiritualism and particularly Physical Phenomena.

'Physical Phenomena – what's that?' I said.

'Well the definition of physical phenomena is that it is something which everyone in the room witnesses. Unlike Mental Mediumship[5] which is only relevant to the recipient of a message, with Physical Phenomena everyone sees it'.

'Sees what?' I said.

'Well the phenomena – it's where something physical is happening, like objects moving or a voice speaking out of the air, or knocking on the wall and in some cases the Spirit Person actually materialises.'

'Really?' I'm sure he could hear the disbelief in my voice.

'There's a group in England called The Scole Group – that's a wee place in Norfolk. It involves only two couples who have been sitting together in the basement of one of their houses in total darkness and they've been doing this for a number of years. Apparently they're getting all sorts of physical phenomena like lights that float about in the dark, apparitions and direct voice'.

'What's direct voice?' came my immediate reply.

'Direct Voice is where the spirit person speaks directly out of thin air – no Medium is involved, but everyone in the room can hear it and it can be recorded – apparently they are doing this – and I'm hoping to go there to see it myself.'

'Really?' I realised I was running out of ways to ask questions.

'Yes, you see, Professor Roy has been invited to witness the phenomena, and he's investigating it together with Guy Lyon Playfair, Morris Grosse and others of the SPR, but I'm hoping to get an invitation as a representative of SSPR – I'm waiting to hear if I'm to be allowed in.'

'Wow, that's amazing. I didn't know these things happened. I've read about some of this stuff, but I thought it was consigned to history in the Victorian period and perhaps also to a number of frauds that had taken place at that time.'

'No, this is real. It's being kept quiet so that the public doesn't get hold of it and to allow the scientists to investigate.'

'Well, let me know what happens – I'd love to hear more.'

Now for those of you reading this who would also 'love to hear more' let me say that Prof Archie Roy *did* visit the Scole Group[6] together with a number of other leading scientists from around the world who had been invited to witness first-hand the extraordinary phenomena which were apparently taking place there. This was done at the request of those communicating from another world who specifically asked that this should be done so that the scientists could inform the public that the 'other world' existed.

This led to another scientific paper being published entitled *The Scole Report*. The authors were Montague Keen, Arthur Ellison and David Fontana. This report was published in November 1999. It can be found in the 'Proceedings of the Society for Psychical Research', which reports on many of the phenomena already mentioned plus lots of other intriguing and fascinating happenings. To give just one example, the invited scientists were asked to bring a new 35mm photographic film and to keep it unopened in its own container. The scientists had previously built a small wooden box for this experiment with a lid with a latch and hasp so it could be locked with a padlock. The unopened film in its shop-bought packaging was placed into the box and locked. When they arrived at Scole, the key to the padlock was then left in the car of one of the researchers and the box taken with them into the house. In this way no-one in the house could gain access to the box. This box was then placed on a piece of paper which was on a table in the séance room and one of the investigators carefully drew the outline of the box, including the position of the padlock, which was also resting on the paper so that it could be established afterwards if there had been any attempt to move the box whilst they all sat in that basement room in the dark.

After the sitting, two of the scientists took the box away to be opened independently and to have the film processed. Initially, before they built the box, a Jiffybag was used for this purpose with the seal of the bag having been signed by the scientists involved. The Manager of the shop where the film was to be processed was then asked to sign a statement confirming that the bag was intact as he opened it. However as these experiments intensified, the scientists built their own box and brought their own padlocks.

When the film was developed it was found to have various writings on it. Some of the writing was in foreign languages: French, German and Greek; some involved very complex drawings; some had the signatures of long-deceased famous persons whose signatures could be verified by comparisons to those left before they died. For me then (and now with some 20 years' experience of psychical research behind me) this is the most compelling evidence of all. It would be well-nigh impossible to reproduce writing on untouched film without hours of painstaking work and practiced forgery all undertaken in a short time and in a dark room – to say nothing of how this prepared film would then be replaced back into its shop packaging and somehow placed back on the shelves of Boots the Chemist in Wimbledon, so that one of the researchers would hopefully choose that particular film to buy and take to the circle.

There is another strange synchronicity at play here since more recently, in 2017, I would come across The Scole Group[7] again, in a completely different context, and establish a working relationship with Jane Solomon and some of the original group members. As I've said before there's no such thing as coincidence.

6 THE GROUP

After giving up my job I was free to attend various workshops and development groups – something that was restricted whilst a Senior Manager in Financial Services – the two things were incompatible and would have been frowned upon by the 'powers that be' in the Building Society where I had worked. But whilst I continued to attend meetings of the Scottish Society for Psychical Research, which were fascinating, educational and enlightening, it wasn't answering my more practical questions about my own psychic abilities. I still wanted to know whether I could develop those abilities in order to be of more practical help by warning of 'pending doom and disaster' as the Professor had referred to my precognition, or whether I could develop further to be able to speak to dead people, just as I had seen the visiting Mediums do at the SSPR.

As well as attending Weekly Development Classes and Weekend Workshops wherever I could find them, I had also set up my own Home Circle. A Home Circle is simply a chosen group of people who sit together for Spirit communication and usually in one of the group member's homes. I saw this as a way of enhancing and speeding up my own development by getting in some extra practice. The practice involved simply sitting in silence together to form a rough circle shape (or as near as the furniture would allow) and after a period of time telling of any visions, impressions, visitations or messages received whilst in this silent, meditative state. The others would then determine whether the 'message' was for them by either recognising its content and communicator or not.

By 2005 I had held a Circle in my home for the previous two years. Having chosen those whom I thought had the right experience to sit in the Circle I found to my bitter disappointment that these were not the right people as whilst they were happy to come to my home, they were even happier getting together for a chat and a cup of tea. The Circle had descended into a chat room – well-intended but without the focus, drive and determination that I sought. More recently I had been invited to sit in a Circle in Morrison Street Spiritualist Church by Thelma Francis, a very well-respected Medium of international repute. Since both groups were due to meet at the same time I used this excuse to disband my Home Circle; thanking everyone for their time and input. I felt sure they would continue their 'chat room' elsewhere – which they subsequently did.

So now I had the chance to start again – and I instinctively knew that this time it would be right. You see the group that was disbanded was the second such group I had put together but like the second one the first group too had faltered under the weight of commitment. Perhaps I expected too much from this early group. This time it was going to be different.

Come on Ann stop procrastinating get it done, do it now I said to myself. This was a recognised mantra of mine. I was not used to wasting time. The more I thought about that the more frustrated I felt – where had the last five years gone in terms of my Spiritual Development? It had been five years since I gave up my job in the year 2000 to concentrate on my own Spiritual Development.

Wait a minute… It was early December. In a week or two it would be 2006. Ten years since the Dunblane Massacre as it had become known and this had really been the catalyst that eventually prompted me to leave my job. And after those two failed attempts at Home Circles here I was again for the third time going to set up another group – I hadn't been very successful up until now - but this one would be different. And that was because, this time, I had been told whom to invite.

I had never felt very knowledgeable in this area, so much so that I had actually recruited a Tutor to take the second group. I felt it needed someone of knowledge and experience to give it some direction – and I was bitterly disappointed. It was whilst sitting in this second group becoming more and more disgruntled by the lack of discipline that I got the impression (or communication or whatever you like to call it) but what came from the ether was *'run your own group?'* And, *'we'll tell you who to get'*. So now I was being told – *do it yourself*.

Under normal circumstances I would have just dismissed this as not feasible given my lack of experience and my own quest for knowledge – how could I possibly run my own group? Ridiculous. Except I was also hearing *'if at first you don't succeed – try, try, try again'* and *'third time lucky'*. This notion came to me with that same urge to *'do something'* that I recognised only too well from the premonitions of 1996.

I mentioned this to my very good friend, Mayumi. Mayumi was a petite Japanese lady now living in Edinburgh with her family. As well as being physically beautiful with a perfectly proportioned figure she had this inner beauty that just shone from her and she always seemed to have this sense of knowing. I thought it perhaps came from her Buddhist background or her vast knowledge of all things spiritual from the Far East.

Mayumi said, 'I think you should do it.'

As I contemplated this thought I said to her, 'What I really want is just a small group of committed individuals who are passionate and honest in their quest for further Spiritual Development.' Above and beyond anything else they had to be trustworthy. This was the over-riding factor that had always held me in good stead in my Professional Career and I saw no reason to change that well-proven philosophy now.

'So, who would we have in this group and where would we meet?' she said.

My house wasn't really conducive to a more serious committed group. It had too many distractions and if I was going to set a group up it would have to be right. Mayumi was attending a Buddhist Meditation Group that met at the Theosophical Society and so she undertook to ask if they had other rooms for hire and how much this would cost.

We turned our attention to who would make up the group. 'Well, there's you and me', she said, 'and what about Gordon?' Gordon Soutar was another true friend who like Mayumi I trusted implicitly. He had also been with me from day one and had supported me in these past failed groups. Before that we had met at a Development Circle for Mediumship but Gordon's path was one of Healing and so he turned away from Mediumistic Development so he could concentrate on his Healing.

Interestingly Gordon like me had received some paranormal intervention that caused him to give up his job too. Gordon was a Social Services Manager and he had previously had an odd encounter with a stranger in a park which was the catalyst in creating a major change in his life. Now some of you reading this with a more wicked sense of humour could create all sorts of amusing scenarios from this outline of events but what actually happened was a lot more mysterious.

I remember him telling me that he was walking through the Meadows, the large park in the centre of Edinburgh which runs from Tollcross in the West to Causewayside in the East. He said that something compelled him to sit down on a park bench – something he never normally did - he was far too busy for that. Then there came along a stranger, a man who sat down beside him despite the fact there were other free benches in the park. This man told Gordon that he should be a Healer and that there was a new energy which was a higher vibrational energy that Gordon would channel to heal people. Gordon had heard about Reiki but didn't know about this 'Sekhem' which the stranger spoke of. He said Gordon didn't have to do anything, the information he needed would cross his path. The man went one way and Gordon headed off in another and they never encountered each other again. Later the following week after Gordon had forgotten all about the strange encounter he walked into a shop in Edinburgh and there was a business card on a notice board from someone who was delivering this type of healing energy in Edinburgh. This was just as the stranger had described. This caused Gordon to make the momentous decision to leave his job and follow his instincts and become a Healer.

Now I didn't know Gordon's financial position but I did know that he had a mortgage to pay and he was a single chap. I also knew only too well the 'leap of faith' it takes to give up a life-long career and step into the unknown but at least I had a husband who was an income-earner. And although it takes a huge adjustment in life-style to move from two salaries to one at least I had one and I knew I wouldn't starve.

As far as I was aware Gordon had no such safety net – but he jumped nevertheless. So he was definitely in. I called him and he agreed without question. 'Who else?' she said.

'I don't know Mayumi, I'll have to give this some thought. I don't want to mess things up by asking the wrong person. Also we don't need that many people. I'd rather have just a handful of really committed individuals than a room full of 'also rans'.'

We agreed to each think about who else we should consider to be part of this new group and meantime Mayumi would find out about rooms at the Theosophical Society. A few days later Mayumi came back to say we could have a room there for £12 per session. 'And' she said 'what about Mairi Anderson?' Mairi also attended the Buddhist Meditations and Mayumi thought she might be good for the group.

I knew Mairi but not very well. I knew her from attending the Spiritualist Church which I had taken up as part of my further quest for spiritual enlightenment. I said to Mayumi 'I know Mairi is a Healer at the Church but I don't know what else she does.' Although I was aware that she was a regular attendee at the Arthur Findlay College in Stansted, London.[8] I had attended a Course there myself earlier that year at which Mairi had been present and indeed she had recommended the course to me. But we hadn't been in the same group so I didn't really know what she did other than she clearly had a strong commitment to her own Spiritual Development.

'The only thing,' Mayumi says, 'I know she sits in a Development Circle for Trance. So she may not want to take on another group.'

'Well I can only ask and see what she says' I said. 'I'll see her at the Church this Sunday.'

Sunday came and I waited as she came into Church and took up her usual position in the congregation. Mairi was about 50ish divorced and worked as a Librarian at the University. But this was her day job. Her passion was Shamanism and she would often be sporting some form of North American symbolism like a totem pole or a dream-catcher either on her clothing or jewellery.

She seemed to glide into Church and displayed that same sense of serenity that was so often apparent in Mayumi. 'She'll do for me', I thought as I watched all this. Like Gordon, Mairi lived alone and this had allowed her the freedom to use her own time as she pleased but because of financial constraints she felt bound by her job. She balanced this out by utilising nearly all her holiday time going either to the Arthur Findlay College or to other retreats, courses and workshops. She had developed a huge bank of knowledge – she would be a very valuable member of the group – and as I had this thought I got this little tingle from Spirit that tells me I'm right. After all they did say they would tell me who to get – now I was getting the message. But would she agree?

The thought suddenly struck me that I was totally focused on Mediumistic Development and my previous two groups had focused on this too. Now I was going to ask someone to join such a group who possibly didn't need to develop her own Mediumistic Skills – she had done all that through all those Training Courses. And now she was more interested in her healing work and her Trance than Mediumship. As I sat there pondering this and the Sunday Service was about to begin, I heard the Church President say, 'we'll start this service with a moment of silence and contemplation' and in that silence I heard, 'you can do it all.'

I really wasn't interested in Trance at all at this time but I was aware that the requirement to sit for Trance was very different from that required for Mediumship – and Healing was another factor altogether. What was I to do? But if there's one thing I've learned over the time that I've become aware of communication from Spirit it is that they're always right. Anytime when I have disregarded the influences I've had from Spirit I've later learned to regret it. I knew to trust what they said.

I'm not sure I heard much of the Service that day; I was working out how this was going to happen. Just tell her I thought. She's well attuned to Spirit. She knows me and she'll know that my intentions are honourable even if I don't know how to implement them.

After the service as she sat there on her own, I made my approach. 'Mairi I know this is going to sound a bit crazy but I feel I've been inspired by Spirit to set up a small development group. Just a small group of like-minded individuals who possess the drive and determination to work together for Spirit. I know you are more into Healing and Trance but I'm told we can incorporate all these things. The important thing is that we all have respect for one another and are willing to give each other time for their own development.'

'It really depends on which night it's going to be Ann as I have a lot on already', she said.

Immediately surprised that she did not question the validity of the group – only the night it was to take place – I continued, 'Well we haven't got to that part yet Mairi but I feel I've been guided to people I've to approach so I think we'll find a day that accommodates everyone.' On that basis she was in. So now I had four and I was happy with that. We could make a start with this number.

I should say at this point there were many more names suggested and rejected. For me it was of ultimate importance that I trusted each member of the group implicitly. I now know why that was so important but at the time I just accepted it. As well as this implicit trust I needed the little tingle from Spirit when a name was mentioned that told me if it was the right person or not. Also with two failed groups behind me I was afraid of getting it wrong and I'd have preferred to have a small group of the right people than risk jeopardising the integrity of the group just to have a few more participants.

Mayumi agreed we should start with just the four of us but I got the distinct impression she knew that that wasn't the end of it. And she was right. Although I was pleased we now had four willing participants I didn't get that sense of accomplishment that I was expecting. Instead I got a very distinctive and very unnerving feeling that something was not quite right.

I had done enough in my own Spiritual Development to recognise this feeling and for me the only way to get answers to the problem was to sit in the stillness and ask the question – 'what's wrong?'

The answer I got back was – *'someone's missing.'* I thought of this on a practical level: what would we do if someone was ill or on holiday? There would only be three of us, or fewer.

I had considered this earlier but the risk of getting it wrong by inviting the wrong individual just to make up the numbers was too great. I had opted for the solution of not holding the group when others were away or on holiday, but now I was *being told* to get someone else.

As I sat there in the silence I mentally ran through some of the names that had been suggested earlier but all were rejected either consciously or subconsciously because I didn't get the 'tingle' that told me I was correct.

It is a proven fact that the majority of those involved in Psychic and Mediumistic Development are women. I believe this is because females are generally more sensitive to the subtleties in life and instinctively tune into others around them to 'feel' their emotions. It is this ability that is the basis for Psychic Development. Men on the other hand have a reputation for being less sensitive to the needs of others (often their wives or partners) and perhaps genetically don't seem to have the same intuition that is inherent in the majority of women. Maybe women really are from Venus and men from Mars, as Ian Gray would say.

However this is a huge generalisation and there are exceptions to any rule. I know a few women who appear to have missed out when sensitivity was being distributed, and conversely there are a few Male Mediums, very well known in the industry, who are highly sensitive; but most of these latter are gay, which perhaps supports the theory that men who possess the higher level of sensitivity required for Mediumship usually have a higher level of the 'Y' chromosome.

And so it was with astonishment as I sat there in the quiet to hear the advice from Spirit *'the group needs to be balanced'*. *'You need another male to accompany Gordon'. A man* I thought with astonishment. The only other man I could think of was Stuart who had been a member of my first group. And he definitely wasn't gay. In fact he spent so much time trying to chat-up a female member of the group that he was really distracted from what we were supposed to be doing. They now live happily together as a couple.

I knew of no other suitable male. *'Yes you do,'* came the reply from Spirit. Now this was a challenge as I literally could think of no-one else but I was getting that familiar urge to keep at it, keep going, and keep thinking. I started working chronologically, backwards through all the groups I had sat in in the last ten years. All the workshops, all the people I knew from the Church – then it came to me. I remembered a Weekend Workshop I had attended at an Edinburgh college right at the beginning of my quest to find out what was happening with me and I remembered being paired up with a man, a fellow student, to do one of the exercises. I remembered the feeling I had had at that time that there seemed to be an instant connection between us – as if I had known him all my life – although we had only just met. I felt sure he felt the same but protocol and embarrassment prevented me exploring this further at the time. But I remember coming away from the workshop thinking I had met such a really nice man.

There was nothing romantic or sexual at all in these emotions, it was a much deeper connectedness. It was as if he instinctively knew more of who I really was than I did myself. He made a lasting impression. As I allowed my mind to reminisce like this I became aware that my intuition was not only tingling but was ringing bells in my head that would have drowned out Big Ben. This was it – this was the missing link and this was the man I was to get to join the group. But who was he? What was his name? I couldn't remember. I thought he may have been called Jim but wasn't sure. Who would know? What else could I remember about him? I needed something practical to track him down.

I quickly sprang out of my meditation buoyed by this desire and enthusiasm to get 'Jim' to join the group. Gone was any notion that we could get away with four members; gone was the hesitation of getting it wrong – this was so right and I knew it and Spirit knew it and once again had directed operations. As I racked my brains to remember practical facts about this person from some ten years before the more spiritual aspect of this person had been imprinted on my brain and I could 'see' his face in my mind's eye and I could tell of his spiritual integrity, but what was his name? What did he do? How could I find him again?

I started phoning around people who might know. 'Do you remember a guy; he was on that first workshop we attended I think his name was Jim something? He had a beard and I think I remember that he worked for the Health Service in some capacity?' Eventually I pieced the answers together: his name was Jim Cleary and he now attended a closed Trance Group. And he lived in Edinburgh – which was a bonus. And here was his telephone number.

I stood there in my kitchen with the phone in one hand and the scribbled phone number of Jim Cleary in the other hand. What would I say? What would *he* say? Would he remember me?

What if his wife answers? What would I say to her? How would I explain who I was?

'Well I once met your husband on a weekend workshop 10 years ago and I was wondering if he wanted to come out to play?' 'Or to join my gang?' It sounded feeble.

I told myself I've been directed to do this he can only say *'no'*. Or even worse, *'who?'*

I had stood there long enough; nothing ventured nothing gained – so I dialled the number. As it rang I nervously held my breath. Then to my relief a male voice answered, 'Hello'.

'Hello is that Jim Cleary?' I asked.

'Yes it is.'

'Hi Jim you probably don't remember me but my name is Ann Treherne and I met you on a weekend workshop at the college probably about ten years ago now.' I paused for breath.

'Yes, I remember you very well, Ann,' came the reply. 'What can I do for you?'

Phew, he remembered – I continued. 'This is going to sound even more strange but I feel I've been directed by Spirit to get a small Development Group together. Now I know you're into Trance but I'm told we can accommodate all of these things as I've already asked others who are also interested in Trance and Healing amongst other things to join. But for me what is most important is the integrity of the people, their commitment to their own development and that of other group members and above and beyond anything else is their complete trust of one another. And I wondered Jim whether you'd consider joining us?'

'Love to,' came the immediate reply. There was no pause, no hesitation, no requirement to know the logistics or whether it clashed with other commitments; he was in – and with conviction.

I was impressed. I came off the phone and at last came that feeling of accomplishment. I knew without doubt that these were the right people – we were now ready to begin.

7 THE GAME'S AFOOT

I came off the phone to Jim Cleary feeling rather pleased with myself that I had managed to recruit the person whom I had been directed towards by Spirit to complete our Group and so we were now ready to begin. However, my indulgence in self-praise was short-lived as I again received a message from beyond – and the information it contained was the last thing I was expecting: *'This is going to be a Physical Group.'*

I cannot tell you how disappointed I was to hear this message. I didn't want to do Physical Mediumship; I wanted to do Mental Mediumship. I didn't want to be like all those weird people with ectoplasm[9] exuding from every orifice; I wanted to be a Platform Medium.[10] I wanted to bring people messages – and more importantly evidence - from their loved ones telling them that they are still alive, still around, just without a body. All of my development over the last few years since Dunblane had been based on this premise. Now I was being told it was going to be a Physical Group and my heart sank as I also knew that Spirit is always right even when overriding what I thought or wanted to do. I decided to keep this information to myself and just wait and see what developed.

I arranged to get the Group together for a pre-meeting meeting so that they could be introduced to one another and we could lay the ground rules in advance of sitting together in Circle. Since it was December we decided to make it a social occasion and have Christmas lunch together in Peckham's Wine Bar in Bruntsfield, a suburb of Edinburgh. As I was arriving just outside the wine bar I could see Mayumi walking up the street towards me, so I waited for her to join me before going in. As she approached she said in an excited but hushed tone, 'I've had communication from Spirit – I think it's going to be a Physical Group.'

So there it was. I don't know if this message was sent for my confirmation or just to make sure I was actually going to facilitate a Physical Group when it was not what I wanted to do, but either way, now another member of the Group had been given the same information.

'So have I' I said to Mayumi, 'but I think we should keep this to ourselves and not raise expectations – let's just see what happens.' She nodded her head in agreement.

I was very aware of the fantastic results achieved by Physical Mediumship in the Scole Group, but I was also aware of the fraudulent mediums of the past and some of the ridiculous photos of so-called ectoplasm and spirit manifestation that were clearly faked – this brought the whole subject into disrepute and I had no wish to be linked to that. If Spirit wanted to do this, they would be the ones who would have to make it happen.

Christmas Lunch in Peckham's was an enjoyable occasion for our newly formed Group but it also provided me with an opportunity to inform everyone of some - not all - of the background to us getting together and to set some ground rules of how we would operate. I told them, 'I've got you all together at the request of Spirit – I was told who to get in the Group. I am told it is not specifically for the purposes of Mental Mediumship, much to my own disappointment, but that we should get a group of like-minded individuals together who are happy to sit for Spirit – and we will be directed from there. I know that some of you are interested in Trance, others in Healing and other modalities, but I'm told we can incorporate all of that. I'm also aware that there are different levels of experience in this Group and indeed I was reluctant to set up this Group because of my own lack of experience in comparison to others, but again I'm told this is not important. What is important is that we all trust each other and we trust Spirit. We need to be confident that if one of us is getting information from Spirit then that person is conveying exactly what they receive and not exaggerating or making it up. We are looking for honest communication between ourselves and with Spirit. Sometimes we will get it wrong, but with the right intention this is unlikely to happen. We need to create a safe environment where we all feel comfortable in sharing these thoughts from the other world without fear of criticism or ridicule. For this reason, I'm also told the Group should be kept confidential and nothing that is said or done in the Group should be discussed outside the Group – unless it's between Group Members.'

I paused for breath as I asked them, 'Is this acceptable to you?' 'Does anyone have any comments or questions?' Surprisingly, as everyone looked round the table at one another, everyone accepted the modus operandi without question. 'Secondly, the Group requires a Leader – not a Tutor, as we're told to sit and we will be directed – but we need someone to head up the Group, to be the Facilitator.' As I looked around the Group again, I noticed that everyone was looking expectantly towards me, so I continued, 'And, it's not going to be me.'

They looked puzzled. 'I think I probably have the least experience of anyone in the Group and although I have been told by Spirit to 'do it yourself' and 'get your own Group together' - and I'm doing that now - that doesn't mean I should be the Leader. Indeed, because apparently we're going to 'do it all', I feel we need someone who at least has experienced most of these modalities, if not is experienced in them themselves – does this make sense?'

Heads were nodding furiously as I suggested Jim. 'Jim to me represents the Elder Statesman and he probably has the longest experience of us all', the nodding was continuous, 'I suggest Jim as our Leader and Facilitator?' All agreed, thankfully including Jim, so we had our Leader. We agreed that a Thursday Evening at 6.30pm was the best night for all, and so the 'Thursday Group' was born.

We just needed somewhere to meet. Mayumi had undertaken her research at the Theosophical Society, and reported that they had a room they would be willing to rent to us. Mayumi was already attending a Buddhist Meditation Group there, so she already knew the Secretary of that organisation so by the New Year, we also had a venue for our meetings.

And so it was that in January, 2006 we met for our first meeting at the Theosophical Society in Edinburgh. They owned an impressive town house in Great King Street. When we arrived, the rented room we had been allocated was on the top floor, which was a bit of a climb up an ornate spiral staircase with wrought iron railings. However, as their main meeting rooms were on the first floor, it suited us to be out of the way, up the stairs with only one other room next door to ours being rented by the Buddhist's for their meditation and the only other rooms on this floor was the tearoom, kitchen and bathroom.

Our room would probably have been a bedroom when the building was previously functioning as a private house. It was rectangular in shape approximately 20' x 14' with a sash and case window to the far end, with working shutters – obviously to stop the drafts. There was a fireplace with mantelshelf on the right-hand wall. The wall to the left was clear and was the adjoining wall to the room next door where the Buddhists met. It should be said that their meditation meeting started an hour after our own meeting, so we never actually met them. It also meant that there was no-one on the top floor between 6.30pm-7.30pm – the time when we would be sitting in silence – so this was perfect.

The room had a few chairs of different shapes and sizes and a couple of occasional tables, a bookcase full of books and a rather lonely looking plant in a pot. The room was rather like an old-fashioned parlour and had a sort of gloomy appearance with a single overhead light bulb that must have exuded all of 40watts. This together with the wooden shutters and the fact that it was dark outside due to the time of year actually made it perfect for our small Circle to sit in.

One of the occasional tables was serving as a coffee table in front of the fireplace, so we moved this out of the away and formed the two armchairs and three of the old dining-room chairs into a circle in the centre of the room. This is how we sat, in silence, together, awaiting instruction and direction from the Spirit World, just as we had been asked to.

In these early days I felt compelled to give an invocation to start our session and I would say something like, 'Spirit, we are gathered here at your request – the people you have asked for – and we sit in silence awaiting your further advice and instruction. We open ourselves for Spirit contact, asking that those who work with us from the Spirit World come forward, make their presence known so we can receive your communication.' Then we would sit, usually for about 45 minutes to an hour in silence and then we would feedback to the Group any feelings, visions or communications we may have received – no matter how vague or tenuous. We wanted to create that safe environment to be able to share our views.

We found that by doing this we often all received different little bits of the same communication. It would only make sense once each person had given their feedback; only then would we realise that the whole thing fitted together and made sense – almost like a jigsaw of which each person had been given a piece.

We continued like this for the first few months of 2006 and during that time, if I'm honest, I was really still focused on Mental Mediumship – this was the thing that I really wanted to do. Also, I didn't know how or what to do about Physical Mediumship, so I just did what I normally did – and so too did everyone else. In a Closed Circle this would normally involve sitting in silence, connecting with your Spirit Guide and asking for help with something. For those practicing Mental Mediumship you would normally be looking for a contact (Spirit Person) belonging to someone in the Circle to come to you with information to prove their own identity and then to give a message to the recipient in the Circle.

The problem I always had with this while sitting in various Circles and Development Groups over the years was that I never had a Spirit Guide. I can remember numerous sessions when fellow students would give feedback after the meditation session: 'My guide's a North American Indian', or 'My guide is a Nun' or 'Mine is a Franciscan Monk'; there were often Chinese or Tibetan holy men and sometimes Mary Magdalene or even Jesus himself.

I had nothing like that, but I did 'know' that there was a higher intelligence out there somewhere, an entity that could communicate with me to bring me those messages and information of loved ones in the Spirit World who were related or connected in some way with those sitting in front of me who were in need of comfort, seeking solace or seeking peace from their grief. And this worked – I didn't need to know how – I just accepted that it did.

I now have a theory, which is that Spirit can take any form, as it is itself formless – there being no body involved after all. And so it will take the form that is most conducive to allowing communication with the Medium. Thus, if a Student Medium has an interest in Shamanism it is a safe bet that their Guide is going to be a North American Indian. And if the Student is very religious or has come from a religious up-bringing and still has that as their form of reference their Guide is likely to be a Nun or a Priest or some other holy man or woman.

There are not many people who are able to accept the abstract notion of a Spiritual Energy somewhere out there in the ether, or the idea that this Spiritual Energy has intelligence. Indeed most people not only have a need to personalise their Guide but also to know their name. I understand this need – it makes sense to want to know who is talking and what their name is - but I had no such need.

This may have stemmed from my earliest experiences when I received premonitions which subsequently came true. From this I was very aware that information could be passed through the ether accurately – from whence it came I did not know – but I knew it was possible. (Although this is a Psychic Phenomenon I am referring to and not a spiritual one it may have opened up my ability to accept that spiritual information could also be accepted in this way, without the need to know where it came from and without the need for a Guide).

Now, just to be clear, accepting information from the ether in this way is not acceptable when one is working as a Medium to bring evidence of a loved one through to a recipient. Indeed it's the Medium's job to find out exactly who is communicating and to provide evidence of that person. (In my case it's just that I don't do this via a Guide). And so it was that my mind was still in this Mental Mediumship mindset when we began our sessions to sit for Spirit at the Theosophical Society.

In one of the very early sessions as I was sitting with the Group in silence, I became aware of the presence of a man from the Spirit World. I am naturally clairvoyant, so tend to work predominantly with pictures. Now, there in my head, was a picture of a man. A big man, elderly, quite distinguished looking with grey hair and a moustache. He looked like a Grandfather to me. So, in the feedback session, I gave this description and asked, 'Does someone recognise this man as their Grandfather?'

As I looked round the Circle in anticipation of someone recognising this description of their Grandfather – I was met with blank looks. 'Does no-one recognise this man?' I asked.

There were more shakes of the heads, and so I could go no further with any communication. You see in Mental Mediumship the Medium's job is to give sufficient information for the recipient to recognise the communicator (from Spirit) and then to continue with the contact by giving further evidence and then a message for the recipient from the Spirit Person. If the recipient does not accept or recognise the initial information or description there's no point going further and the Medium will have to accept that either the information they have received is wrong or that they have misinterpreted it in some way. I just accepted that I was wrong – and let this man go. It was still fairly early in my development and so if my more experienced colleagues said 'no', I accepted it.

The following week however the man was back again – the same man, with the moustache and grey hair – I recognised him from the week before and so this time I took in a little bit more information: he wore a dark suit with a waistcoat and he had kind eyes and this had given me the feeling that he was a caring man and quite protective. Perhaps this is where I had got the notion that he was a Grandfather. Now I realised I was wrong, he wasn't a Grandfather, he just exuded those qualities, so I realised where I had gone wrong the week before. Also, now he was showing me Surgeon's Hall, in Edinburgh – a place I recognised from my own knowledge of Edinburgh – and I realised that this man had been a Doctor. As well as this I got the message, *'you should know me.'* (Strange, but those words are not heard, but felt – somehow you just know what is being said).

However, once again, I was to misinterpret his message. When it was my turn to give feedback from our silent session, I felt confident I knew exactly who this man was trying to make contact with – the message had to be for Jim. Jim was after all a retired Psychiatric Nurse; he would have visited Surgeon's Hall from time to time through the course of his work and therefore by my deduction he was the person who would know my communicator, just as he had said. And so I said to Jim, 'I've got the same man as I had with me last week, but I know now he's not a Grandfather; indeed he's not a relative of anyone's. But he is for you, Jim, as he's showing me Surgeon's Hall and I know he is a Doctor. He also said, 'you should know me'; so Jim, I think you are the one who will know him, you must have worked beside him or met him when you were in Surgeon's Hall as I know he would have worked there too.'

I watched as Jim mentally scrolled through his memory banks, visibly searching for someone he had known who matched this description.

'I can't think of anyone like this, Ann. I only visited Surgeon's Hall once, and although I knew many Doctors, I didn't know anyone who worked there. Most of the Doctors I came into contact with were at the hospital where I worked. Surgeon's Hall is mostly a museum now and sometimes used for meetings, but I don't know any Doctors who worked there.'

I was deflated. I felt I had got really relevant information this time and my logic was telling me that Jim was the obvious recipient since he was the one member of the Group who worked in the medical profession yet he didn't know a Doctor from Surgeon's Hall. So once again the message and the communicator went no further as, again, I sent him away.

So, another week went by and, 'that man is back again,' I said. 'And this time, he's showing me Edinburgh University' – actually he was showing me the McEwan Hall, which is the building used in the student graduation ceremonies – this was to have even more relevance much later, but for now he was letting me know that he had gone to Edinburgh University. As well as this, there was a second image of a bookcase which seemed to focus in on a shelf of books and I immediately knew that this man was an author – and had written not just one book, but several.

My logic kicked in again – I knew who this man was trying to make contact with now – he was for Mairi. It couldn't just be coincidence that we had a University Librarian in our Group – she must know this man, she must have worked with him, or at the very least, know of his books.

As I gave this feedback, Mairi was looking puzzled.

'I don't think I've met any authors,' she said. 'I know a few people who have published papers, but I can't think of anyone who has authored a shelf of books or who would look like that, I'm sorry, Ann.'

As I dejectedly let this man go for the third time, I was beginning to strongly question my own Mediumship. How could I get it so wrong? I was sure the information was correct. As these thoughts were traversing across my mind, I'm sure Mairi must have picked up how I was feeling, as she said, 'Could he be for you, Ann?' She was being kind I was sure and trying to bring me some comfort, but I didn't know any Doctor or Author who had a shelf of books at Edinburgh University.

Well he was nothing if not persistent, and I recognised him once again as I sat in Circle the following week. This time he showed me a vision of King Arthur – and the Knights of the Round Table. He also said, *'I'm a knight of the realm.'* Well, as I looked at this picture in my head of King Arthur sitting at that round table – I was in two minds as to whether I should even share this with the Group as I decided that my Mediumship had hit new depths. This time I had no idea who the message was for and was preparing myself for further rejection.

As I recounted my vision – from that man again – to the Group, Mairi again said, 'I think this man is for you, Ann?'

However, this most recent piece of information clinched it for me – he was definitely not for me – I didn't know anyone who had been knighted – and I told Mairi so. However, I also told the Group that I was aware that the name Arthur was significant which resulted in us all trying to wrack our brains to try to remember who had written the book of King Arthur and the Knights of the Round Table and was it possible that the author's name was Arthur – no-one could remember, not even the Librarian. So, as once again I concluded that something was going badly wrong with my Mediumship, I let this man go yet again.

By now I was beginning to re-examine why my Mediumship was failing so miserably. Was it because I had been told that this Group was going to be a Physical Group? Was I clinging on to Mental Mediumship when I was supposed to be doing something else? Was I somehow being taught a lesson? Yet I knew that the information I had received was correct – so, why was it not accepted? Why did no-one know what I was talking about? I didn't have the answers – I was confused and dejected.

As I attended the Group meeting the next week I had mentally decided that I should somehow be open to receive a different type of communication – I didn't know how this would work - but I would somehow set the intention not to receive Mental Mediumship.

It didn't work. He was here again – that same man. But…I liked him, he was nice, somehow familiar even although I didn't know who he was, and he had those kind caring eyes. As I looked into those eyes again (in my own mind's eye), feeling saddened that I couldn't get his message across for him, he showed me another picture. This was Sherlock Holmes!

As I looked at this vision of the famous detective, my heart sank. Why was I once again seeing images of fictional characters? How would I explain this one to my colleagues? I decided this was absolute nonsense. It couldn't possibly be a message for anyone in the Group – so best not to even mention it at all.

As the Group all gave their feedback, they then turned to me to ask what I had received. I answered, 'Nothing.'

'Come on,' Mayumi said, 'I know you received something.'

'Nothing worth mentioning.'

'Was that man back again?' asked Mairi.

'Yes, he was here again.'

'What did he show you this time? asked Gordon.

'Another fictional character,' I said, feeling dejected.

'Who was it this time? says Mairi.

'Would you believe – Sherlock Holmes,' I said with exasperation.

There was a stunned silence, as I think most of the Group were thinking along the same lines as me – that this was nonsense, until Mairi said, 'I think it's Arthur Conan Doyle.'

Everyone was looking rather puzzled as Mairi continued, 'He was a Doctor, he went to Edinburgh University and he wrote the Sherlock Holmes Stories; in fact he wrote a number of books – just not sure if he was knighted or not?'

As she looked around the room for an answer to her question, you could almost hear the pennies dropping as we all realised she could be right. But no-one knew if he was *Sir* Arthur Conan Doyle or not. The feeling of excitement and anticipation was almost palpable in the room as we considered the possibility that Arthur Conan Doyle was actually communicating with our Group. We all resolved to go home and investigate.

It is strange to look back upon this now. Back then I couldn't identify Arthur Conan Doyle if he was in a line-up. Now I recognise him immediately and at different stages of his life, but back then – I didn't know him from Adam – although, as we heard, he clearly thought I should.

The following week we all returned to the Group with renewed vigour and enthusiasm as everyone had searched the internet to find that it was true – he was *Sir* Arthur Conan Doyle. Mairi added to this by telling us that she had discovered that Arthur Conan Doyle had actually worked in Surgeon's Hall where he was Clerk to his Tutor, Joseph Bell, himself a Surgeon and President of The Royal College of Surgeons. 'Of course, Joseph Bell', she added, 'was also the inspiration for Sherlock Holmes.'

Wow. Could it be possible? Was Arthur Conan Doyle really communicating with me? My mind was racing. All the bits fitted. Each piece of information which had been given over several weeks had all been rejected when considered separately. Also, I was focused on someone in the Group recognising and accepting this information from a relative or someone they had known – and no-one could. But when applied to Arthur Conan Doyle, each piece of evidence was correct, and it was indeed for me.

The excitement in the Group was at fever pitch as they excitedly chatted about our new member and what he might bring to the Group – this was going to be good. I was a bit more circumspect. Was this *really* Arthur Conan Doyle? Or had I somehow just made him up? I considered the question. The information given had all been correct. It all fitted. I considered, did I somehow know this information? Did it come from the deepest recesses of my mind?

I pondered this question and began to analyse the answer. What did I know of Arthur Conan Doyle? Answer – not a lot. If someone had asked me who wrote Sherlock Holmes, I could have given them the correct answer and if I had thought about it, I could probably have told them that he was born in Edinburgh, but other than that my knowledge was sparse. I then considered my theory that Spirit can take many forms – had they created someone from a background that I would have a particularly interest in? He was a Doctor, an Author and most famous for Sherlock Holmes. Did any of that resonate with me? Not really. I did like watching detective programmes on TV, but really did not like Sherlock Holmes, had never read the books, and particularly disliked the films. I concluded that I really didn't know much about Arthur Conan Doyle – therefore it was unlikely I would have created him as a hero – or even a Guide.

To quote that famous detective: "..... when you have eliminated the impossible, whatever remains, however improbable, must be the truth.'

8 LET'S GET PHYSICAL

At the same time as we were receiving the information that we eventually deduced came from Arthur Conan Doyle we were also receiving further instruction on how we should sit, what the conditions should be like and the purpose of our Group.

This information would come to me usually whilst I was at home, thinking or preparing for our next meeting. And it was on one such occasion very early on in the Group's existence that I wondered, given that each member of the Group had a different discipline or interest, how would I satisfy their needs and desires. More generally I needed to maintain their interest in our meetings. I had already decided that, unlike in most Physical Groups where one person is deemed to be the Physical Medium and all other members of the Group sit for the benefit of that one person, we would all sit for one another and each of us would have a 'turn' at doing our thing – whatever that happened to be.

This was an easy decision for me to make because I didn't want to be a Physical Medium anyway. And, although Spirit had told me (and Mayumi) that it was going to be a Physical Group, I had also been told we could 'do it all', and I took that to mean that we should just sit for Spirit and see what emerged or what we were drawn to do each week. And almost immediately the answer to this question - a question that I wasn't even conscious of asking – came to me from Spirit: *'They weren't chosen for their mediumistic abilities – they were chosen for their ability as public speakers.'*

I thought this was extremely odd and I couldn't think why it should be. And again, came the answer to that unspoken question: *'We have chosen ordinary people whom everyone can relate to; for at some future stage you will be required to take this message out to the general public. Until that time, we will train you, so you can speak from experience - until that time this should be kept confidential.'* This was another new revelation for me. Quite apart from the surprise of us being a

Physical Group we were now going to be Public Speakers as well.

So, when I sat with the Group at our meeting I voiced nothing of what I had received. Instead I silently sent a thought to Spirit to ask for some form of confirmation that what I had received was correct. As the Group came back from sitting in silence, some reported that they saw themselves speaking on a stage, some at out-door festivals, others saw themselves speaking to group meetings and still others saw themselves standing on stage in a theatre-type environment. All seemed as confused as I had been and this seemed quite a disturbing thought to some in the Group who did not relish the prospect when they could see themselves standing on a platform speaking to hundreds of people. But all accepted that this was our purpose – eventually to communicate our message out to the wider world.

By the end of April other details from that earlier communication had been downloaded, so much so that my invocation now read something like this: 'Spirit have got us together, a chosen Group of like-minded individuals who have absolute trust in Spirit and each other. We have been chosen not for our mediumistic abilities (that was a pre-requisite) but because we are all capable of public speaking and at some future stage we will be called upon to do so. In the meantime we will be taught the various forms of Spirit communication, both going back to some of the old-fashioned methods of the Victorians and also bringing us up to date to show us that things have changed now and that Spirit too has evolved. The custom in the past of sitting in the dark behind screens and cabinets had permitted charges of fraudulent mediumship to be brought against even some of the top Mediums, but we would be different. Spirit would show us how to handle some of these different forms of Spirit intervention, but we would learn to do this in the open without all the old paraphernalia and in doing so the public would realise that these were genuine phenomena that were being produced and, ultimately, that there's another world out there to be taken account of. In doing so, we would be able to talk not only with knowledge but from our own experience.

Spirit tell us that it has been more than 150 years since the Fox Sisters[11] heard the rappings on the wall of their house in Hydesville, in 1848 in New York State, which brought Spiritualism to the attention of the masses – but little progress has been made during that time and today people are much less aware of the other world than they were then. Spirit tried to communicate using the basic intelligence of young girls in a log cabin just as they tried by using the brilliance of Swedenborg[12], but still the message hasn't got through – so now we are trying again, they say. We are using ordinary people that everyone can relate to and they (we) will be used to disseminate the message. But for now, we must keep it quiet, keep it confidential and Spirit will tell us when the time is right to communicate it to the wider world.'

This communication to the wider world was apparently to take an additional form too, when I was also told by Spirit that I should record our sessions as I would need the information later as I was to write a book about our experiences. Whilst I was very clear about what I had received, I felt sure that it would not be me who was to write the book, as there were others in the Group far more qualified and experienced than me to handle this task. I felt sure this responsibility would be sorted out when I was able to check it out more fully back in the Group – especially as a new member of the Group had joined us who just happened to work for The Times Newspaper on their Educational Supplement, Scotland.

During my years of preparation, as I saw them, I attended various classes for Mediumistic Development at a number of venues and at one such class my Tutor was Gill Muir. Gill was a very good Medium and a certified Spiritual Healer. She had developed her skills over the previous 20 years (whilst maintaining her day job) and more recently she had been invited to become a Tutor and to take evening classes. Although she was a good Tutor and was very well-liked by her students, this new role did not sit comfortably with her – something which I had been totally unaware of as I sat in her class. It was after one such occasion, that she asked if I fancied going to the pub for a glass of wine after the class.

Now I didn't know Gill that well, other than the relationship once a week between Tutor and Student, but I could tell that something was troubling her and so I happily agreed to go to the pub with her. Gill had rescued me from an earlier Tutor who had cast me aside and Gill had invited me into her class, so I felt I wanted to return the favour and help her in any way I could.

As we sat in the Rutland Bar at the end of Princes Street, sipping our white wine she confessed to me about her lack of confidence as a Tutor – something which I found hard to believe but which she was finding hard to bear. 'I just want to work for Spirit. I'm happy to help others and to see them progress', she said, 'but now that I'm a Tutor I'm missing out on my own spiritual work.'

As she talked, I was listening and feeling quite sorry for her but at the same time I was wondering why she had asked me to the pub. There were others in her class that she had a longer and stronger relationship with than me – I hardly knew her. And then it came. 'What I miss the most is not being able to sit for Spirit. Now that I'm a Tutor, I can't attend classes and groups any more. I wish I could find a group of nice people where we could just sit for Spirit, somewhere quietly, with no agenda – just sit - that would be great – but that's not going to happen is it?' As she was speaking I realised why I was there and why she had inadvertently chosen me. My body was also giving me the little tingle from Spirit that says 'pay attention – something going on here you need to take notice of' – and I recognised that. And that was how Gill was invited to join the Thursday Group. So now, we were six, and Gill with her journalistic skill seemed to me to be the obvious candidate for the task of writing our story.

When we started to sit together in our group of six we would form the chairs into a circle and sit in silence after the invocation and wait to see what we could sense. We had already received some of the Mental Mediumship that conveyed the presence of Arthur Conan Doyle and foretold of the purpose of the Group. So now we were waiting to see what he had in store for us and for this promised training.

As we sat in the quiet of that gloomy room on the topmost floor of the Theosophical Society it started. Firstly we just heard odd sounds in the room. This was usually explained away as creaks in an old building or the pipes expanding, or if we heard a knock on the floor others would just assume that someone in the Group had moved their feet or some such thing. This continued regularly over the early first weeks as Mayumi and I kept quiet about what we had been told about the Group being a Physical Group.

However, the volume of the noises increased until they couldn't be explained away. There were very loud bangs on the wall and they usually came from a position very high up on the wall where there were no pipes or other possible sources of sound. There would be bangs on the floor as if someone had jumped down on it from a great height and we could feel the vibration of this noise through our feet, on the floor. And strangest of all there would be loud snaps and cracks as if someone was cracking a whip in mid-air and this would be coupled with a sense of an electrical crackle of the sort you sometimes hear from high-voltage overhead cables.

This of course alerted other members of the Group to the fact that something out of the ordinary was happening here and it was Mairi who said, 'This is Physical Mediumship!' I still remember the looks of shocked disbelief on the faces of each member of the Group as the realisation struck home that the only possible explanation for what we were experiencing was Physical Mediumship.

Physical Mediumship was extremely rare then and still is today although there are a few young Mediums who profess to demonstrate it. However, there has recently been a very public exposure of one of those mediums as a fake and a fraud just like earlier times, so I didn't want our Group exposed to public criticism and ridicule before we had even begun. I also felt that if Spirit really wanted to do this it was likely to take some time to manifest itself as something more tangible. We would have to be patient and wait and watch. Suffice to say that we had a very excited and apprehensive Group – all waiting to see what was going to happen next.

During one of the following weeks, Mairi and Mayumi both came back from their meditation with the same vision – that the small table that we had initially moved out of the way, should be replaced back in the centre of our Circle as we sat. The following week we followed these insights and placed the table in the centre of our Circle. After the meditation Gill and I opened our eyes simultaneously as we looked at each other with a knowing stare – we needed to place our hands on the table, all of us, but just our fingertips - and as we did this the table sprang into life like a bucking bronco bouncing around the centre of our Circle so much so that it was difficult for all of us to keep our fingers on the table. As it continued bouncing around the Circle we had to stand up to keep up with it as it pushed through between the chairs and headed over towards the left-hand wall with various members of the Group either left behind or tripping over chairs trying to keep their hands upon its surface.

As it hit the wall it stopped momentarily. This allowed the excitement and nervous laughter of Group members to subside as they recomposed themselves around the table which was now positioned up against the wall. No sooner had all fingers been placed back on the table than it started rocking furiously back and forth, banging against the wall as it did so. The noise of this banging against the wall was loud and the ferocity with which it was hitting the wall made us feel sure that this rather old and rickety table belonging to our hosts was most likely to fall to pieces at any moment.

I had seen table-tilting[13] before and experienced it in earlier workshops; it is normally what is known as kinetic energy[14] but this was different; I had never seen a table so animated before, almost as if it had a life of its own. Jim suggested that perhaps it had got stuck against the wall and that perhaps we should place it back in the Circle and start again. We did this about three times and each time it would end up in the same position against the wall and begin the ferocious banging all over again. Somehow it seemed strangely purposeful in some way, but no-one knew quite what to make of it.

Other members of the Group started making suggestions: maybe the room wasn't big enough and that's why it kept hitting the wall; maybe the wall was in the way of the direction of travel and we should move the table to the next door room and see what happens; maybe we shouldn't use it at all as what was the point of all this anyway? And then Gordon Said, 'why don't we ask it?'

No sooner had the words left his lips than the table reacted like a rapid-fire machine gun rattling against the wall far faster than any of us could have mustered physically. 'There's your answer,' he said.

And so we realised that the table could be used as a means of communication with the Spirit World. Gordon, an experienced dowser, took charge of the situation and asked, 'Can you indicate your signal for 'Yes'? The table swung to give a loud but single bang on the wall. 'One knock for yes', said Gordon. 'Can you indicate your signal for 'No', he says. And as we all anticipated the 2 knocks – nothing happened.

'What happened there,' Mairi said.

Gordon repeated, 'Can you indicate your signal for 'No'. The table remained silent.

'Maybe we're not supposed to do this', Jim says as we all looked at each other rather puzzled.

Undaunted, Gordon says, 'Do we have permission to continue this session?'

To everyone's surprise the table swung into action again with another loud bang on the wall. Gordon explained to the Group, 'There's no point using energy unnecessarily – this seems to be one knock for yes and silence (no knock) for no.'

He now addressed the table and asked, 'Is this right?'

The table once again swung out from the wall and crashed back into it with another loud bang. 'I think we've got our answer.'

Buoyed that this new form of communication appeared to be working, Jim decided to ask for further clarification: 'Does the table need to be in this position to utilise the energy between this room and the one next door which is used for Buddhist Meditation?'

The table was silent as Gordon instructed Jim, 'You have to formulate your questions carefully.'

Gill took over: 'Is this wall important?' *Silence* = No.

Gill: 'Would any wall do?' *Yes*.

Gill: 'Is this the best wall because of the available space?' *Yes*

Gill: 'Are you ready to communicate with us?' *Yes*

Jim: 'Is it the same Spirit Team who are around us?' *Yes*

Jim: 'Do you approve of the Origami figures?' *Yes* (Mayumi had made paper origami figures and brought them to the Group as at a previous meeting an umbrella had suddenly 'fallen' and there had been a feeling within the Group that Spirit may make an attempt to move objects. She decided that paper figures would be the easiest to move).

Jim: 'Could you at some future stage do something to move these figures, or something else?' *Yes*.

Jim: 'Last week an umbrella appeared to move and fall. Was that of your volition?' *Yes*.

Jim: 'Was it easier to shift the large umbrella, albeit that it was on the other side of the room, than the small figures?' *Yes*

(Little did we know that weight was no obstacle to Spirit moving inanimate objects – but we had to be patient for a few more months before Jim was to get his wish).

Jim: 'We acknowledge that event and thank you.' The table knocks *'yes'* in response.

Jim: 'Would it be in order for us to move the table away from the wall so as not to disturb the people next door with the knocking?' *No*.

We were puzzled by this response – surely Spirit would not wish to disturb the Buddhists whom by this time must have arrived and were probably meditating next door?

Gill: 'Then would it be in order for us to check that we are not disturbing the people next door?' *Yes.*

Gill leaves the room to go next door and check on the people next door – only to find that there's no-one next door and the room is empty.

Jim joked and addressed the table, 'This does not mean that you can play a tune on the wall'. The table knocked on the wall excitedly, to everyone's amusement. As we noticed this further animation, Jim says, 'It's amazing that the table (Spirit) actually knew that there was no-one next door?'

The table knocks a *'Yes'*. 'It also seems to respond to human voice.' The table again rocks in response.

Jim: 'That being the case, maybe we should sing to the table – to raise the vibration.'

Mairi: 'You've got to be joking.'

Gill: 'I can't sing.'

Mayumi: 'No-ooooo'

Gordon: 'Well since it seems no-one can sing, doesn't look like this idea is going to work.'

This ended with us all laughing at the possibility and this seemed to once again animate the table as it appeared to respond to our laughter.

Jim: 'Let's get down to more serious business. Ann, do you want to ask a question?'

'Yes', I did want to ask a question as we appeared to be getting the correct answers from Spirit via the table and I was impressed by the fact that apparently they knew there was no-one in the next-door room while we didn't. (The Buddhists normally arrived an hour after us – so just as we were finishing our period of silence and beginning to feedback, they would arrive). I felt that more testing questions would be required to conclude that the Spirit Team were indeed using this method of communication. But, what would I ask? I wished I had been a bit more prepared for this. I needed to think of something that no-one else knew about. Then I remembered what I had been told about needing to record the session and about writing the book – no-one knew about this. I started my questioning by asking if what I had received from Spirit about the purpose of the Group was correct. The table knocked its confirmation but I noticed that the table actually started knocking its affirmation before I had finished voicing the question. This was interesting. I tried again, 'Am I correct in what I have received……' Again, I hadn't finished the question yet the table was already knocking its confirmation. I stopped, and said to the Group, 'what do you think the rest of this question is, as the table has already responded?'

Mayumi: 'Oh yes, so it has.'

Mairi: 'That was clever, wasn't it?'

Jim: 'Is this something new you have received, Ann?'

Ann: 'Yes'

Jim: 'Well how would we know what it is then?'

Ann: 'I know, I know. I was just trying to find a way to test that what we're getting is not being unwittingly influenced by any of us.'

Jim: 'Unwittingly – that's the right word, because none of us have a clue what you're going to say next Ann – but we're all waiting to hear.'

The Group laughed in response to Jim's exasperation.

Ann: 'Okay, well this isn't going to work out as a very good test, but I'll carry on anyway. 'Am I right in what I have received, that these sessions should be recorded?'

Gordon: 'Ah, that's a good idea.'

Mairi: 'Yes, why didn't we think of that?'

Once again the table had started knocking its response halfway through the question.

Jim: 'For posterity?'

Ann: 'No, it has another purpose.'

The Group all look at me in anticipation.

Ann: 'Am I correct in saying (the table is already knocking the wall in response) that these sessions are to be recorded (the table continues its affirmation) to enable someone in the Group, at some future stage, to write a book?'

As the table continues knocking, the other group members let out an 'ahhhh' in unison at this revelation, as I continued.

Ann: 'And, the person who is to write the book is Gill'.

I felt Gill would be the most obvious candidate to choose by those in the Group – including me. But the table fell silent.

Gordon: 'Well that answer is clearly, No'.

Ann: 'Sorry, my mistake, the person who is to write the book is Mairi.'

As the Librarian, she would be the next best guess of the candidates present, I thought. Once again, the table fell silent.

Gordon: 'Well, it's not me?'

If this was a question there was no response from the table.

Gordon: 'Is it Jim?' That was a reasonable guess, given he was the patriarch of the Group, but again the table remains silent.

Mayumi: 'It is you, Ann?' again, as soon as she had started speaking the table was rocking in response.

'Apparently so.'

Ann to Spirit: 'There are others in this Group with more experience and who would be better qualified to write a book than I; can I ask one of them to write the book?'

The table remains silent.

Ann: 'Can I get someone else to write the book on my behalf?'

Again the table remains motionless.

Ann: 'Do I have to write the book myself?'

Suddenly the table springs back into life again banging relentlessly against the wall, as I sigh in anticipation and say to the Group, 'this is really not my thing.'

And as they all laugh at my disappointment at being handed this task, the table continues to rock to their laughter.

Our first recorded session took place on 27th April, 2006. After each session the recording was transcribed by me and circulated by email to the Group so they could add any further comments or amendments.

So all that you read in this book - no matter how incredible it may seem to you – actually took place and was both recorded and documented. This book has been created from those transcripts; the recordings having been independently verified by the Editor. So what you read in this book is the record of actual happenings as they took place. *[Wherever the text is indented and in a different font, it is a verbatim record of actual events]*. Now I understand why I was instructed to record these events, unbelievable as they were - although I'm still not feeling confident about having to write this book.

And Spirit would keep their promise to Jim to 'do something or move something!' we just had to wait a little longer.

9 RECORDED TRANSCRIPTS

I regularly sat in silence at home for my own development. I would sit in my bedroom and allow my mind to quieten. As I dropped into an altered state (probably into theta brainwaves) I would become aware of Arthur. I would sense him by my side. As if, were I to open my eyes I would see him standing next to me – although I knew that he wasn't physically there. I began to know the 'feel' of him, the size of him – and he had quite a stature. The smell of him and occasionally I would get the whiff of tobacco – pipe tobacco. All of this I now found strangely comforting. I liked this man. He was somehow familiar, protective, supportive, guiding my journey.

My husband and I had converted the attic in our house into a large open-plan bedroom that also had a small sitting area with TV and my computer desk - where I would work into the wee small hours. When we did the attic conversion we had bought two of those armchairs that swivelled and were designed to support your posture – ideal for watching TV but even better for sitting in silence. In May 2006 as I sat there in my silent meditation after Arthur had made his presence known to me a distant memory came into my head. It was a little brass bell which my Grandmother used to have on her mantelpiece. When a vision such as this pops into your head, somehow you just know that it hasn't come from your own thoughts – someone else has put it there. I wondered if I were being directed to find a bell to take to the Group so that Spirit could use it to create sound. But that thought wasn't getting enough resonance from the other world so I ignored it on the basis that if it were important it would come back again. Now I was seeing a much clearer vision - of stones, those crystal/quartz stones that were so popular at that time and still are today. Mine looked like black-coloured stones. I wondered whether I was being directed to bring crystals into our séance room[15], perhaps to help boost the energy. But no, that didn't feel right, either. As I subconsciously asked what they were for, I saw them form into a circle of stones and was immediately aware that this signified our unity and the trust that existed in the Group.

I liked the sentiment and was very comforted by that thought; it felt as if it signalled that we were 'solid as a rock'. But I wondered whether this was merely symbolic or whether something more practical was required. Again, no sooner had that thought materialised than the circle of stones turned into a bracelet. It looked like those 'power bracelets' of crystal beads that were readily available in most holistic and alternative health shops. But along with the image came the message that we should all wear them as a symbol of our unity.

My feeling of comfort disappeared almost as quickly as it had come – I thought this was a rather trivial path for us to follow. I've never been the sort of person who needs designer labels, brand names or personal number plates – in fact I'm positively against them – and I think such things are needed by some people to impress others – to shout out 'look at me'. I'm perfectly comfortable in my own skin and have never had need nor desire of these accessories - and I was certainly not inclined to display my heart on my sleeve. I realised I was being challenged – with something I particularly did not want to do. Spirit was testing my trust.

This testing had already been established in another format too. Since realising that Arthur Conan Doyle was communicating, I had started to read his book, *The History of Spiritualism*[16]. The book documents how Spiritualism came to be and how various phenomena became recognised and adopted by Spiritualists and I began to realise that our experiences in the Group were following the flow of information contained in the book almost Chapter by Chapter. So, after the last session using the table as a means of communication, the Group asked me 'what happens next in the book?'

'After using knocks on the wall, Spirit goes on to use letters of the alphabet to communicate, so that they can move on from just 'yes/no' answers.'

'So, Ouija Board?' says Mairi.

The thought filled me with dread. I had already done enough Paranormal Investigations with my fellow investigators from the Scottish Society for Psychical Research to know that dabbling with the Ouija Board[17] seems to allow an opportunity for lower level entities to emerge. This had caused endless problems, usually with students or teenagers who thought this would be a bit of fun only to realise they had bitten off much more than they could chew by facilitating a haunting or at the very least allowing a dark energy to emerge. I was very wary of using the Ouija Board and my advice to anyone who would listen had always been not to touch it. Now we were being encouraged to use it – we were being tested. Perhaps that's why a couple of weeks before this I had also been given a vision of a 'circle of light' when I saw the Group sitting inside a circle of candles. I was made aware this was for protection. I thought this was unnecessary at the time but since it looked pretty and helped create a nice atmosphere we had gone along with it and got the candles. Now that the suggestion of an Ouija Board was being considered the reason for the circle of light was becoming very clear.

As we had continued to record our sessions over the previous weeks it became apparent that there was another advantage to doing this. For just as in the case of the information which eventually identified Arthur Conan Doyle, we were able to note how information was being fed through to us week by week and although initially most of the information would not make sense to us, when we reviewed our recordings from earlier sessions we were able to realise that a pattern of evidence was emerging. Again, almost as if to help establish the genuineness of this information, it would often come through various members of the Group and not just through one individual. The following excerpts from the transcripts[18] demonstrate this:

> THURSDAY GROUP – 4th May 2006 (Excerpt from Transcript)
> Ann became aware of a Male Spirit with her …. she felt that he was on a Penny-Farthing Bicycle and he was cycling through a park with a little dog running alongside. ….. He was well dressed in tailcoat, waistcoat and top hat and he kept impressing his face upon her as if she or the Group should recognise it.
> Jim asked Ann if he was involved in Psychical Research or had anything to do with the Theosophical Society. She said she didn't know.
> She then said he was taking her into a hospital, not because of any illness, just to show her around. Jim asked if he worked in the hospital. Ann says no. Jim asked what does he do there. Ann immediately answered that he was a scientist. She then began to struggle getting more information from the man.

I was aware that the Penny-Farthing was being shown simply to give me a time frame for this man – as well as his dress – top hat, tailcoat, etc, but I didn't know who he was.

By the following week, I had formed an idea of who he might be, but clearly I was wrong: -

> THURSDAY GROUP – 11th May 2006 (Excerpt from Transcript)
> *(Responses by Spirit are typed in italics, as are comments by the author).*
> The Group convene around the small square (yes/no) table to begin.
> Ann: 'Is the same Spirit Team present with us this week, as had been with us last week?' *Yes.*
> Ann: 'Is Sir Arthur Conan Doyle with us again tonight?' *Yes.*
> Ann: 'Last week when we were sitting in Circle, I was aware of a spirit presence with me……'
> *At this point the table began moving excitedly, as if it knew the questions that was about to be asked. Everyone noted this and was amused by the*

table's movements.
Ann: 'Was that person, Sir William Crookes?'
The table suddenly fell silent, to everyone's surprise – this was not the answer expected.
Gill then became aware of another communicator:
Gill: 'I'm aware of another person who is with you, and would he be of a journalistic background?' *Yes.*
Gill: 'Was he connected with the Spiritualist Movement?' *Yes.*
Again the table became excited as if those on the other side were gaining the recognition that they desired.
Gill to the Group: 'At this point I just want to ask the others in the Group if they know who I'm referring to?'
Ann to Gill: 'Is it Barbanell?'
Gill to Spirit: 'Is this Maurice Barbanell?' *Yes.*
Ann: 'The person who was with me last week was a Scientist?' *Yes*
Ann: 'And, was this Sir William Crookes?' *No.*
Mayumi asks between ourselves if this person could be Sir Oliver Lodge.
Ann: 'Is this Sir Oliver Lodge?' *No.*
Ann: 'Can we establish how many are in your team? Will you tell us that?' *No.*
Gordon: 'Is it true, just like this side, that the numbers present vary in number?' *Yes.*
Gill: 'Is there a well-known Medium working with you on the other side?' *Yes.*
Gill: 'Would this well-known Medium be one who I personally would have known?' *Yes.*
The table became very responsive again to Gill's questions.

Gill had clearly tuned in to the person communicating and felt she knew who he was.

Gill: 'Were you with me at Stansted[19]?' *Yes.*
Gill: 'You're in the Library, aren't you?' *Yes.*
Table again becomes excited as Gill says she doesn't want to say the name; she wants others in the Group to tune-in. Table knocks in excited anticipation.
Gill: 'If I remember rightly, you never made it very easy for those Mediums you were training?' *Yes.*
Gill: 'So, why make it easy now?' *Yes.*
Gill: 'Would you be able to spell it out for us on the other table? Is that what we're looking for?' *Yes.*
Gill: 'It may be appropriate for us to move around the other table – is that what you're trying to get us to do?' *Yes.* 'Yes.' *(Table knocks twice repeatedly, in confirmation).*
At this point the Group moved away from the small wooden table and reconvened around the circular table with the brass top. They had

earlier placed the letters around the edge of the table and the upturned glass in the centre.

This was our first attempt at using the Ouija Board. Although I was very wary about using it I also wanted to test the information that would come from it. In order to rule out human intervention the information needed to be intelligent and better still be information that was unknown to those with their fingers on the glass.

> Gill: 'Can you carry on friend; we've got into position?'
> *The upturned glass moves around the table top in a circular movement. Then spelt out – Gordon*
> Gill: 'Can you spell out the letters of your surname?' *H,I,G,G,I,N,S, ...*
> Gill: 'Have you got tired spelling out your name, because you know we know who you are? Is it Gordon? Gordon Higginson? That well-known Medium and President of the SNU?' *Yes.*
> Ann: 'Can we ask who else is here tonight?' *Yes.*
> Ann: 'Could the next person spell out their name?' *Yes.*
> Gill: 'Thank you. Gill verbalises the table's movements. That's an *A,R,T,H,U,R*.'
> Gill: 'Yes, continue.' *D,O,Y,L,E.*
> Ann: 'Are you Sir Arthur Conan Doyle?' *Yes.*

Up until this point, although the information coming through was accurate, it was already known to all those present. Therefore any critical Psychical Investigator could not rule out human intervention – yet.

> Ann: 'Yes, thank you. Can we have the next person, please?' *Yes.*
> Ann: 'Would you care to spell out your name?' *Yes. G,I,I,L*
> Gill: 'I'm sorry, Friend, we don't understand what that is. Can you be more precise and do it again, please?' *G,I,I,*
> Gill: 'Friend, this is just not making sense.'
> Gordon: 'Are these initials?' *No.*
> Ann: 'Gill?'
> Gill: 'Is your name Gill?' *No.*
> Ann: 'Okay, carry on spelling then, we've got G,I,I,L, what's next?' *F*
> Gill: 'Are you referring to me, at all?' *No.*
> Gill: 'That's fine, are you referring to someone from a different country?' *Yes.*
> Ann: 'Is that the end of the name? Have you spelt it all out?' *No.*
> Ann: 'Okay, so we've got G,I,I,L,F, what's next?' *E,A, ...*
> Gill: 'The country you come from, can we establish that, please.' *Yes.*
> Gill: 'Would you come from a Northern Hemisphere Country?' *No*
> Gill: 'Germany?' *No*
> Gill: 'Would you come from a Scandinavian Country?' *No*

Gill: 'Russia?' *No*
Gordon: 'Can you spell the name of the Country, best you can, so we can understand it?' *B, H, A, H, I, A.*
Ann: 'Is it Bahia?' *Yes.*
Gill: 'Is that from one of the Eastern, Indonesian Countries?' *No.*
Gordon: 'Would it be what we used to refer to as an Eastern Block Country?' *No.*
Gill: 'Is it a warm climate, Friend?' *Yes.*
Gill: 'Could it be Mexico?' *Indecisive.*

This comment of 'indecisive' was usually appended where the glass would move very slowly towards its answer. This felt as if the communicator was considering the answer, almost as if to say, 'nearly' or, 'you're not quite right, but almost'. Gordon's comment below identifies this slow movement. We came to realise when we saw this movement that we were on the right tracks.

Gordon: 'That was very slow, that didn't seem to be so definite. Could it be an Island?' *Indecisive.*
Gordon: 'Peninsula?' *Yes.*
Ann: 'Is the Peninsula off California?' *Yes.*
Ann: 'So you're American?'
Ann: 'Spanish?'
Ann: 'Indian?' *Yes.*
Ann: 'So we've got from you G,I,I,L,F, - Is that your name?'
Gordon: 'What about Geelf – as a different pronunciation?'
Ann: 'Are there more letters than that?' *Yes.*
Ann: 'Okay, give us the rest?' *E,A,T,H,E,R.*
Ann: 'Giilfeather (pronounced Geelfeather)?' *Yes.*
Ann: 'Thank you Giilfeather, we are happy to have you with us.' *Yes.*

I was happy with this. Here apparently was a new communicator who was not known to anyone. He gave us a name which initially everyone struggled with; therefore it was unlikely that any of us made it up. He gave us a place name – was there a place called Bahia? Was it a peninsula? And, was it off the coast of California? I had got California psychically as I tuned into the communicator, but now we'd have to go and find out if such a place existed. Meantime what else could we glean from this new method of communication: -

Ann: 'We got an earlier indication via the table that there was a stone that was important to the Group…It looked like a black stone.' *Yes.*
Ann: 'And it was to be used in a bracelet of some type? Is that correct?' *Yes.*
Ann: 'I was tasked with getting theses stones and the bracelets for this Group. Was that correct?' *Yes.*

Ann: 'So, the message via the table, was, that I'd recognise the stone when I saw it. Is that correct?' *Yes.*

After getting my early vision of these stones whilst sitting at home I had checked out my vision via the table at the next Group meeting. I had asked if my vision was correct and if we were to get these awful bracelets - not only that but, as if to rub salt into the wound, I was told it was me who was to go and get them. I was sure this was Spirit just having another go at me – not only was I to wear them but now I was the one who actually had to go and buy the darned things. This testing was pushing my buttons. However, when asking these questions via the table, I would test them (Spirit) by firstly asking if Mayumi was to be the one who should get the bracelets. When I got a 'no' to that question, I would substitute the names of Mairi, Gordon and Gill - all were much more knowledgeable about crystals than I so it was logical that one of them should be tasked with getting the stones. This was my test of the table responses – to see if human intervention, human logic would kick-in. But no, no-one was influencing the movements of the glass.

(When doing this, I would always remove my finger from the glass so as not to influence the result myself and since the others did not know what I was going to ask this was a further test that what I was receiving psychically was correct or at least being confirmed via the table).

Since I genuinely had no knowledge of the stones I was being shown in my vision I asked how I was to recognize them and I was told I would recognize them when I saw them. Mayumi had very helpfully brought in a book of crystals with pictures and descriptions of each one – a very comprehensive directory - but I couldn't find anything there that resembled what I had seen in my head. Undaunted Mayumi had taken me to visit a number of specialist crystal shops where she felt sure I would be able to identify a stone and recognize it as being the same as the one in my vision. We had set off to do this on the day of the meeting in the hope that we could buy the stones and bring them with us to the meeting that evening. On exiting the third such shop having failed to identify the correct stone after viewing their entire collection we started to walk away dejectedly. But something made me turn and look back at the shop we had just left. There in the plate-glass window was one of those large globes of the world, turning continuously on its axis driven by some sort of electric motor. Its surface was made entirely of crystal stones – each country inlaid in a different stone in a different colour. I walked back towards the shop to have a closer look at it and as it turned, there, I saw my stone. 'There it is, Mayumi – that's the stone I saw in my head'. We rushed back into the shop. 'What's that stone called', I asked the shop assistant – she didn't know. She went to summon more help. The Manager told us he thought it was called Blue Goldstone, but it may also have another name, he wasn't sure because it wasn't a stone he kept

— nor, it seemed did any of the other specialist shops we had visited. This was the extent of the information we had gleaned before going directly to our meeting together.

>Gordon: 'Can I ask, was it a collective thing so that *we* would recognise the stone, rather than an individual?' *No.*
>Gill: 'Friend, can I ask you: on my holiday last week, were the stones that I came into contact with on the beach, for this Group?' *No.*
>Gordon: 'Is the depth of black important in the stone? Is the stone very black?' *No.*
>Ann: 'Is it a black sparkly stone – the one you impressed upon me?' *No.*
>Ann (realizing her mistake): 'No, of course not, because when I saw it today in the shop I realised it was actually blue. Its dark blue isn't it?' *Yes.*
>Ann to the Group: 'I just realised what I was saying there, I was talking about black stones, because it looked black when I saw it in my head, but it's actually blue sparkly. The shop tells us that it's called Blue Goldstone, but it may have another name, is that correct?'
>Gordon commentating: 'It's moving back and forward again.'
>Ann to the Group: 'There's something not quite right.'
>Gordon: 'Is it an Obsidian-type stone?' *No.*
>Ann to Group: 'So, we know it's a dark blue sparkly stone...'
>Gill to Ann: 'No, you didn't say sparkly, you just said dark blue?'
>Ann to Gill: 'You're right.'
>Ann: 'Is it a dark blue sparkly stone?' *Yes.*
>Gordon: 'Is it a dull stone.' *No.*
>Gill: 'Is it a stone that is specifically geared towards protection?' *No.*
>Mayumi: 'Is this the Falcon's Eye, which is Blue Tiger's Eye?' *No.*
>Ann: 'Does it matter what stone it is?' *Yes.*
>Ann to the Group: 'That's what we got the last time, and remember I was to go and get it and was told I would recognise it when I saw it.'
>Gill: 'Is it of a symbolic nature that we have a circle of stones?' *Yes.*
>Gill: 'As the circle from Spirit working with the circle of us?' *Yes.*
>Ann: 'Well that's good actually – at least we know.'
>Gordon: 'Can we again just verify that Ann believes that it would be totally up to Ann just to go and select a stone which she would be drawn to?' *Yes*
>Ann: 'And let's just clarify again, is it to be a bracelet?' *Yes.*
>Ann: 'Okay I will go and do that; I will buy bracelets in the appropriate stone.'
>Ann: 'The important point is that they signify our unity as a Group?' *Yes.*
>Ann: 'And our unity with you in the spirit world?' *Yes.*

There it was again, that confirmation that it was me who was to go and get the blessed bracelets in this stone which I had seen in my head, which I would recognise when I saw it – possibly the Blue Goldstone as it had been called by the shop manager that day, although he wasn't at all sure – nor were we.

You will note that there were significant challenges to this instruction from other members of the team – particularly those who would know the quality of each of the stones as they viewed them. But on each occasion the table responded by rejecting the suggestions of the various types of stones forwarded by my colleagues and confirming that, unfortunately, it was me who had to go and get them.

Now that we had a form of communication that went beyond the yes/no of the other table, Gill suggested we try to get more information on what was to happen next:

> Ann: 'Now, from last week, we were very impressed to realise we had such eminent individuals with us from the Spirit side as, Sir Arthur Conan Doyle and others. And, we asked last week... our intuition told us that you had got together to teach us the various steps of spirit development. Is that correct?' *Yes.* (The glass is moving excitedly.)
> Gill: 'That's definitely a yes.'
> Ann: 'And you were going to take us back to the beginning and allow us to experience each step of spiritual development. Is that correct.' *Yes.*
> Ann: 'So in that development our Group started by sitting in meditation and then we got some clairvoyance and then we built up the power one week with the 'circle of light' – was that your instruction?' *Yes.*
> Ann: 'And after building up the power we were drawn to using the (yes/no) table. Was that the next step?' *Yes.*
> Ann: 'Now we've moved on from the table – last week you instructed us to use this table using letters – is that correct?' *Yes.*
> Ann: 'And you asked us to do this specifically so you could communicate more effectively with us?' *Yes.*
> Ann: 'Now, back to Gill's questions. So, we've established where we've come from up to date, so we have the table and we have the letters so we're expectantly waiting to hear your next instruction.'
> Gill: 'Can you tell us what our next step can be, Friend.' *Yes.*
> Gill: 'Can you spell it out for us, please?'

You could feel the anticipation in the room as everyone waited to hear what was going to happen next. The anticipation grew as we anxiously waited for the glass to spell out the answer:

> Gill: 'If you'd like to begin? If you're ready.'
> *There's a slight delay, then the glass circles round in wide circles and the ceiling light starts flashing at the same time.*
> Gill: 'Okay, Friend. Will we get physical phenomenon?' *Yes.*
> Gill: 'How do we achieve this?' *D,E,D,I,C,A,T,I,O,N.*

I smiled at this answer that cleverly deflated our heightened sense of anticipation in hoping that we were about to be told what to do to achieve Physical Phenomena – clearly, it wasn't going to be as easy as that.

> Ann: 'I get the impression that rather than telling us, you're asking us to use our own learning and intuition for the next step?'
> *No response.*
> Ann: 'So are you are going to tell us then?' *No.*
> Gordon: 'You are going to assist us?' *Yes.*
> Gill: Should we sit in the quiet for longer? *No.*
> Gordon: 'Is what we do at the beginning to build the power, just what we should be doing?' *Yes.*
> Gill: 'Would you prefer us to use music?' *No.*
> Gill: 'Am I correct in thinking that this would detract from the simplicity of the power?' *Yes.*
> Gill: 'Would you like particular things to be placed within the room that you could perhaps use to communicate with us? By things I mean, perhaps a bell that you could perhaps ring? Or anything else?' *No.*

I was intrigued by Gill's statements and wondered if she too had received a vision of a bell in her personal meditation at home as I had done. And she was voicing the same thought I had had that Spirit might use it to make a sound in the room. Either way, we were both wrong as the answer was still 'no'.

> Gill: 'You will make your own? Is that correct? You will use whatever is available to you?' *Yes.*
> Gill to Ann: 'Do you have anything else to say?'
> Ann: 'I feel you want us to experience each step of development and that we will use this table for a few weeks of our development, is that correct?' *Yes.*
> Ann: '…and **then** we'll move on?' *Yes.*
> Ann: 'Okay, thank you. We look forward to next week and we will set up this table again, as instructed. Will you be with us again, this same Spirit Group, next week?' *Yes.*
> Ann: 'Thank you. Now we'd just like to thank you all for being with us tonight, it's been a very exciting evening, we're delighted with the progress and we're really looking forward to working with you again next week. Thank you so much for being with us.'
> *The glass circles the table widely and noisily.*
> Gordon: 'The table has been circled several times by the glass, quickly and noisily whilst Ann was speaking and it has now come to a halt.'
> Gill: 'It's such a noisy table.'
> Gill: 'Goodnight my Friends, and thank you again for being with us.'

Discussions within the Group:
Ann to the Group: 'Does anyone want to say anything whilst the tape's still running?'
Gill: 'Maurice Barbanell was an investigative journalist, who was sent out to a séance to investigate and he was so impressed by what he saw that he continued to investigate and ended up setting up the Psychic News (newspaper) and became involved in a Psychic Group involving a very strong group of Mediums and his wife Silvia was also involved in Spiritualism and would conduct séances at secret locations.'
Ann: 'For the benefit of the tape, the light is flashing on and off whilst Gill is speaking.'
Gill: 'And, Gordon Higginson was a very well-known Medium within the Spiritualists National Union. His mother Fanny was a Medium and was a very hard disciplinarian in Gordon's development. Gordon attended a meeting and was told by the Medium that his mother was communicating from the Spirit World to him. He said this was not correct as his mother was still alive, but when he got home his mother had died. Giilfeather, is someone we will have to investigate. Sir Arthur Conan Doyle is the author of Sherlock Holmes, but his involvement with Spiritualism was not commonly known at that time but his diaries revealed his deep involvement with the movement. From my point of view, I felt there were another two people within the Group that have yet to reveal themselves.'
Ann: 'Yes, I feel that too. And the light flashes again.'
Ann: 'And, I have to find out who the Scientist is.'
Gill: 'I think there are as many there, as there are here. And, the lights flash again.'
Ann: 'I feel we've had another step forward in our experiences. We were told we were going to experience things right from the very beginning. So, we've had the table-tipping, then the table banging against the wall, now we've moved on to this table with the lettering, which was the next step in the original Spiritual Development. It seems we will be experiencing this for the next few weeks then we'll be told what the next stage will be. Anyone else got any comments?'
Gordon: 'It's been very revealing and a worthwhile experience this evening, for which we're very grateful. And it has been quite a clear way, certainly, to communicate with us when compared with the type of communications we have had previously.'
Gill: 'Has anyone noticed that the temperature had just dropped significantly.'
Ann: 'Yes, let's bring this to a close.'
Ann closed in prayer.

It was several weeks later that Mairi advised the Group that she had investigated the name Bahia that Giilfeather had informed of. 'It's part of

Mexico', she said, 'do you remember when we got that slow movement of the glass, when someone suggested Mexico? Well, it is part of Mexico and it is a peninsula, just as we were told, and, would you believe, it's called the Baja California Peninsula (spelt baja but pronounced baha – not actually bahia - in Spanish), so California is correct too, and the indigenous people there were the Baja Indians - everything we were told was correct.'

We were yet to find out who the Scientist was and where we were to find those elusive stones in the bracelets.

10 THIS PLACE AINT BIG ENOUGH FOR THE BOTH OF US

At the following meeting, on 18th May, 2006, my initial anxiety about using the Ouija Board was given a worrying boost.

That session began by me telling the Group that I had made a mistake. When they had asked me the previous week what came next in the book I was reading, Arthur Conan Doyle's History of Spiritualism, I had said that Spirit was using letters to spell out words and names for communication. This was correct, but in fact it wasn't in the normal Ouija-Board fashion that Mairi had assumed - it was by calling out the letters of the alphabet and waiting until a 'knock' of response was heard by Spirit to indicate which letter was being chosen.

When I had gone back to look at the book again after the previous week's session I realised my mistake – this form of calling out letters was actually referred to in the book as being 'laborious', so our method had actually been much more efficient – and I was aware that it was indeed intended that we use the Ouija Board method, as Spirit had confirmed that via the table, and I was also aware that it was being used as a test of our trust to see if we would follow these instructions and use the Board even although we were wary of doing so.

'So what did come next?' says Mairi.
'Would you believe – North American Indians!'
'No – I don't believe it', says Gill.
'Yes – believe it – and we already got that last week with Giilfeather without even knowing it'.
'It's just as well there's someone more intelligent than us up there directing operations', says Jim and we all laughed in agreement.

Jim welcomed everyone to the Group and asked that they all go into a silent meditative state. Afterwards Jim outlined his thanks to Ann on behalf of the Group for the work she was undertaking in transcribing the tape – 'a very difficult job, but one that is appreciated by us, and I'm sure also, by our friends in the Spirit World.'

Ann: 'Last week we started with an invocation, and Gordon did it. I wonder if maybe we should do that again?'

Gordon: 'We are gathered here as a Group to welcome Spirit this evening. We have been gathered for a few weeks now, and have made good progress we feel. We have made a particularly good connection with the Spirit Group on the other side. And, Spirit has said that they would contact us again in this way and that they would come back this week and work directly with us, which is very much appreciated. And just to clarify that we were asked to move to the table with the letters, (away from the table on the wall), which we have done, and now we are ready to proceed. And, would like to think that you will come forward and we will have a very good communion as we have had in the past. We are a bit uncertain as to how to proceed, at this stage, but based on what was said last time, I'm getting an idea that we ought to just place our fingers on the glass.'

Ann: 'Could I also add, that we also call on our Spirit Friends who are with us to keep us safe and protected and grounded as we carry out this exercise. We are trusting in your safe-keeping because none of us were keen to use these letters in this way, but we have trusted in your instruction and have done as you asked, and we ask and trust you now to keep us safe and protected in your bright white light whilst we carry out this exercise and we look forward to hearing your further instruction and guidance tonight.'

All present placed one finger on top of the glass.

Ann: 'Good Evening Friends, are you with us tonight? Can you just indicate by moving the glass that you are present and with us again this evening?'

The glass is still for a long while and then very slowly begins to move, ever so slightly.

Ann: 'Thank you. Thank you for confirming that you are here with us. Can we just establish that we have the same Spirit Team with us this week as we had last week?'

The glass is painfully slow and edges towards 'yes'.

Ann: 'We're slow this week, aren't we?'

Gordon commentating: 'The glass circled around the table first before stopping at 'yes'.'

Ann to the Group: 'Does anyone detect that there's something different from last week? The glass is slower and the energy is heavier?'

Jim: 'It may be because our make up is different tonight. We've got one more male in our party.' (Jim was absent last week).

Ann: 'We detect that the energy from Spirit is different this week. The question from Jim is, is this because there's a change in our group

members this week?' *No.*
Ann: 'Could that be because there is a change in your (Spirit) Group members this week? Is there a change in your group members this week?'
The glass moves very slowly again, but the answer is unclear.
Ann: 'Can you confirm that that is a 'no'?'
The glass moves towards 'yes' but stays there and does not return to the centre of the table, as usual.
Jim: 'Could you go back to the centre of the table, and we'll ask that questions again?'
The glass does not move.
Ann: 'I'm going to lift this glass and put it back into the centre of the table, and replace our fingers so we can get a clearer indication of what you're saying.'
The glass remained stationery and then slowly edged towards, 'no'.
Gill: 'Thank you for that. Are our energies low this evening?'
The glass remained in its previous position over 'no', and did not move further.
Gill: 'Now you're going to have to move away from there and move into the centre of the circle and then move back again. You'll have to show us what you mean.'
Ann: 'Each time you give us a 'yes' or a 'no' would you please return to the centre of the table, please?'
The glass moves slightly, then moves to 'yes'.
Gill: 'Yes, I know, you have to build on it, my Friend, once you've started you have to keep the energy going, you have to keep the momentum going. Okay?' *Yes.*
Ann: 'That's a bit better.'
Gordon commentating: 'The glass now is moving between 'yes' and 'no'.'
Gill: 'So, can you now, go back to the middle of the table, please?'
The glass moves to the centre.
Jim: 'Should we keep the tape on throughout our sitting from the word 'go' including our periods of silence?'
The movement of the glass is slow and nondescript.
Jim: 'We had a discussion before we started this evening. It's very helpful to have a 'yes' and a 'no'. Do you require a period of time for the group on your side to give us an answer, in other words a period of silence, perhaps before you answer?' *No.*
Ann: 'Are you just taking time to build up the energy on your side this evening?'
The glass spells T, D, Q,
Gill: 'Too damned quick. Is that too damned quick?'
The glass continues: B, P, A, O, Q,
Gill: 'Continue Friend, we are with you.'
The Group jokes that Gill must be dyslexic!

The glass continues: B, Q,
Ann: 'B, Q, are you saying Be Quiet?'
Jim: 'Could we go back to the beginning of this evening, Friends. Did we not....'
Ann: 'There's something not right. Can you tell us who's with us? Can you spell out your name? Tell us who's with us. Spell out your name for us?' *O, A, Q, D, P,*
Gordon: 'It's going back and forward almost directly opposite each time.'
Ann: 'I don't like this, there's something not right.'

My fear of using the Ouija Board was rising – I knew what could happen, I had experienced the aftermath of unskilled tampering with the Ouija Board before and at best, it was not nice, at worst, it was downright dangerous.

Gill: 'Okay Friend, we're not understanding your meaning, and what we're asking for this evening, as we do always, we ask that we have the highest and best and if we are going to communicate better, then we need you to help us. So, we ask for those who are in the higher realms to work with us this evening and we ask for them to come forward, please?'
Gill: 'Are you there?'
Glass moves slowly to N,A,O,B,O,B.....
Ann: 'No, No. Hold on, let's stop that's not right. Let's sit again.'
(Group sit in silence).
Ann: 'Dear God, Great Spirit we call on you now to be with us and to come again and protect our small gathering here. Keep our small Group safe and protected and grounded in your bright, white light as we open up our senses to the highest and the good and those of positive intention and more specifically to those in our Spirit Group who have been working with us to guide our learning and our development to come forward and be with us again tonight. If this be your purpose, then please let it be.
And we ask you dear God to keep us safe and protected from those in the lower realms who we do not want to communicate with this evening. We are gathered here at your request – at the request of Spirit and we were called by those in the higher realms to get together as a group to sit with you for the development of this Group and we have done so. We have shown our commitment and we are calling on you now to come forward and be with us again this evening. Please let it be.'
Ann to the Group: 'Can we just sit for a minute to build up the power again?'
Gordon again leads the Group in building up the power.
Ann: 'Do we have the original Spirit Team who were with us last week, here again tonight, are you there?'
Gill: 'Friends, do you require one communicator this evening?'
Gill: 'Do you wish us to communicate through the table?'

No movement from the glass.
Jim: 'I think we take charge of the situation at the moment and we go back to the other table.'
Ann: 'It doesn't feel right. It's completely different from last week.'
Gordon: 'It's not right tonight, it's very, very different.'
Jim: 'It's maybe our changes. I'm here this week and Mayumi's missing?'
Ann: 'No, I don't think so, it's not us.'
The Group moves from the round table with the brass top to the original square, wooden table which is still placed against the wall.
Gordon wonders about possibly space-clearing, but the Group decides against that, since the room is used by others in our absence.
Gordon: 'Is there something about the use of the brass table that is wrong?'
Ann: 'By using the brass table tonight have we allowed others in to influence the Circle?'
Jim: 'Have we influenced the circle adversely?'
Ann: 'So, just to confirm, we have **not** opened up to any malevolent spirits? *Yes.*
Ann: 'So, we have **not** done that?' *Yes.*
At last we get some movement from the table.
Ann: 'Okay, good, good. We are a bit confused here, as we have been following your instructions, you, and the rest of the Spirit Team and we were asked to move on from this (wooden) table to the brass table using the letters to communicate because you told us that would be more effective. Is that correct?' *Yes.*
Ann: 'So, we've moved back to this table(yes/no) tonight, was that the correct move?' *Yes.*
Ann: 'Was that because there was some problem in using the brass table tonight?' *Yes.*
Ann: 'Was the problem on our side? Did we create the problem?' *No.*
Ann: 'Was the problem on your side? Was there a problem on the Spirit side?' *No.*
Gordon: 'Was there a problem with the equipment?' *No.*
Ann: 'No, there's something not right.'
The Group struggle to think of what else might have caused the problem.
Jim addressing Gordon Higginson (in Spirit): 'Do you approve, Gordon, of us recording this event?' *Yes.*
Jim: 'So, can we establish what the problem is?'
Ann: 'Has the room been rectified now? Is it okay now? Have you sorted the problem with the room now?' *No.*
Gill: 'Right now, are you trying to get across to us what the problem is?' *Yes.*
Gill: 'Is it the situation of the room?' *No.*
Gordon: 'Should we clear the space and make it sacred space?'
Ann: 'Has something happened in this room between us being here last

week and us coming back this week, that you're not happy with that has affected the energy?'
Gordon: 'Is it a lack of energy in the room?'
Mairi: 'Is it because of influences outside of this room?'
Gill: 'Is it the noise outside? We're aware that we don't always have quiet?'
Jim: 'Well we were aware this evening that there was another meeting.........'
The table begins moving.
Jim: 'Can I just finish my question, I'm not sure what you're responding to. Are you responding to Gill's last questions?' *No.*
Jim: 'Are you unhappy that there's another meeting, the nature of which we can only surmise, is occurring in this building at the same time?' *Yes.*
Jim: 'Thank you. Is that because the other meeting, and it's no concern of ours, but you are concerned when you see particular groups wearing particular apparel?' *Yes.*

Jim, our elder statesman, had hit the nail on the head. He had discovered the problem.

Gordon commentating: 'The energy is building now.'
Jim to Gordon Higginson: 'I'm sure, from my understanding of you, that you were never in favour of Robes of Office?' *Yes.*
Ann: 'But they are nothing to do with us and they are not in this room, so hopefully we can continue unaffected by them?' *No.*
Gill: 'Are you saying that the energies that emanate from others is making it difficult for you to get a clear link?' *Yes.*
Ann: 'Do we need to change our meeting place altogether, would that help?' *Yes.*

I'm not sure now, why I leapt to this suggestion – perhaps I was picking it up psychically but here, for the first time came the suggestions that we should move. This would become a recurring theme in the Group from this moment on over the next five years before we finally found our place.

Ann: 'So it would please you if we found a place that was specifically for our own use and not influenced by others?' *The table sways.*
Ann: 'I'm getting a shoogle.'
Jim: 'Could I be more specific. It seems clear to me that the energies are not mixing well. On previous occasions when there have been Buddhists working with us, that has never had any adverse effect, is that correct?' *Yes.*
Gill to Jim: 'But, how do you mean, working with us. They weren't working with us.'
Jim: 'Well they had the same relationship with us as the other group tonight, (they were in the room next door)'. 'But you are unhappy with the

group tonight but you weren't on previous occasions?' *Yes.*
Jim: 'So just to be clear, you want us to meet in a place where spiritual philosophy is pre-eminent?'
Gill: 'Would you prefer a Home Circle?'
Gordon: 'Would it be appropriate to move to a different room in this building?'
Jim: 'Should we understand more about their philosophy?'
Ann: 'Do you want us to find a space that is solely for the purpose of communicating with you?' *Yes.*
Gill: 'Has this got to be a place solely used for spiritual purposes?'
Jim: 'Would you be happier if we met in somewhere like the college?'
There was no response to any of those questions.
Ann: 'Well I get the impression.... Am I right in thinking that you want us to find neutral ground? Neutral ground which may be used for other purposes e.g. other domestic purposes or something else, but when we meet once a week it will be solely for our purpose and will not be used for any other, out with this Group, is that correct?' *Yes.*
Ann: 'So we need to find a space, it doesn't necessarily need to be.........'
The table begins rocking back and forth again excitedly.
Gill: 'Is it in a house?'
Gill: 'Is it in a place of tranquility?'
Gordon: 'Sanctity?' *Yes.*
Ann: 'Is it us who will create the sanctity?' *Yes.*
Ann to the Group: 'You see, I don't think it needs to be in a particular location, I think it needs to be special to us.'
Gill: 'Is it a place of learning?'
Jim: 'Do we have to go back to the drawing board on this one, Gordon? Are you aware, that there is a place, and you know Edinburgh well as Mary (Duffy),[20] does. Is there a place that we could find?' *Yes.*
Gill: 'Is it in Edinburgh? Is the place we could find in Edinburgh? *Yes*
Jim: 'Albany Street Church. Would that be an appropriate place to meet?'
Jim: 'Because you and Mary have worked there and found it conducive to this type of thing?'
Jim: 'But that's only one place in Edinburgh, there may be others.'
Ann commentating: 'That's not very definitive, is it?'
Gordon: 'Is the place itself, really important, like the name of a specific place? Have you somewhere in mind specifically?'
Gordon: 'So the place isn't really important as long as it meets criteria?' *Yes.*
Ann: 'So, in the meantime do we continue meeting here?' *Yes.*
Ann: 'Okay so we will continue meeting here and at the same time we will each look out for an alternative venue where we could meet in the future which would be more conducive to this, is that correct?' *Yes.*
Ann: 'Could it be that the external group along the corridor, who have influenced us tonight, will only affect us tonight and other nights may be okay?' *Yes.*

Jim to the Group; 'Well that's a 'yes', but I'd be interested to know what that was that affected us tonight.'
Ann: 'Have the negative influences that have affected this Group tonight been caused by an interaction between one of us and one of those along the corridor before coming in to this Group tonight?
The table gives a much more decisive, 'yes'.
Ann to the Group: 'Because I met who I think you were referring to, in the hat and robes, and she was complaining about a smell in the room along the corridor. (Now addressing Spirit), is that what's causing the problem?' *Yes.*
Ann to the Group: 'Before our Group began, I was coming up the stairs and I met the woman in the long robes and the hat and she just started saying to me that the room they had rented smelled and had been left in a mess and she was asking me to look at it. I just thought it was surprising that she should speak to me, since I'd never seen her before and she didn't know me. My thought was that she was being particularly negative.
Whilst Ann was talking, the table began rocking violently in a 'yes' movement.
Ann: 'Oh right, right, that's it.'
Jim: 'Was the smell Spirit induced?' *Yes.*

Our Elder Statesman was right on the button again.

Gill: 'Because you don't want them to be there, would that be correct?' *Yes.*
Gill: 'Have we got it, then?' *Yes.*
Gordon: 'Is it something to do with the philosophy to do with the Wheel of Life?' *Yes.*
Gill: 'Well we could investigate that?'
Ann: 'Well, wait a minute, **should** we investigate that?'
Ann to Group: 'I just wondered if we should stay away from them.'
Gill: 'No, I think we should find out what it is that they're about.'
Gordon: 'The wheel of life would seem contrary to our thinking – to ascension, is that correct?' *Yes.*
Gill: 'But we have to be tolerant of other people's view point?' *Yes.*
Gill: 'And we can learn from it? We have learnt?' *Yes.*
Ann: 'Yes, but it was the smell in the room, the bad influence that was causing the problem wasn't it?' *Yes*
Ann: 'It was affecting our Spirit Team, wasn't it?' *Yes.*
The table continues rocking whilst Ann is speaking.
Jim asks Ann: 'What type of smell was it?'
Ann: 'It was a musty smell, sort of stale, it could well have been a Spirit smell I've smelt that before on some of my investigations.'
Gill: 'Were you trying Gordon (Higginson) to get them to move?' *Yes.*
Gill: 'Ah, right. So Gordon, you would prefer if we were in here on this

floor by ourselves, without their interruptions and vibrations on the energy?' *Yes.*

Jim: 'We have been grateful to this organisation for allowing us to use this room and can in no way influence how they wish to use the other rooms, we can certainly disassociate ourselves from them, would you agree?'

The table continued swaying in a 'yes' movement whilst Jim was speaking.

Jim: 'Well I'm aware of time, folks, so before we terminate, I'd like to feel comfortable in the knowledge that we can continue here in the meantime, and we will come back to this subject from time to time just to have the confirmation that all is well with us.'

The table sways in a 'yes' repeatedly.

Jim: 'And before I go, was it the right thing that Ann insisted upon, having an invocation?' *Yes.*

Gordon: 'Earlier, the vibration seemed very different. Was there someone else through and in contact initially?' *Yes.*

The table is still dancing around from leg to leg.

Jim: 'And was that the influence that was affecting us or was it the influence from next door?'

The Group respond to Jim: 'That's two questions. Jim:'

Jim: 'Okay, when we set out, was it the influence of what was happening next door having an effect on what we were trying to do?' *Yes*

Gordon: 'Was that to do with a change in the energy that caused a difficulty in you coming through?' *Yes.*

Gordon: 'Is that why it allowed others to come through earlier on?' *The table responds with a definite 'yes'.*

Gill to the Group: 'That was a lesson.'

Ann: 'Yes.'

Gordon: 'Should we do anything in the room to protect the room from outside influence?'

Jim to the Group: 'I have some difficulty with that, as I don't think we can leave our influence in the room either, as it is used by others.'

Gordon commentating: 'The table's moving back and forth in agreement with you.'

There was a sense of disappointment in the room as we left the building that night. We had only just started our Circle and although we had just been sitting since January – nearly five months – we were surprised and pleased with the phenomena already experienced and witnessed and there was a reluctance to leave this place – not because anyone felt particularly attached to the building but more because of concern that moving might disturb the energy already built up in the Group and that we might have to start to build it again somewhere else. There was relief that at least we could continue there until we found somewhere else.

We never did investigate the group that the Theosophical Society had rented the other room to that night. I didn't see the woman in the long robes and huge hat again, thankfully. So I'm not sure what that group were doing, but I do recognise a Spirit Smell when I encounter it – and this is a clear signal that Spirit is present, usually not a friendly Spirit. In this case the smell was being used to dissuade people from using the building and maybe it worked, who knows? They were never seen again.

My fear of using the Ouija Board however, was to be realised a few months later. But for now, … I was just pleased I was going off on holiday.

11 BLUE GOLDSTONE

I really hadn't been happy about witnessing that strange energy that came through the Ouija Board and the random letters that were being attributed to it – I was going on holiday and I was glad. Mayumi and I had visited several other crystal shops in the interim trying to track down the elusive stone that I had seen in my head – hoping that I'd be attracted to one in the shop as had been foretold and that somehow I would recognise it from my vision. This didn't happen.

I was going away for the next couple of weeks, so I resolved to continue my search for these blue/black stones with the name that no-one was entirely sure of, in Spain. I was also kind of pleased that I wasn't having to work with the Ouija Board and maybe by the time I got back the Group would have worked things out.

When I returned to Scotland and got back to the Group on 15th June 2006, they were telling me that not much had happened whilst I was away. Except, as Jim said, 'We have been most undecided over the last 2-3 weeks. With the help from the Spirit Team it was confirmed that they were dissatisfied with whatever was occurring here and we were able to establish that we were most definitely to consider a move – I don't think there was anything else of significant importance that's occurred over that period of time?' And he turned to the others for confirmation.

Mayumi and Gordon were nodding in agreement – Gill and Mairi were on holiday. 'What about Mairi's trance?' says Mayumi.

'Ah, yes', says Jim, 'I think I was so consumed by the fact that we're having to move from here – and I like it here – that I've completely overlooked Mairi's trance. Since we were not getting much from the table, Ann, we decided to sit for Mairi, to see if anything would come from that'.

Mairi was an excellent Trance Medium and she seemed to slip into an altered state of consciousness with remarkable ease. The communication that she could deliver in this way was always very profound.

'On the first week you were away she seemed to be overshadowed by the presence of an old man, he was in a monastic order and towards the end of his life he may have been imprisoned. This overshadowing continued in the second week with the same man and she felt that he was a Monk in Italy. But she saw him almost like 'Merlin' from *King Arthur and the Knights of the Round Table*', so he would be mixing potions, medicines, maybe even spells of some sort and she thought he would be involved in alchemy. She saw him creating something in a cauldron but it was very hot and she thought there was molten metal involved. Something like turning lead into gold, she said'.

Jim continued, 'It didn't mean anything to anyone Ann, so we agreed that we would just document it, as we're doing now, so you can record it in the transcripts in case it meant something at some future stage. Does it mean anything to you, Ann?'

'No, it doesn't'.

Gordon says, 'I've got a monk as a guide but all this alchemy didn't mean anything to me, and she says her monk is from Firenze – that means nothing to me'.

'That's the Italian name for Florence', I said.

'Oh, that's right; Gill told her that, but Mairi just said that she knew that her Monk was not in Rome but somewhere else in Italy'.

'Well we've recorded it. Now – let's just see what happens'.

> The Group sat in silence. Then Jim asked for the normal feedback:
> Jim: 'I was aware of something happening with you, Ann.'
> Ann: 'Well I was getting strange images of battles between religious groups; between churches; the Church of Rome, the Catholic Church and other Christian religions. I was aware of persecution of one religion over the other and I got the feeling it was to do with the inability to express views which were different, and this led to battles. I felt I was actually struck quite hard across my face and that was part of the violence that was going on.'
> Jim: 'Anyone else got any views?'
> Gordon: 'I was aware that the energy was higher, this week.'
> Jim: 'Can you define, 'higher', Gordon?'
> Gordon: 'It's the level of energy, the intensity. I felt I may have had someone with me, but the person was a mystery. This mystery person was very tall.'
> Ann: 'Was he heavy footed?'
> Gordon: 'Tall.'
> Ann: 'It's just that I was aware of heavy footsteps walking across the room and the floor and the chair actually vibrated.'
> Mayumi: 'I felt the energy was heavy. I felt the footsteps and vibration that Ann was talking about too and I felt strange in that I couldn't get into a meditative or a trance state as I felt like I was actually going to fall

asleep. I felt this feeling of expectation but I couldn't get anything further.'
Jim: 'Were you aware of who was there?'
Mayumi: 'I wasn't aware of anybody there, just aware of the feeling of expectation.'

These images of religious battles, the Church of Rome and so on made me wonder if I had been influenced by what I had heard of Mairi's trance, at the beginning of the evening – so had I just imagined the whole thing? What was certainly sure was that I hadn't imagined the footsteps – heavy footsteps, the unmistakable sound of someone walking right through the centre of our Circle and the floor vibrating with each step taken. I was pleased that Mayumi was able to confirm that she too had experienced the same thing.

Throughout the next week whilst at home I was continually being drawn to images of bells – even objects that were the shape of a bell - and it was beginning to annoy me. Being aware that I was being directed, I brought in a collection of objects that looked like bells. I was also prompted to bring a piece of turquoise and more candles.

> THURSDAY GROUP – 22nd June 2006 (Gill Muir and Mairi Anderson are both on holiday). Ann opened by giving a short prayer and invocation.
> Ann: 'I'm now going to light a candle to signify our safety and protection. I'm going to create a Circle of Light.'
> Ann then proceeded to light small candles in the form of an outer circle enclosing our physical Group. She also lit the larger candle on the table in the centre of the circle and asked everyone to enter into the silence, in meditation. Then Feedback:
> Mayumi: 'I could see us in cupped hands, and we were all inside them. This hand was also a lotus flower. And, the inside was all white light and the outside was lilac and pink – just like a lotus flower. Also, I heard a voice saying, 'Dear Chosen Ones', so I thought that was for us but I thought my mind came in, so I didn't want to make it up.'
> Ann: 'I sat at home today before we came here and I felt the energy with me instantly. I felt something was happening but I couldn't get what I was supposed to do, so I thought I'll just have to go with my intuition, so I thought I'll bring candles and then for some reason a bell came into my head. Now I've had that before, a bell, and this part of the candle-snuffer came to mind – I know it isn't a bell, but it looks like one – so, I thought I'd bring it with me. Also, it was next to this little candle and it's sort of bell-shaped, so I've brought that as well and then my eye fell on the crystals and I knew in particular I had to bring turquoise – and I just felt there was some sort of Shamanic connection, so I brought my Dream-catcher too.'
> Gordon: 'Your selection of turquoise in particular, did you get a feeling

it was necessary for its protection qualities or was there something significant about it?'
Ann: 'The only significance I thought was; it was to do with American Indians.'
Jim: 'Does the turquoise come from a Copper Mine at all?'
Ann: 'No, not as far as I'm aware?'
Gordon: 'No, I don't think so.'
Ann to Jim: 'Why?'
Jim: 'Because it's significant to me that colour.'
Ann: 'Is it?'
Jim: 'Yes, it is.'
Ann: 'Why?'
Jim: 'Just let me not say just now, Ann, in case something comes out later on.'
Ann: 'Yes, that's okay.'

I thought this was a strange thing to say – I couldn't see any reason to think that a Copper Mine would have any connections with turquoise – but Jim clearly thought so. And we would later find that our patriarch was once again on the ball.

Mayumi: 'I just got the words in my head, 'open a portal'.'
Ann: 'A portal?'
Mayumi: 'I don't know what that means.'
Ann: 'How do we do that? A portal – is a door or doorway, an opening.'
Ann: 'I've got something or somebody here from Spirit, and it's a powerful presence but they're not making themselves known.'
Mayumi: 'I'm aware of it with you too.'
Ann: 'Oh, this is weird. It's sort of swirling.'
Ann: 'Good Evening, the person who is trying to communicate with us here tonight, please draw close and communicate with us by helping to move the table.'
Ann: 'I'm feeling a strange sensation; I seem to be in motion. Do I see you moving too, Gordon, or is it just me?'
Gordon: 'Yes, I seem to be picking up the motion of the table and it's coming through me rather than the table.'
Ann: 'So am I, so am I.'
Gordon: 'And, I'm very conscious of the fact that my hands are just resting on the table and they're not pushing it.'
Ann: 'It's as if they're pushing us instead of the table. And you're going that way and I'm going this way.'
Gordon is swaying from side to side in his seat whilst Ann is rocking back and forth. Mayumi laughs in amusement at the spectacle.
Ann: 'I'm away again.'
The rocking movement starts up again stronger this time.
Gordon: 'Just wondering what's happening, it's a different sort of

movement. I'm just finding - and Ann's finding - that we're both moving, without so much as the table moving and I just wondered if it's us that should be moving the objects rather than them (Spirit) moving the table?'
Jim: 'That's an interesting thought.'
Ann: 'Gordon, you're still swaying away there and so am I, yet we're not managing to move the table.'
Jim: 'Well just a suggestion, Mayumi, but if you stood behind Ann and put your hands on her back and I stood behind Gordon and we could see what happens.'
Jim to Gordon: 'Gordon, if you can, can you concentrate your energy on the table.'
Ann laughs as the rocking becomes even stronger with Mayumi's energy on her back, and she has to ask Mayumi to take her hands off.
Gordon: 'When you connected with me Jim, the motion stopped with me and now that you've taken your hands off, I'm away from side to side again.'
Ann: 'Well I would say it was stronger with Mayumi here.'
Mayumi: 'Well I'm shaking here.' *(Mayumi indicates her shoulders).*
Ann: 'You're shaking?'
Mayumi: 'Yes.'
Ann: 'It's quite powerful. I'm away in a swirl now.'
Ann: 'Oh, it's got stronger again.'
Ann with eyes shut asks Mayumi: 'Can you feel it again?'
Gordon: 'You're moving from side to side now, Ann.'
Ann: 'I am, I'm swaying.'
Jim: 'It's okay now, Ann, take your time. Now you're in unison, you two.
Ann with eyes shut: 'Are we?'
Mayumi: 'It's going faster though.'
Gordon: 'It's a sort of sickly sort of motion, actually.'
Ann: 'Yes, do you feel you're on the sea?'
Gordon: 'Well, it's too fast for the sea, but it's that sort of feeling, as if you're on a swell for a while.'

After much questioning, we couldn't establish the reason for this motion of Gordon and I whilst the table remained stubbornly still. I believe now that this was the first attempt by Spirit in experimenting with moving us physically, rather than inanimate objects. Some final confirmation that night:

Gordon: 'As I indicated last week, I was just a wee bit disappointed with the turn of events for the two weeks when you were away Ann as there was nothing definitive, but I thank you for tonight, Arthur.'
The table rocks in response to Gordon as he is talking to Arthur Conan Doyle.
Mayumi: 'Yes.'
Ann: 'Have you come, to communicate through this table, specifically to give us some encouragement?' *Yes.*

Ann: 'Yes, I thought that. You are still not happy with the conditions in this room but you are tolerating them for our benefit to keep us going until we find something better, is that correct?' *Yes.*
Ann: 'So, you have specifically come back to boost our spirits?' *Yes.*
Ann: 'Thank you for doing that, I know the conditions aren't exactly right for you or for us, we were becoming a bit downhearted.'
Table rocks in recognition.
Ann: 'Has having the candles here tonight helped you to come back, to come forward and use that energy here tonight?' *Yes.*
Ann: 'Okay. So, it was significant to bring the candles here tonight to help you to do that?' *Yes.*
Ann: 'Good, I'm glad. Was it significant to bring the turquoise?'
Table rocks a 'yes' but not so aggressively.
Gordon: 'Was the purpose of the turquoise to do with protection?' *Yes.*
Ann: 'So did you guide us then, for this evening, to bring the candles and the turquoise to help you come back this evening?' *Yes.*
Ann: 'Was it your direction as well to bring the crystal and the bell-shape?' *Yes.*
Ann: 'And the Dream-catcher?' *No.*
Ann: 'Oh, no, not the Dream-catcher – well I wasn't sure about that anyway. Well that's not bad, I got most of it right. Two out of three ain't bad.'

I was relieved that the Group had moved on from using the Ouija Board; some may say that we had actually moved backwards to using the yes/no table, but at least we were again getting answers to our questions that seemed logical and that confirmed information received by other means. Also, we seemed to have moved forward with a new phenomenon – this swirling movement that Gordon and I had felt – albeit we didn't understand the purpose of it at the moment.

I decided it was high time that I procured those bracelets of crystal stones that I had been instructed to get. I had exhausted all the crystal stockists within a reasonable drive time of my house. None had bracelets that resembled the stones I had seen in my vision. None had loose stones that I felt drawn to and no-one had heard of 'blue goldstone', it didn't seem to exist in those crystal directories that each shop consulted to see if they could order them for me – not even in Spain.

I hadn't considered searching for them on the internet. Principally because I was told I would know the stone as I would be 'drawn to it' – this couldn't happen on the internet. However, this was my last chance. The nearest I had got to it was the tiny bit of stone I had seen inlaid on a globe of the world, as the country of Italy.

Now was the time to see if the stuff really existed or whether it was all a figment of my imagination. I typed in 'Blue Goldstone' – and couldn't believe what I found. No wonder the crystal shops didn't have it – it's not a crystal – it's man-made. It's actually formed by melting down glass and adding – would you believe – copper, to make it sparkly. I wondered whether Jim actually picked this up when asking me if turquoise could be found in a copper mine?

There was more: *"Urban legend says goldstone was an accidental discovery by unspecified Italian monks or the product of alchemy"*

Unfortunately Mairi was still away on holiday as I had this urge to call her up and tell her that her Italian Monk of two weeks before seemed indeed to be dabbling in alchemy. And all this had taken place whilst I was in Spain – looking for the stones. And, the other name for those stones – Monk's Gold! Here's an excerpt from Wikipedia:

One original manufacturing process for goldstone was invented in seventeenth-century Venice by the Miotti family, which was granted an exclusive license by the Doge. Urban legend says goldstone was an accidental discovery by unspecified Italian monks or the product of alchemy, but there is no pre-Miotti documentation to confirm this. A goldstone amulet from 12th- to 13th-century Persia in the collection of the University of Pennsylvania shows that other, earlier artisans were also able to create the material. The most common form of goldstone is reddish-brown, containing tiny crystals of metallic copper that require special conditions to form properly. The initial batch is melted together from silica, copper oxide, and other metal oxides to chemically reduce the copper ions to elemental copper. The vat is then sealed off from the air and maintained within a narrow temperature range, keeping the glass hot enough to remain liquid while allowing metallic crystals to precipitate from solution without melting or oxidizing. Another common name for the material is aventurine glass, based on the original Italian name avventurina (from avventura, "adventure" or "chance"). It is also sometimes called "stellaria", "sang-e setareh" or "sang-e khorshid" (sang means 'stone', 'khorshid' means 'sun' and setareh means 'star' in Farsi) for its starry internal reflections, or "monk's gold" or "monkstone" from folkloric associations with an unnamed monastic order.

I couldn't believe it – the information about the stones had come to me in early May. In my absence on holiday, Mairi was entranced by a Monk talking about alchemy. Her Monk was in Italy (coincidentally the same country depicted in Blue Goldstone in the globe I had seen in the shop window). Just a few days before this, Jim is talking about copper – when everyone else was talking about turquoise. Then suddenly all the pieces of the jigsaw fall into place. It is times such as this that you know you are getting absolute proof that there is a higher intelligence communicating with us. Whatever you may call that higher intelligence is not important. The important thing is to know that it exists and can influence us – if we will just listen.

12 THE CADUCEUS AND THE PORTAL

Now that we had unearthed the significance of the 'stones' which we had been directed to we could understand that the bracelets had a much more important meaning than just their symbolism of unity and comradeship. These 'stones' symbolised alchemy and the ancient wisdom of an unknown monastic order – had one of these monks been directing us towards this source?

I didn't have the answer to this but what I did know was that despite my own personal aversion to the thought of these bracelets they obviously had greater significance than I had realised. I was going to give them much more credence and since I was tasked with getting them I had better get on with it.

Having tracked down Blue Goldstone on the internet I could find no source for ordering bracelets made of it. Just as the crystal shops had intimated, they were nowhere to be had. There was nothing else for it, I would just have to order the loose beads, some elasticated thread, and make them up myself – it shouldn't be too difficult.

And so it was that by the following week, as I drove into the Theosophical Society for our next meeting, I was sporting my own Blue Goldstone bracelet – and was feeling quite proud of myself. I had ordered an initial small quantity of beads and thread to try out my skills as a 'jeweller' and to see if the stones really were what I had 'seen' several weeks before. I also wanted to look at the size of the beads, since there were different diameters to choose from and also to determine how many more beads I'd have to order since the men would obviously need larger sized bracelets than the women. I'd measure them up tonight and order up the right quantity that I would need to make up another five bracelets.

It was Thursday, 29th June, 2006. Just a day before the annual Edinburgh Trades Holiday – the traditional period when many factories and workplaces would close for two weeks. Unusually for Scotland at this time of year it was a glorious summer evening as I drove through the centre of town from my home at Fairmilehead, which is on the south side of Edinburgh, towards the Theosophical Society in Great King Street, to the north. My route took me straight down 'the bridges', over Princes Street, towards the north side of Edinburgh. The views from here towards Fife and over the Firth of Forth were simply stunning that evening.

However, as I drove to 'the bridges' (the main arterial route towards the East end of Princes Street), the traffic was very busy as people were either heading home after work or engaged in Thursday late-night shopping when the shops were open till 9pm. Although my car was crawling along slowly because of the volume of traffic I had to be especially vigilant as people were weaving between the moving traffic, either running for buses or just jay-walking rather than crossing at the zebra crossing just ahead.

As I sat in the queue of traffic edging slowly forward, I glanced down at my new-found symbol of unity, this bracelet of Blue Goldstone which had proven to be so elusive but which was now glinting in the summer sunshine as it sat proudly on my wrist. I could see that those stones really were blue and not black as I had originally thought when I first saw them, but it needed the strong summer sunshine to determine the difference.

But as I glanced at my wrist I 'saw' something dangling from my bracelet that was clearly from the etheric realms. I caught a glimpse of what looked like a charm, like those you would see dangling from a charm bracelet but only the one, which would be unusual on a charm bracelet.

I had already returned my gaze to watching the road ahead and was puzzling over what I had just seen when I quickly returned my gaze towards the bracelet, but the image had gone and the bracelet had returned to sparkling prettily in the sunshine.

What *was* that? I didn't know. I immediately brought it back into my mind's eye to try to analyse what I had just seen. I knew this image was important and I instantly knew I had been given another message. But what was that message – I wasn't sure. I comforted myself in knowing that if I tried to remember what little information I could glean from what I had seen and bring this information to the Group they would be able to add to it and hopefully make some sense of it. This was how it usually worked and we had become accustomed to this piecing together of the 'jigsaw'. This was just the latest challenge.

When I got to the Theosophical Society I decided to keep this latest piece of information to myself to see if someone else received anything similar during our period of sitting in silence, that begun each session.

> The Group then sat in silent meditation for some time. Jim asked the Group for a brief comment as to how they felt.
> Mayumi: 'I felt somebody just behind that wall, not physically, because

we talked about portals, and I could see them there (Spirit People) waiting, as though they are ready to come in but I don't know how to open the gate, as you say, but that's how I felt it.'

Mayumi was always very quiet in the Group and wouldn't speak much, but she had such a good connection with Spirit that meant she could see things, most of the others couldn't –and this subject of the Portal had been raised already and would come into play again.

Mairi: 'I just felt very still and quiet.'
Gordon: 'Like Mairi, very quiet, very still and peaceful, in fact I almost dropped off.'
Mairi: 'I think I nearly dropped off myself; I was just on the borderline.'
Ann: 'I felt strange again, like last week, I felt that motion again, not that it was physically making me move but I could feel that swirl again and it was making me feel quite sick again, and I also felt like I was a bird, or at least, I had feathers, my wings were very prominent and I felt I could open my wings and I could fly, and the song, 'the wind beneath my wings' came into my head. The energy was very powerful.'
Jim to Ann: 'You didn't physically move at all. But I was very aware of strong presences and strong energy with you.'
Jim: 'So shall we try and see where that takes us? I guess we should move the table.'
The small square table is moved across to the wall, as had been instructed last week.
Ann: 'Great Spirit if you are with us here tonight, would you indicate your presence by moving the table for us, please – any direction at all.'
The table beginnings to move.
Gordon: 'Will you please indicate 'yes'.'
The table rocks and knocks against the wall.
Gordon: 'And, for a 'no'.'
The table remains stationary.
Jim: 'I think, Ann, you had something you wanted to ask?'

It was strange how Jim always just seemed to know that something was going on. So, it was my turn to address our Spirit friends and see if I could gain some sort of confirmation about what I had 'seen' earlier.

Ann: 'Oh, it's just a small thing? You'll notice that I've got the bracelet on tonight that you asked us to get, is that correct?' *Yes.*
Ann: 'Can you confirm that these are the right stones?' *Yes.*
Ann: 'Now, I wanted to ask – and I really don't mind if you say, 'no''.
Everyone laughs as they wait in anticipation of what Ann was about to say.
Ann: 'I got the indication when I was driving in tonight, and I happened to look at the bracelet on my wrist, that there's something else which is

to be attached to this bracelet, is that correct?' *Yes.*
Everyone laughs, as they are aware Ann is being tested to get things for the Group that she personally would not do, nor choose to wear!
Ann to the Group: 'This gets worse!!!' *Again, everyone laughs.*
Jim: 'Excuse my sense of humour, but does that mean it's attached to an arm?'
Again the Group laugh but the table answers – No.
Ann: 'Am I right in thinking it's some sort of silver charm?' *No.*
Jim: 'Is it the tie that joins both ends of the bracelet together?' *No.*
Jim: 'Mayumi's suggested, that there is something more sophisticated than just a knot, is that correct?' *No.*
Jim: 'Should we also attach a clasp to both ends of the bracelet?' *No.*
Jim: 'Is a knot sufficient?' *Yes.*
Ann: 'No; the impression I was getting, was that there was something else that would be attached to the bracelet?' *Yes*
Ann: 'And, it looked to me like it was something silver, is that correct?' *No.*
Ann: 'Okay, it looked to me like it was silver-coloured.....' *No.*
Ann to the Group: 'I'm getting this wrong. As I was driving in tonight, my hands were on the steering wheel and I glanced down at the bracelet and I just saw this thing, and I thought, oh, there's to be something else attached to it like a wee charm or a wee something...'
Gordon to Ann: 'Was it a particular shape?'
Ann: 'Well, I'm calling it a charm, and that signifies luck and maybe that's what's wrong, that's not the way to describe it. What I mean is....'
Jim to Ann: 'Would an icon be too strong a word? Is it something perhaps in the shape of perhaps a Masonic Symbol or something?'
Ann: 'It is symbolic, yes.'
The table knocks, in agreement.
Jim: 'Yes, thank you.'
Ann: 'Am I right in thinking it symbolises our spiritual connection?' *Yes.*
Ann: 'Thank you. You see it's a further symbol, the bracelet.....'
Gordon to Ann: 'What about an Ankh?'
Jim to Gordon: 'What's an Ankh?'
Gordon: 'An Ankh is like a cross with a loop across the top.'
The table starts rocking.

The table was rocking, but not banging against the wall for its signal for 'yes'.

Gordon: 'Now, that's interesting, as that's the first thing that popped into my head when you mentioned it. The table seems to be happy about that.'
Ann: 'But why is it moving in that direction?'
Jim: 'And that being the case, should it be of either silver or silver-type material?' *Yes.*

> Ann: 'Now what's not clear about that, is that's what I asked, and I saw it as silver.'
> Gordon: 'Is it important what the material is made of, for this Ankh?' *No.*
> Mayumi: 'Or is it just symbolic? Is it the symbol which is important?' *Yes.*

Mayumi had made sense of it, it wasn't the material that was important – but the symbol.

> Gordon: 'Are we right in assuming however, that you wish an Ankh, no matter what material, to be attached to the bracelet?' *Yes.*

Although we got a positive response from the table, we were aware that two questions were asked here.

> Jim to Ann: 'So what's the significance of the Ankh? Are you not too happy with it, Ann?'
> Ann: 'No, I just knew I saw something else dangling from the bracelet and I could see it, this other thing dangling from my wrist,......you see, (as *the table starts banging against the wall as she's speaking*) if it's an Ankh, it's an Ankh, but I'm just not sure.'
> Jim to Ann: 'But have you any idea in your mind what it could be?'
> Ann: 'I saw it as silver – charm - that's how I'm putting it. I couldn't see it as an Ankh. I would see it as more oval shaped. Like a disc with a symbol in the middle which signifies......'
> Mayumi to Ann: 'Maybe it could be a disc with the Ankh inside it?'
> Ann: 'Could be, could be. That's what I saw, more as an oval shape dangling from the bracelet with some symbol on it, or in it?'
> *The table moves in agreement with that.*
> Jim: 'What comes to my mind is when one goes to lectures about auras and things, there's a template of a body surrounded by the aura –is that the sort of thing?'
> Ann: 'That's the sort of shape. As I said, I couldn't see what was in the centre of it, I just knew it was symbolic and it was a symbol of our link with Spirit and it further endorsed and confirmed our membership of this Group and our link with Spirit. You know, it was adding further to what has already been said about the bracelet.'
> Gordon to Ann: 'Would the Ankh do until you get it to really show you, if that's okay?'

In my frustration, I decided to address the table directly.

> Ann: 'Right, table (Spirit), I'm just going to speak and I'm not going to put my hand on the table, so I don't influence anything and just move if I'm going in the right direction. What I saw in the car when I was

coming down the road, was a silver-coloured metal disc-type object, oval in shape, that was attached to the bracelet that seemed to have some form of emblem contained within it that signified our link with Spirit. Am I correct?'

The table had already started rocking as Ann was speaking and continued to do so.

Jim: 'Yes.'

Ann: 'And I couldn't quite be clear what the symbol inside was, as I only got a fleeting glance, is the symbol inside an Ankh?' *No.*

Ann commenting on the table: 'That's a 'no'. I didn't see it as an Ankh.'

Gordon to Ann: 'Is it important?'

Ann: 'I don't think it's an Ankh. It didn't feel right to me somehow?'

Jim to Spirit: 'The other thing that comes to me is, could it be in relation to the Healing Symbol?' *Yes.*

The table was now rocking and knocking very excitedly.

Jim: 'That's the staff with the serpents and snakes?' *Yes.*

Ann to Jim: 'Now that feels much better to me, actually.'

Mayumi: 'I've forgotten the name of it......'

Ann: 'I should know the name of it as well.'

Jim: 'Is that symbol, something that I may previously have worn?' *Yes.*

Jim: 'Would that have been on a Uniform?' *Yes.*

Jim to the Group: 'Yes, it was my RAF Uniform, I was a Medic in the RAF and I had two of those.'

The table rocks in agreement.

Ann: 'That's good; that feels better to me than the Ankh, that's really good.'

Ann: 'So, table (Spirit), are you telling me that as well as getting the bracelets, I've also to find this silver disc with the medical emblem on it?' *Yes.*

Ann: 'Or, can someone else get it?' *No.*

The Group all laugh.

Ann: 'Well, why not???'

The Group was laughing at my frustration as it was always me who seemed to be instructed to obtain things for the Spirit Team, when some of the others could have done it equally as well, and possibly more easily than I could – I don't think making it easy was their plan.

Jim: 'Well could it be that if we had one of those in the Group as one of our icons and had it present in our Circle, just like the turquoise, would just one of these badges or emblems present... would that be sufficient?' *No.*

Ann: 'No, I knew that, because I know the feeling; it's further endorsing the properties of the bracelet and it's linking us all together with one purpose and one cause and the link with Spirit – that's what it's to do with. So, we'll all wear them individually but when you see then

collectively, you'll know we're part of the whole.'
Mayumi: 'Something just came into my mind. You know these tourist places where you can put a coin in a machine and you pull the lever and it stamps it and it comes out as a souvenir – is that what you mean?'
Ann: 'That's the sort of thing, yes.'
Jim: 'I think there's one of these organisations that use it as a medical alert; you know if you're epileptic or diabetic, and they wear them as chains round their necks – I think they may use that symbol.'
Ann: 'Yes, I know what you mean. Right I'll see if I can get it somewhere.'
Jim to Spirit: 'The important thing that you're saying about the bracelet and the emblem is that it's the symbology that's the important thing for us?' *Yes.*
Jim: 'So, are we now establishing that part of the function of this Group is that it's a healing group, as well as other things, but healing is important?' *Table is unclear.*
Jim: 'Well I take the view, Friends, that ultimately all that we do in Circle work is about healing, would you agree?' *Yes.*
Ann: 'Yes, I think that's why you're getting a nondescript answer, first time around.'
Jim: 'Yes, it's not a healing circle, its only one of the ingredients.'
Ann: 'Yes, and also that symbol wasn't originally the healing emblem, it was adopted as the healing emblem, it didn't start off that way.'
Jim: 'And, what it is Ann, is that it is most definitely the Architects symbol worldwide.'
Mairi: 'It's possible that its original meaning was to do with ....'
Mayumi: 'Yes, like the High Priestess or something?'
Ann: 'Yes, I would have said it was something like that, like Alchemy or something.' *The table rocks as Ann talks.*
Ann: 'Is it Alchemy? Was that the original association?' *Yes.*
Mayumi: 'The topic for my Course this year at Stansted was Alchemy.'
Ann: 'Was it?'
Mayumi and Mairi: 'Yes. Alchemy and transformation.'
Ann: 'You see it's interesting how all these things fit together.'
Ann to the Group: 'Okay, next subject, I've done mine.'
(The Group laugh).

Now that I had my confirmation of what I had seen en route to the venue, and I had accepted the outcome of the debate with Spirit, that this emblem was indeed the Caduceus, I made a mental note to attempt to source these via the internet along with the additional stones required for the bracelets. For now, the Group returned to Mayumi's vision of the portal.

Ann: 'Is this a Portal that you are opening for us?' *Yes.*
Ann: 'Well done, Mayumi.'
Mayumi: 'Yes, I knew that.'

Ann: 'Mayumi was correct in her assumption about the Portal?' *Yes.*
Mairi: 'What are the implications of that if we move – is the portal with us, or the building?'
Gordon to Mairi: 'You'll need to separate out these questions.'
Mairi: 'Is this portal linked to this physical location?' *No.*
Ann: 'So if we move location, the portal will move with us, you will see to that will you?' *Yes.*

It is interesting to remind myself of this transcript recorded in the first year of the Group's formation (2006) for it would be another five years before this phenomenon of a portal would be experienced and photographed in our new venue. For now, we continued to investigate.

Mairi: 'Must be some kind of energy.'
Ann: 'Yes, they're creating it, somehow.'
Ann: 'Is it important for you to create the portal at a wall?' *No.*
Ann: 'It just happens to be at the wall in this particular building, is that correct?' *Yes.*
Ann: 'Is that because the energy lines are helping you to create it in this particular position, is that correct?' *No.*
Gordon: 'Last week, I dowsed for the best position for the table in this room and from several points within this room the pendulum pointed out that this location where you are now was the best. Is that to do with the fact that I found energy lines that crossed at this significant point?' *Yes.*
Gordon: 'One of these energy lines was positive and the other negative, is that important?' *Yes.*
Gordon: 'Is that because this crossing creates a spiral of energy?' *Yes.*
Gordon: 'And this would be important for the portal?' *Yes.*
Ann to Gordon: 'And what happens if we don't have that in our next location?'
Gordon: 'Well, if we select the location, then presumably we are selecting it with guidance, and I would hope that we would receive their acknowledgement or guidance in the selection of things.'
The table rocks in agreement whilst Gordon is speaking.
Gordon: 'I was at a Fair operated in a little room which was off a Church at Holy Corner, at the other side of the Eric Liddle Centre. There is another room that we might be able to use. I was wondering if that might be worth checking out?'
The table continued to rock in agreement throughout Gordon speaking.
Ann: 'I think you've got a 'yes', to that, Gordon.'
As the Group enters into a discussion about the exact location of this room, the table suddenly starts moving quite excitedly.
Gordon: 'Hello, what's happening?'
Ann: 'It likes you Gordon, you've come up with the location for our next venue.'
Gordon: 'Do I take it that I try for this new location?'

The table rocks violently in agreement.
Gordon: 'Okay, I'll do that.'
The table starts moving quite excitedly towards Ann.
Gordon: 'It's jumping towards you now, Ann?'
Ann: 'Oh. Okay, well..... I'm wondering what the table wanted me to do just now?'
Jim: 'You moved over to Ann, is that correct?'
Mayumi: 'Were you just excited?' *Yes*
The table moves excitedly.
Gordon: 'It's like a dog, isn't it?'
Jim: 'Are you excited because after many weeks of deliberations, it looks like we've found a venue?'
The table spins around on one leg and then rocks - yes.
Gordon: 'Was that a sort of Group attempt to say, yes?'
The table rocks and swings again.
Ann: 'I was trying to think why the table was coming towards me, as it did earlier, and so I'm going to ask a question... Is it necessary, or would you like me to go over the purpose of this Group again?' *Yes*
The table was rocking throughout Ann speaking.
Jim to Ann: 'For their benefit or for our benefit?'
Ann: 'Don't know. It was the only thing I could think it was coming forward for.'
Jim: 'Right.'
Ann: 'You know, re-stating why we were here.'
Jim: 'Yes, right, right.'
Gordon: 'I'd like to establish something, just before we go over it. Are we part of a greater collective of other small groups with particular tasks?' *No.*
Jim: 'So, you have a specific purpose for us?' *Yes.*
Jim: 'And it's up to us to try to establish what that is?' *Yes.*
Jim: 'Right, now Ann is now going to give you a sort of resume.'
Ann: 'My influence and recollection from the beginning was that I was to get a Group together of likeminded individuals, who had complete trust in one another, is that correct?' *Yes.*
Ann: 'Okay. No sooner had I put the phone down on the last person, when I did the phone round, than you acknowledged that I had the right people?' *Yes.*
Ann: 'And you acknowledged that again, last week?' *Yes.*
Ann: 'Okay. You then influenced us with the information that this Group would be a physical group, was that correct?' *Yes.*
Ann: 'And the purpose of getting us together in this way was to use us to further the aims and knowledge of Spiritualism – when I say Spiritualism, I mean it in its broadest sense, not necessarily the religion – is that correct?' *Yes*
Ann: 'Now, other recollections were that the Group was to remain secretive and the information was to remain closed – you've already

responded positively to that question, so I'll move on. And, the information collected and gleaned whilst in this Group was to be recorded, and not only was it to be recorded for our own purposes within this Group, but I did get the impression that you would want a book to be written about these experiences at some point?' *Yes.*
Ann: 'Yes, thank you for acknowledging that.'
Jim: 'And, Ann was going to do that?'
The Group laughs and the table responds positively.
Mayumi to Jim: 'I was going to say that, too.'

The Group always found it amusing that I was the person singled out to write the book, especially when they knew it was really something I did not want to do.

Ann: 'The other influence I had was that you would use each one of us in our own special way to further this aim of promoting Spiritualism (again in its broadest sense) for example I did get the impression that I would see some of us on the platform speaking about this subject and perhaps teaching it too.'
The table was rocking in appreciation of what Ann was saying up until the last few words and then fell stationary.
Ann: 'Oh, it's stopped.'
Jim: 'Just as Ann has been nominated and we've all seconded it and thirded it and fourthed it, about being the Author, would there be a spokesperson for this Group that would perhaps emerge in due course, when the time was right, that would speak and perhaps broadcast the views and philosophy, with your permission, I might add, would that be right?' *No response from the table.*
Ann: 'There's something not quite right, but I know we're on the right track because actually I saw specifically Mairi on the platform.'
The table rocks in response.
Gordon: 'When we're talking about platform, we're used to referring to it in the Spiritual sense but what we meant was a floor or some sort of gallery or forum, some sort of meeting in other words – not a platform in the spiritual sense.' *Yes.*
Ann: 'Yes, good, thanks Gordon.'
Jim: 'Could you be more specific on that; would Mairi be that person, in due course?' *Yes.*
Jim: 'So, now we're getting down to ………'
Ann: 'Oh, wait a minute, hold on. Would Jim also be that person in due course?' *Yes*
Ann: 'And, would Mayumi also be that person in due course?' *Yes*
The Group laugh as Jim thought he had found the spokesperson in Mairi, only to find he was being given equal responsibility. The table rocks an acknowledgement.

It was my turn to gloat now as they were all delegated a collective responsibility instead of it falling to one individual – for once letting me off the hook.

> Gordon: 'Would the whole Circle have that responsibility?' *Yes*
> Ann: 'Yes, it's all of us, that's my influence. We are all going to be used in our own way to promote this and…..'
> Jim: 'Right, right.'
> Ann: 'Okay, having set that scene, and that's what you got us together to do. You would then take us through step by step, the development of Spiritualism to allow us to experience how Spiritualism came to be so we could experience that and learn from that and we would use that experience in furthering your aims.'
> *The table rocked forcefully throughout Ann speaking.*
> Ann: 'I take it that's a 'yes'. *Yes.*
> Ann: 'So you are taking us through each stage of the development of Spiritualism but we're stuck at the moment because we can't go any further with the Physical Phenomena until we get suitable premises to allow you to take us to the next stage? I'm taking your rocking as a 'yes'.'
> *Table rocks violently as Ann talks.*
> Jim: 'When we go to the new premises, if it's for Physical Mediumship, I'm taking from that, we're really talking about Physical Mediumship in terms of ectoplasmic developments and things of that nature, is that right?' *Yes.*
> Jim: 'That being the case, is there any individual you think is most suited to be the person in this Group to perform that function that you think has the innate ability?'
> *No response from the table.*
> Gordon: 'Anyone in the entire Group?' *No response.*
> Mayumi: 'Can I ask a question, because I just got this thing through. Is it right to say that each one of us will develop a new Physical Phenomenon which is different from the old style?'
> *The table rocks an excited 'yes' in acknowledgement of Mayumi's question.*
> Mayumi: 'I don't know what it is, but I just got it through.'

Little did we know, but we were just about to receive a demonstration of this new form of Physical Phenomena.

> Jim: 'Well, but could that be, doing things in light, or various types of light, which has not been accepted before?' *Yes.*
> Jim: 'Sound perhaps? Is there something with sound we could do? *Yes.*
> Jim: 'Is there something to do with healing that has perhaps not been done that perhaps we could do?'
> *The table rocks and moves in response to Jim.*

Jim: 'You're now sending us very definite answers.'
Gordon: 'You seem to be going around and around, so I take it that it's a Group effort and that we have to take it as it comes?' Yes.
The table is moving in a sort of circular movement on one leg and then resting back on all four.
Gordon to the table (Spirit): 'Are you getting close to trying to levitate?'
Jim: 'That's not giving an answer.'
Ann: 'Right, what is it doing then? We've got this rocking rolling movement.'
Mayumi: 'Do you want Jim to sit and you would like to talk via Jim?'
The table is rocking and swaying in towards Jim.
Jim: 'Is that after I've been decapitated – kneecapitated!'
The Group laughs as the table knocks against Jim's knees.
Mayumi to Jim: 'Do you want to sit?'
Jim: 'Well, you never say no to Spirit, but I can't figure out myself what's happening.'
Ann: 'Right, people in the Spirit World, can you settle down again so......'
The Group gives out an exclamation as the table spins round on one leg.
Gordon: 'The table is going around erratic.'
Mairi: 'I think it really is going to levitate.'
Gordon: 'Well, that's your answer to that, Ann.'
Mairi: 'Oh, it's nearly there. I think it's actually trying to get off the ground.'
Jim: 'I think we should stand up.'
The Group stands and moves the chairs out of the way.
Gordon commentating: 'The table is going around in circles rather animated, one leg after another, we're also heading towards the centre of the room.'
Jim commentating: 'We're going clockwise now, then anti-clockwise, one leg, do you want to lie down?'
The Group again let out a collective exclamation as the table bows down low towards the ground until the top of the table is resting on the floor and the table is on its side, then all four legs of the table are lifted from the floor and then it quickly rises again.
Gordon: 'Oh, hello. That was clever, the nearest thing to a summersault we've seen.'
Gordon commentating: 'Although everyone's hands were on the top of the table which was lying down on its side, all four legs were lifted off the floor, and there's no known way which we could be making that happen. That happened twice. I didn't really comment the first time, because we couldn't believe what was happening.'

The Group was nervously laughing through disbelief of what we were witnessing.

Ann: 'You like the laughter though, don't you, you like the energy?' *Yes.*
Gordon: 'Having two hands on the table seems to help. I think it gets more energy that way.'
Mairi: 'It's just so difficult keeping your hands on it when it's moving so fast, and it depends what it's going to do and which way it's going to move.'
Jim: 'You would like us to stand still now, and see if you can rise?'
The table stands still in response. The Group stands around the table, each with both hands on the table waiting to see what's going to happen.
Mayumi: 'Do you feel the energy? There's a sort of tingling and it's underneath as well.'
Mairi: 'Yes, I feel it too.'
Ann: 'Mmm.'
Jim: 'You feel it's eventually going to take off don't you.'
The Group agrees.
Gordon commentating: 'We've adopted a posture with our hands cupped above the table, projecting energy towards the table.'
Jim: 'Did you come into the middle of the room to demonstrate something to us?'
Ann to the Group: 'Can you just indulge me; can we link pinkies with one another and join our own thumbs. Don't know why I want to do that, but.... '
The Group link hands as Ann has asked. This forms a sort of frame around the top of the table, but above it, not touching the surface.
Gordon: 'I'm starting to get the same phenomenon that I get in my scrying mirror. I see the fogginess I get in my scrying mirror.'
Mayumi and Mairi: 'Yes, yes.'
Gordon: 'This reminds me of free-falling.'
Ann: 'I can see a face in there. Can anyone else see it?'
Mayumi: 'Yes.'
Jim: 'Can we lay our hands down on the table like this, without losing the linkage?'
The Group does as requested, but the table had stopped moving.
Ann: 'Do you want to move to the wall?'
Ann: 'Do you want us to try to sit to see if we can get some communication from this spirit person trying to communicate?'
No response, the table was suddenly stationary.
Jim: 'Perhaps we've taken enough of your time this evening?'
Ann: 'Maybe we've had our lesson this evening.'
Gordon: 'Perhaps we've exhausted a chunk of the energy that's available?'
Gordon: 'Would you like us to bring the Circle to a close?' *Yes.*
Jim: 'Is that why you brought us back next to the centre of the Circle, gave us the demonstration of movement and that was the finale, was it?' *Yes.*
Gordon: 'We are just human; we always want more of a good thing.'

The table rocks in acknowledgement.
Jim: 'Final question, have you been trying to place a face upon the table for some of us to see?' *Yes.*
Ann: 'Okay, we'll try harder next time.'
Gordon: 'Would it be useful to bring a scrying mirror next time? Would it have a purpose to bring it here?' *Yes.*
Ann: 'Good, Gordon, good.'
The Group all thanked Spirit and Jim closed in Prayer.
The Group then had a small discussion over the preceding this evening: Gordon said that he thought it a pity that we didn't have this session on video.
He then explained that he wanted to carry out an experiment to provide proof that it would not be possible for us to lift all four legs off the floor whilst the table was lying on its side on the floor when we all had our hands on the top surface of the table. If this was the case, then it would prove that there was some other force which was causing this phenomenon.
Gordon then placed the table on its side on the floor, as it had been positioned earlier, the Group members all placed their hands on its top surface, again as before, and tried to move it in such a way to lift the legs from the floor, but this proved impossible. All that happened was that the table slid along the floor, it was not possible to lift the legs from this position.
The Group agreed that what was witnessed tonight was quite phenomenal.

The Group had experienced another very fascinating and enlightening evening and we were all stunned by the movement of the table, which had been literally unbelievable. We were all still very excited about what we had witnessed and no-one seemed quite ready to go home. So, someone suggested that we go for a drink just to chat about the night's events. Because this was the last meeting before the summer break and we wouldn't see each other for the next couple of weeks, it seemed like a good idea.

The Group hadn't socialised with each other since our inaugural meeting at Peckham's Wine Bar, so everyone seemed keen on this impromptu idea. But where would we go? There are no pubs in this part of town - it's a terrace of Georgian Town Houses. There were no commercial or retail outlets here.

Gordon said he thought there might be a pub in the street that ran parallel to Great King Street, just further down the hill. So we set off walking and found a bar which was extremely busy with drinkers on this balmy summer evening. As it was so crowded some people were sitting outside. We went inside and eventually managed to push ourselves towards the bar and ordered our drinks. We had hastily organised a kitty. I had been given the money, so whilst Gordon – who was the tallest in our party – was able to shout the order to the barman over the heads of all those hogging the bar all I had to do was hand the money to Gordon to pay our bill and then put the change back into an envelope I had in my bag, just to keep it separate from my own money. We stood there discussing the movements of the table in the Group that night and how amazed we all were with this gravity-defying phenomenon. As we continued our animated chat, someone noticed that a table had become available over near the window, so we quickly commandeered it so we could all sit together.

As we settled down, drinks still in hand, the conversation changed direction, 'And what about the Caduceus?' Jim says.

'If that's what it is', Mairi questioned, 'it could've been an Ankh'.

'Yes, it could've been, but that didn't feel right', I said, 'but, you know me, I always like to have a bit more proof'.

The Group laughed as they knew I wouldn't just accept the first answer that came – it had to be right.

'But the table confirmed it was a Caduceus', Mayumi was on the same wave-length as me.

'Yes, but we have to be sure – I would've liked a bit more confirmation', I said.

'Well', says Gordon, 'you wanted confirmation – there it is'. As he pointed to a glass screen that separated the seating area from the entrance door, there, engraved on the frosted glass was a Caduceus that must have been six feet tall and about three feet wide.

As we all gasped in amazement – 'What are the chances of this?' says Gordon, 'You wanted confirmation, it couldn't come any bigger than this'.

'Wow', there was a simultaneous exclamation as both Mayumi and Mairi took in the sight of this giant symbol. 'You've got your answer, Ann'.

When I got home and checked out The Caduceus on the internet, here's what I found from Wikipedia:

The caduceus (☤; /kəˈdjuːʃəs, -siːəs/; Latin cādūceus, from Greek κηρύκειον kērúkeion "herald's wand, or staff")[2] is the staff carried by Hermes in Greek mythology and consequently by Hermes Trismegistus in Greco-Egyptian mythology. The same staff was also borne by heralds in general, for example by Iris, the messenger of Hera. It is a short staff entwined by two serpents, sometimes surmounted by wings. In Roman iconography, it was often depicted being carried in the left hand of Mercury, the messenger of the gods, guide of the dead, and protector of merchants, shepherds, gamblers and thieves.[3] Some accounts suggest that the oldest known imagery of the caduceus have their roots in a Mesopotamian origin with the Sumerian god Ningishzida whose symbol, a staff with two snakes intertwined around it, dates back to 4000 B.C. to 3000 B.C.[4] As a symbolic object, it represents Hermes (or the Roman Mercury), and by extension trades, occupations, or undertakings associated with the god. In later Antiquity, the caduceus provided the basis for the astrological symbol representing the planet Mercury. Thus, through its use in astrology, alchemy, and astronomy it has come to denote the planet and elemental metal of the same name. It is said the wand would wake the sleeping and send the awake to sleep. If applied to the dying, their death was gentle; if applied to the dead, they returned to life.[5] By extension of its association with Mercury and Hermes, the caduceus is also a recognized symbol of commerce and negotiation, two realms in which balanced exchange and reciprocity are recognized as ideals.[6][7] This association is ancient, and consistent from the Classical period to modern times.[8] The caduceus is also used as a symbol representing printing, again by extension of the attributes of Mercury (in this case associated with writing and eloquence). The caduceus is often incorrectly used as a symbol of healthcare organizations and medical practice, particularly in North America, due to confusion with the traditional medical symbol, the Rod of Asclepius, which has only one snake and is never depicted with wings.

13 SOMEONE'S KNOCKING AT THE DOOR - SOMEONE'S RINGING THE BELL

The Group returned to the Theosophical Society in mid-July after a couple of weeks break. Mayumi was still on holiday but everyone else was back and there was a sense of renewed enthusiasm and expectation. The sounds we had experienced before when it seemed as if someone had walked across the room came back, and this time in such a way that it couldn't fail to grab our attention:

> *The room was set up again by having candles and turquoise present – these were set up along the top of the fireplace. There was a larger candle-jar (a candle moulded into a glass jar). Gill placed this in one of the corners of the room on an upturned vase. About 5 minutes into the meditation Ann got up and quietly moved the candles from the top of the fireplace and placed them around the room, encircling the Group members, and retook her place. Also during the meditation, the door made a loud crack as if someone wanted to enter the room and had tried the door handle.*

Ann opened in prayer and the Group then sat in silent meditation for some time. Jim then asked the Group for a brief comment:

Gordon: 'I don't know if other people heard what I heard?'

Ann to Gordon: 'Someone walking across the room?'

Gordon: 'It was like an animal snorting. In that direction (he pointed directly opposite himself to a position between where Gill and Jim were sitting). Like a big animal, a big beast. I heard that about three times all in a very short period of time – that's why I looked up. I was just hearing it for the third time and I thought, I am going to look and see what's happening.'

Gill to Ann: 'Did you walk across the room?'

Ann: 'I did, yes, but after I sat down again I thought you (Gill) had got up and walked across there (she pointed to a position directly opposite Gill, between Gordon and Mairi) because there was definitely movement, but someone walked from there across and through there and I could hear distinctly the movement and the clothes, the only thing is that it wasn't the clothes you (Gill) are wearing; they were more rustling than yours would be if you were to move. (Gill was wearing jeans and a t-shirt?). Did anyone else hear that?'

Gordon: 'I felt there was some movement, here (he indicated the same position that Ann had referred to), but that blended into the background as a result of this very loud snorting sound that I perceived. Did anyone else hear any of this?'

Gill: 'All I heard was the door.'

Gordon: 'It was after that.'

Jim: 'Did the door open – was it the door?'

Gill: 'I thought it was as if someone was coming in the door.'

Gordon: 'Yes, I thought someone had put a hand on the handle of the door and tried it. Were you aware of it, Mairi?'

Mairi: 'Yes, I was aware of it but I was also aware of Spirit with Jim and I turned and looked, shortly after you did (Gill).'

Jim: 'I think there may have been a female (Spirit) with me; there was a very strong presence, a very strong energy, but I didn't feel like speaking, there was nothing there to say.'

Jim: 'Do you have anything, Mairi?'

Mairi: 'No, I didn't really feel like speaking, it seemed to be very quiet. I was in and out of a very strong quietness; I was disturbed by the door and it sort of rattled me awake and then I became aware of what was happening with you (Jim), then there was a huge amount of heat and I felt it quite difficult to stay with the breathing, my breathing seemed to speed up and I felt I wanted to get up and move and I thought no, I can't do that, then the heat seemed to move over to you (Jim), that's when I opened my eyes to see what was happening with you.'

Gordon: 'I was aware of a presence to my left (indicating towards Jim). As for the other thing, I'm not one for audibly hearing things and it was unusual, that experience. I can only liken it to one other experience I've had before and it was when I was doing a Shamanic Journey and I was aware of the Buffalo, and heavy footsteps; it sounded as if it was going round the ring quite quickly and I became aware of footsteps from four feet and then there was some snorts at that time, right up at the back of my neck, and I can only assume that that was the Buffalo, and that was what this sounded like to me tonight over in this corner and I'm not used to getting that.'

Jim: 'Just for the benefit of the tape, shortly after we sat, probably five or ten minutes into it, Ann got up and walked around the room placing candles. It seems to me that the noises we have experienced and are discussing took place *after* that event, and if there are footsteps or whatever, that happened after Ann had actually sat down.'

Ann to Gordon: 'Were you aware of me getting up?'

Gordon: 'Yes.'
Ann: 'That's good then, so you can make the distinction?'
Gordon: 'Yes. I'd just be interested in the tape when playing back if it has captured anything, as I don't normally hear that type of thing.'
(It should be pointed out at this time that the tape was switched off whilst the Group were in silent meditation – as is the normal procedure. It is usually considered a waste of the tape to record the silence, but given what occurred here, it may be something to consider for future.)
Ann: 'I was sitting trying to go into the silence, but I wasn't allowed to. I was getting prompted by Spirit to move these candles; *they've got to be around us and particularly in the corners of the room.* But I was replying, that I couldn't move now, because we'd started and we were in Circle and I was trying to ignore this and say, carry on, I'll do it later, but I was not allowed to, I was experiencing just what you were saying Mairi, it was like, *you've got to get up, you've got to get up.*'
Mairi: 'Yes, yes. I was experiencing that at the same time.'
Ann: 'I felt *I know I have to do this* and I got the impression that the energy was not going to build properly unless I did it. I also thought it may have been something to do with protection and so I thought, well I'll have to do it, so I got up and moved the candles and I thought, well if they've to surround us, I'd better do it.'

Interesting that both Mairi and I had been influenced very strongly to get up – in my case, to move the candles. Etiquette states that once a Circle is sitting (in silence) no-one should move and certainly not get up and walk around the room. This urge felt by both Mairi and I was going against all protocol. Perhaps Gordon's Buffalo was serving the same purpose, he was just experiencing it in a different way. What we do know is that very shortly afterwards the handle of our door was turned giving out a loud crack as if someone was going to walk into the room.

> Ann: 'I was then aware of the movement (in the Circle) and thought, oh, Gill's got up now, and I could distinctly hear the movement of clothes but when I think about it now, it was like a rustling of someone moving with....'
> Gordon: 'Petticoats.'
> Ann: 'Yes, skirts or something. I could hear the movement and it went from there, (indicating a line through the centre of the circle) through between Gordon and Mairi, which made me think again, someone's moving.'
> Ann: 'Oh, the other thing I should mention is that when I went to turn on the tape after the meditation, I noticed that the buttons were sticky, and my fingers aren't sticky. It's gone now, but there was a stickiness to the buttons on the tape recorder.'
> Jim: 'Does anyone have a feeling of what we should be doing?'
> Ann: 'Well, we're supposed to be moving the table over there.'

Jim: 'For the purposes of the tape we have now moved the table to a position against the wall, which we had previously been directed to do and we'll see where that takes us.'
The Group all sat round the small upright table with their hands lightly on its surface.
Ann to Spirit: 'If we have a Spirit Communicator with us tonight would they please make their presence known by moving the table – any direction at all, just move the table for us, please.'
The table began to vibrate slowly.
Gordon: 'Please move in a direct manner.'
The table moved more positively.
Gordon: 'Thank you.'
Jim: 'We are making the assumption that your 'yes' and 'no' will be the same as in previous occasions. If you could give us the 'yes', please.'
The table remained stationary.
Jim to the Group: 'That was a very garbled question, wasn't it?'
Ann: 'Show us your 'yes'.
The tabled moved in a rocking motion from side to side.
The Group laughed at the simple questions that got the positive response.
Jim to Ann: 'Smart arse!' *The Group all laughed again.*
Mairi to Jim: 'This is the woman who edits the tape.'
Ann: 'Exactly!' *The Group all join with laughter again.*
Gordon: 'I like that, yes. The table's quite happy too; it's rocked against the wall.'
Ann: 'Can you show us your 'no''.
The table is suddenly stationary. 'Thank you.'
Gordon: 'Can we ask for confirmation that we have the same Spirit Group that was with us last time?' *Yes.* 'Thank you.'
Mairi: 'We've maybe got more people with us tonight, as they're not at the college.' *Everyone laughs and the table rocks in appreciation.*
(Mairi was joking about the fact that the Psychic College had an evening of clairvoyance on at the same time as our meeting last time and suggested that some of our Spirit Team would be required there).
Ann: 'Now that's interesting, because, did anyone notice from the last notes that, what I think helped made a difference last time, was the laughter?' *The table knocks in acknowledgement.*
Mairi: 'Yes, that's right.
Ann: Because, if you remember, there was quite a lot of laughter and it just seemed to raise the energy again and again.'
Gill: 'Yes, and you like to hear us talking as well?' *Yes.*
Gill: 'You don't like the long periods of silence.'
Mairi adds: 'While we think.'
Ann: 'You can smell the wood burning!'
The Group laughs again and the table rocks as Ann makes a joke about the Group thinking.

Gill clearly has her own agenda and comes in with a more serious question:

>Gill: 'I have a question. Regarding the other person who is with you, is he of a medical background?' *Yes. (The table continues rocking excitedly, almost as if perceiving the next question).*
>Gill: 'And, this person was a colleague of Sir Arthur Conan Doyle?' *Yes.*
>Gill: 'Thank you. Did he work in Edinburgh?' *Yes.*
>Gill: 'Would I be correct in saying there has been a recent newspaper article about this?' *Yes.*
>Gill: 'Am I correct in saying there has been a special exhibition regarding this?' *Yes. (The table then tilts over till the top of it is resting in Gill's lap).*
>Gill: 'Can you just go back to your position now, so I can ask another question.' *The table returns to an upright position as the Group realise that Gill is receiving further information that the others are unaware of.*
>Gill: 'Would this gentleman's name be – now I'm not putting his title in - Joseph Bell?' *Yes.*
>Ann: 'Well done, well done, I'm glad you're back, Gill. She's obviously been doing her homework whilst she's been away, that's good.'
>Gill: 'It was actually in tonight's paper.'
>Ann: 'Oh, excellent, well there's synchronicity for you.'
>Jim: 'Who's Joseph Bell?'
>Gill: 'Joseph Bell was the Professor at Arthur Conan Doyle's university, and Arthur Conan Doyle worked as his clerk, isn't that correct?' *Yes.*
>Gill: 'And he is reputed to have been the model for Sherlock Holmes, and if you see a photo of him, you'll see that apart from the white hair, he looks exactly like Sherlock Holmes – don't you?' *Yes.*
>Ann to Gill: 'Does that mean he's tall and thin with a wee goatee beard?'
>Gill: 'Yes, with white hair – isn't that correct? Well you had white hair – you may have gone back to your younger days, but you had white hair, isn't that correct?' *Yes. (As the table tips forward towards Gill again.)*
>Gill: 'Yes, thank you, I'm glad to be back.'
>Ann: 'Is this the same person that came through very early on in our deliberations?' *Yes.*
>Jim: 'With the bike [the penny-farthing]?' *Yes.*
>Ann: 'Right, so you're also the scientist?' *Yes.*
>Ann: 'So, we've pinned him down now?' *Yes.*
>Gill to Ann: 'Maybe you should rephrase pinning!' *(The Group laughs).*
>Gill: 'So, if we could establish this evening, please......'
>Ann in exclamation: 'Bell, his name's Bell!'
>Gill to Ann: 'Are you listening outside?'
>*Outside the Group become aware that an alarm bell (like a burglar alarm) has started ringing.*
>Ann: 'Yes, but also, ...' *the table rocks and tilts towards Ann.*
>Ann acknowledges the table: 'Okay, that's fine, thank you.'

Ann to the Group: 'Do you remember the other week I kept seeing a bell and I was to bring a bell-shaped object and I kept asking for the name?'
Jim: 'Yes, yes.'
Ann: 'Was that…….. Oh, you've already answered the question' – *as the table was rocking continuously as she spoke.*
Ann: 'Was that your influence to get us to recognise your name?'
Table rocks an excited, 'yes'. And, there's another bell ringing outside.

The Group is amazed by yet another example of the intelligence of Spirit, using visions, inanimate objects and now external sounds to get their message across.

From the time that we discovered that Arthur Conan Doyle was communicating with me, each time I sat in silence thereafter he would give me a quick flash of a vison of his face to let me know he was with me – this was by now a regular occurrence. There was no need for the convoluted clues, pictures and messages now that I had accepted him. Now, it would seem that Joseph Bell was following this same rule of thumb.

Gill: 'Yes, there's an alarm gone off outside, well done.'
Gordon: 'The ringing of the alarm bell is a bit of a coincidence.'
Gill: 'There's no such thing as coincidence.'
Ann: 'So, can I just clarify then, there's no need… I was influenced by you about the bell-shape and I thought I had to bring a bell-type item here….' *Table responds, yes.*
Ann: 'Yes, thank you, but that was to allow us to grasp your name, it wasn't for any other purpose, you don't actually want a bell here, is that correct?'
Gill repeating Ann's garbled question: '…you don't actually want a bell here???'
Ann: 'Do you want a bell here?' *No.*
Ann: 'The bell-shaped item was to signify your name, that was the sole purpose of it, is that correct?' *Yes.*
Ann: 'Wow, that was clever – it just took us longer to figure out what was happening.'
Ann: 'Would I be right in thinking ………… we've pulled together a group of like-minded, trustworthy, committed individuals, you've already acknowledged that… but, in bringing this particular Group together, each member has their own specialism. So am I right in thinking that just like that, each member of the Group in the Spirit World who are linking with us, also have their own specialisms and have been brought together to link with each one of us? In other words the Group in the Spirit World, their specialisms mirror the specialisms of each one of us here in this Group?' *The table was continually rocking in the affirmative as Ann was talking.*
Ann: 'The reason it's making me think this is that we have healers here and you have healers there. Also, Giilfeather would perhaps be a

Shamanic person and Mairi and Gordon are both into Shamanic things?' *Yes.*
Jim to Gordon and Mairi: 'And Gordon and Mairi agree with that too?' *Both nod in agreement.*
Ann: 'And there's probably more linkages and connections and more to find out too, is that correct too?' *Yes.*
Jim to Ann: 'Could you try and establish if there's someone to work with the three who have not been mentioned?'
Ann: 'Well I'm just glad that there's an author up there, because there's not one down here!' *The Group all laugh and the table rocks excitedly.*
Jim: 'Well Mayumi would be a healer, and Ann you would consider yourself a healer too? My impression is that the main aim of this Group – now you've answered this before – but I feel quite strongly that this is what this is about, this Group – would you agree?' *No.*
Mairi to Jim: 'You got the same answer last time.' *Table is stationary.*
Ann to Jim: 'You just need to rephrase your question.'
Jim: 'We are all of us, in the course of our everyday lives able to offer healing to individuals, and do. Would that be correct?'
After a long pause the table rocks a 'yes'.
Gill to Spirit: 'Took you a while to understand that one, eh?'
Jim: 'I'll explain to the Group afterwards what I mean by that.'
Ann: 'Thank the Lord for that!' *The Group all laugh.*
Mairi: 'Is he here too?' *The Group continue to laugh.*
Ann: 'Well, I'm trying to help the humour.'
Jim: 'Yes, the Lord is here.'
Mairi in jest: 'Well hello there!' *As the table responds to the humour excitedly.*
Jim: 'Just refer to him, as JC.' *The Group continues to laugh, as Jim refers to his own initials JC.*

Once again our session had proven the intelligence of the spirit world in getting its message through – in this case in using inanimate objects to signal the surname of a communicator – the impressive Joseph Bell, inspiration for Sherlock Holmes. Some would say his talents were not solely confined to observation and deduction – he might well have achieved some of his remarkable results because he himself was psychic.

Also, the 'circle of light' which was created by the candles was another vision previously downloaded which was said to be for the protection of our Group; with the candles encircling us we would be sitting inside this 'circle of light'. So it was strange that both Mairi and I were prompted to get up and in my case move those candles to provide this protection; did Spirit know that someone was going to try to walk into the centre of our Circle and try the door handle, or was it a Spirit person who had walked through the Circle – perhaps wearing petticoats?

14 LEVITATION

There are a number of religions which include the ability to levitate as some of their recognised miracles. The most obvious example is Buddhism where Buddha is reputed to have levitated cross-legged –especially over water. This walking on water or levitating over water appears in many other religions including Hinduism, Judaism and of course Christianity where Jesus walks on water. Some other examples include St Theresa of the Roses, St Francis of Assisi, as recent as the last century, Padre Pio and from Spiritualism, Daniel Dunglas Home, mentioned earlier in this book. It is interesting that by far the majority of these examples come from Christianity and in most cases those individuals involved are later made Saints by that religion. However when it occurs in Spiritualism it is usually decried either as the work of the occult or the devil and normally the Medium involved is accused of fraud and trickery. So, I'm not sure what the sceptics would think of inanimate objects levitating when those Mediums present are as surprised as anyone else!

Back at the Theosophical Society we learnt a lot more about table-tilting over many of the following weeks. In previous weeks we had been surprised by the table's movements which had defied gravity. Amongst some Group members there had also been an expectation that the table would actually levitate, a huge expectation and not one that I thought we would actually see; but how wrong I was. At the next session of the Group this is what transpired:

> Gill: 'Right, can you give an indication of which way the Group should direct its energies please?' *No.*
> Gordon: 'Should we continue with the table this evening?' *Yes.*
> Gordon: 'Well, previously you obliged us very much by showing the amount of energy that was within the table; it was rolling all over the

floor and made a partial elevation by moving all four legs off the floor; is that correct?' *Yes.*
Gordon: 'This week, should we expect something similar?'
The table vibrates slightly.
Gill: 'Mmm, the energy's different.'
Gordon: 'Okay, we stick with the table just now and we see what happens?'

The other point that had emerged was that the previous demonstration (with the Buffalo and the ringing of the bell) was not only to identify a surname but also to demonstrate Clairaudience – Jim had asked about Clairaudience and if we were going to hear something. Spirit had asked him to continue his line of questioning.

Jim: 'Right. Was it also for Clairsentience?' *Yes.*
Ann: 'Before we move away from the animal, can I just ask one question? Was it a positive Spirit that was creating that energy?' *No response.*
Gordon: 'Maybe it's the term 'positive' that's causing the problem. Maybe a 'good' energy Spirit is better?'
Ann: 'The Animal Spirit that was creating that image, was it of good intent?' *Yes.*
Ann: 'Okay, that's fine.'
Jim: 'But why would an animal want to come through to us?'
Gill: 'It's not.'
Ann: 'It's the Clairaudience – it's been used as a demonstration'.
Mairi: 'Well, I would like to turn that questions around and ask, do animals want to come through and communicate with us, as part of what we're doing in this Group?' *Yes.*
Ann: 'Well done, Mairi, that's good.'
Gordon: 'We've already experienced animals coming through this Group and indeed quite regularly in the beginning, is this a reminder to us not to forget this and for us not to get too caught up with only humans?' *Yes.*
Gordon: 'Yes, thank you for that remembrance.'
Gordon: 'Has that got us to the root of it now? Maybe not quite but we're much closer anyway.'
The table continues to rock and then tilts over into Gills lap.
Jim: 'What were you thinking Gill that made the table tilt over in that way?'
Gill addresses the table: 'Yes, would you like to move? Could you go back to position so I can stand up please?'
The Group all stand and move their chairs to the side to allow more space in the room. The table moves away from Gill's lap to a position in the centre of the room.
Gill: 'I feel that the purpose of this Group is that we're trying to bring

back the basics of what this is about, the good basics, of trying to prove the continuance of life, is that correct?' *Yes.*
Gill: 'So we have to use this opportunity to get our link stronger with you, is that correct?' *No movement from the table.*
Gill: 'Would you like to use this opportunity to do more physical work?' *Yes.*
Gill: 'Okay, so if you would like to move, just move. Okay, so you want to go down on to the floor?'
The table tilts downwards on two legs and slowly and gently lowers itself down on to the floor. All Group members have their hands on the table top.
Jim: 'For some of us here: it's easy to get down but not so easy to get back up again.'
Gill to the table: 'Come on, go, go, go.'
Jim: 'That's it.'
Mairi: 'That's it. Lovely, lovely... up... up.'
The table now uses the wall as a lever to right itself again and is standing on two legs with the other two propped up against the wall. Everyone has their hands on the table top except Ann who has returned to the tape-recorder to record this excerpt.
Gill: 'Can you do a twirl on one leg? You seem to be wanting to dance? Come on then, on you go. I think you want to get the momentum up, is that correct?'
The table knocks loudly against the wall.
Gill: 'Are you wanting to go up the wall?'
The table moves away from the wall.
Gill: 'Are you wanting to move into the centre?'
The table moves towards the centre of the room.
Mairi exclaims at the movement: 'Oh!'
The table has now lowered itself to the floor again and slid along the floor again and is now revolving on one leg.

This was similar to the movement we had previously witnessed, but tonight something different was happening.

Jim: 'I wonder if we assisted it, and let everyone know that we are assisting it, simply by two of us placing our hands on the bottom, at the legs.'
The table has now gone on to the floor again on its side.
Gill to Jim: 'Well it could perhaps use that to build up the energy.'
The table is lying on its side on the floor, Gill, Gordon and Mairi all have their hands on the table top, Ann and Jim are on each side of the table, each have placed their hands at the table legs and are trying to build up the energy there.

The Group held this position for several minutes, commentating on how they were feeling the buildup of the energy, especially around the table legs – our hands had never been placed around the legs before, so this feeling was very new.

> *Suddenly the table elevates to about 2 feet from the floor level and then turned right upside down and then came back to lying in the same position on its side, back on the floor again. (Almost like turning a summersault).*

As you might imagine, we were aghast – especially me because whilst the others had an expectation of levitation, I didn't think it would actually happen; yet here was a table turning summersaults a couple of feet off the ground.

> *There are various gasps and expletives as well as commentary amongst the Group as they again become aware of the energy building. Then, the table elevates again, about 2-3 feet from the floor and quickly moves across the room and comes to rest upside down on one of the chairs that had been pushed back to the side of the room near the window. The Group members were left standing round the chair on which the table had come to rest, except Gill who had dropped to her knees in front of the chair as she had tried to keep up with the table and keep her hands on the table top whilst it moved across the room.*
> Gill: 'I have to say, that the sweat is now pouring off me, here. And I have a genuine, genuine fear that……. you eventually will be off the wall?' *The Group all laugh.*
> *At this point, as if in response to Gill, the table tilted from the chair it was resting on and tilted over to a position so that it had captured Gills head between its legs. Gill was now facing the underside of the table top. This was done in a slow and gentle movement so that Gill's head was encapsulated within the relatively small inner space of the table without it ever touching her face or head as it did so.*
> *Again the Group all laughed in surprise at this move.*
> Gill: 'Oh, thank you very much. Right, come on then, let's move. Where are we going then?'
> *The table then begins moving forwards, legs first, in doing so it is pushing Gill so that her back is being pushed backwards as if she was a limbo dancer.*
> Gill: 'Now I can't do that, and I can't lift that.'
> Jim: 'It's all right, we've got it.'
> *The Group retained their hands around the table as before until Gill 'limboed' so far backwards that the table cleared her head whilst remaining at the same height – about 2 feet from the floor. It then righted itself to stand again upright on four legs in the centre of the room.*
> Mairi: 'Ohhhhhh!' *As the table elevated upwards and went entirely upside down and moved over towards the wall and then back towards*

the centre of the room and has now come to rest upside down with the table top resting on top of Gill's head.
Jim: 'Now, could you raise yourself off Gill's head?'
Gill: 'You're on my head. Right okay, concentrate you've got to keep the energy – I know it's easy to say but you've got to move yourself.'
Gill is on her knees and the table is now above her head and her hands are underneath it. Gill then takes one hand away as she wants to hold on to Gordon. Jim asks the others if they can take their hands away, which they do but the table becomes unsteady. Jim then asks Gill if she can take her hands away, but she says no. The others return their hands to the table and take its weight to return it to the floor right way up.
Gill to Spirit: 'Are you still there?' *Yes.*
Gill: 'It was a lapse in concentration, I'm sorry.'
The table continues to rock positively. (Gill refers to herself as she felt she had lost concentration momentarily when the Group had to take the weight of the table).
Gill: 'Would you like to go back to the wall, please?'
Ann: 'The last time it wanted to finish in the centre of the room.'
Gill: 'Right, would you like to finish in the centre of the room?' *Yes.*
The table moves back to the centre of the room. The table was almost galloping whilst the Group were talking and then came to rest.
Mairi: 'It's stopped.'
Gill: 'It's concentrating. There's a change.'
Jim to the Group: 'Can we change position just a wee, wee bit if possible. Let's try this connection that Ann suggested we did last week.'
The Group all have their hands on the table top and link their pinkies together with the person next to them and connect together their own thumbs, making a circle on the table top.
Mairi: 'Yes, they liked it last week. It made a circle.'
Jim: 'Yes, it was scrying.'
Gordon: 'Yes, I apologise for that; I forgot my mirror.'
Ann: 'Remember the face that appeared last week?'
Gill: 'Have you finished for the evening?'
Gill: 'Is it symbolic, the linking of the circle?'
Jim: 'Before you go, can I just ask a question. It would have been extremely good to have recorded this photographically. What I want to ask is if we bring a camera along next week, with the strict understanding and agreement that we know we are taking a photograph of a re-enactment – could we recreate this event next week – if that makes sense.'
Gill: 'Do you mean a still camera or a video camera?'
Jim: 'A still camera. And, it would be clear to all of us that we are actually recreating the scene for the purposes of the photograph - it was not photographed when it was actually taking place - and it would be labelled accordingly.'
Mairi: 'How would we get into those positions?'

This comment from Mairi demonstrates how difficult some of the positions were that the table had got into, such that even trying to recreate them for a photograph would prove difficult. Later, when typing up this transcript it was noted that Jim did not actually receive permission to his suggestion to recreate the event and during the Group Discussion (towards the end of this transcript) he appeared to change his position and warned against this course of action. Meanwhile, something else was happening.

> Ann to Gordon: 'Can you see something in there?'
> Gordon: 'Again, like last week, there's an element of the fogginess coming in again and I was just wondering if they were going to show us something, as they are still very much here, you see, they didn't go.'
> Ann: 'There's something in there. Do you see it right in the centre?'
> Mairi: 'There's something in the centre.'
> Ann: 'Yes it's a sort of swirl.'
> Gill: 'Is it not just the residual energy of the table?'
> Ann: 'Well when we did this last week we stood for a while and let it build up and we began to see a face, and we had that confirmed that they were trying to show us a face.'
> Gordon: 'My eyes are going out of focus to allow them to direct something at me.'

Suddenly the energy was gone – even quicker than it had arrived – we surmised that table movements like this used up a lot of energy.

> Gill: 'They've gone now.'
> *Ann closed in Prayer.*
> <u>Group Discussion:</u>
> Mairi: 'Well, how do you explain that away?'
> Ann: 'Right, can I have a quick summary from each of you of thoughts or impressions?'
> Gill: 'When the table was... not liquefying, but changing its molecules, I was very conscious of using the energy. My solar plexus was getting pulled on quite strongly and they were using the energies of all of us to build up an extra support to allow the table to change and there were moments of stillness, and then there was this surge and I was getting told, we're going to go now, and then it would move. When it was on its side on the ground, it was almost as if there was a debate going on on the other side; it was like, *we're down here, so how do we get back up?* That's when it changed; they changed it to doing that other thing. When it was on my head, it was unbelievable, I could feel the power, it was like high voltage electricity. Thing is it was just so concentrated and I was sweating and I don't usually sweat like that.'
> Mairi: 'Well it was just mind-blowing. You wouldn't believe it if you

hadn't seen it yourself, that it could move as freely as that and get so high off the ground and get out of such impossible situations. And we tested it previously to see how much energy it took to move it and it was considerable and I just thought it was incredible.'

Ann: 'Jim, do you want me to come back to you?' *(Ann has become aware that Jim is being overshadowed again).*

Jim: 'Yes, please.'

Gordon: 'The other amazing thing to me that I witnessed was that, like Gill, I felt the stillness and I knew it was going to move and I knew it was going to shoot off before it did, and on one occasion I knew it was just about to go and that's when it moved towards the wall. Even on its biggest move, or biggest first move, although it would appear if you were looking at the table that there wasn't anything happening, it certainly didn't feel that way and the table certainly felt strange and then there were four distinct cracks that were heard loudly. And to see Gill taking part in the way that she did with the table sitting the way that it was, was something to behold.'

Ann: 'Yes, I wished I had had a camera.'

Jim, [in a voice that is not his own]: 'You should not make the assumption that you'd be allowed to use the camera.'

Ann: 'Oh, no, I just mean, I might well have actually had my camera with me tonight, and I could have asked permission.'

Jim: [speaking still with a slight overshadowing]: 'I think if we try and replicate that next week it will be very difficult to do as we will have to physically try to hold the table in place whilst we take the photos. This is not the purpose of the Group. But we have to acknowledge here and now that what took place tonight was NOT by us holding anything physically at all; we just placed our hands upon it. But, one will argue, especially if they see staged photos, especially when they see Gill on her knees and when she stood up she will be seen to have her hands on the table... inevitably people will say she was supported. We know that did NOT take place, but for the purposes of recording accurately, having made that statement, I think this should be recorded: The room, the table, and the movements of the table are all important for historical documentation and we should undertake that now. I for one, am very happy to be associated in what took place here this evening and I'm absolutely, 100% sure, that wherever the energy came from, the table was NOT held in place by ourselves. This is my testimony. A Camera is not necessary.'

Ann: 'Thank you for that, and I concur with what you've said. The only thing I would add to what Gordon has said is that I agree that when we were both down at the bottom end of the table, near the legs, I could feel them cracking and at one point I thought the leg had come apart; it became fluid almost and I thought it had come away completely from the table, and I could also feel energy coming out from the bottoms of the legs as it was tickling the backs of my hands, it was like invisible hairs of something streaming out from the bottom of the legs. I was also amazed how quickly the table moved as well.'

Gordon: 'Yes, I think someone used the term, 'rods'[21] and I used the term as well and it did actually feel like there were rods of energy coming out of the legs of the table. One other aspect with regards to what Jim was saying about the photographs – it may not come out as exactly as it did tonight, and would diminish what actually happened.'

Jim: 'I think, Gordon, it's almost difficult to say; at one point this table actually went over to that chair and actually sat on the chair upside down, which in itself is a bit of a feat when you hear all the other things it did. It then acknowledged all the requests that it was asked to do.'

Gill: 'Yes, it was mind-blowing really.'

Jim: 'It was just amazing to see it.'

Further discussion took place after the tape ended, including Jim's request that there was a need for Ann to type the transcript of the tape verbatim because of the significance of the events this evening.

And as that transcript is reproduced here for the same reasons, you will now begin to realise how amazing and unbelievable these experiences were.

15 DIAGNOSIS

As we reconvened the following week after the remarkable feats of the table the week before there was a palpable anticipation that we might be privileged to enjoy a repeat performance – we lived in hope. But before we started I again had that feeling that something was not quite right in the room. The need for protection that had struck me before was back. I had previously decided that my unease was the residual feeling of concern I had about using the Ouija Board but the feeling was back this week. Discussing it with Jim before the others arrived we felt that the circle of candles gave some comfort against this feeling of vulnerability, but we realised that, although we had the candles, our box of matches was empty. The Group sat in silence again as usual then Jim asked for feedback:

> Mayumi: 'I feel two very different activities. This side is very calm but I was feeling as if I was being pulled at this (other) side – quite a strong pull.'
> Ann: 'The first thing I got was Red Feather, and I thought, as well as Giilfeather, there's also Redfeather, but I don't know if that's a person or an object. Then I was aware of a male presence with me and I saw his face and he reminded me a little of Sean Connery - thinner in the face but that sort of type – short grey hair and I think he had a beard. I felt he was trying to highlight something, draw our attention to something, some connection that we're missing; but I don't know what it is. He was showing me something and it looked like one of those highlighter pens. I don't know what all of that was about but I think it was the same person as last week. I feel there's some connection we're yet to find, but I don't have any more than that at the moment.'
> Gordon: 'At the beginning I felt a lot of energy very quickly and then I felt a presence very close and then it dissipated, and I don't know if that's when he went off in your direction (indicating Ann), but then I became

aware of something happening over here (pointing towards Gill) and I opened my eyes and saw that Gill had bent over in a sort of scrunched up position and I didn't know if she was, a) okay physically, or b) whether Spirit was with her and Spirit was in a frightened state, or a disabled state, or c) whether it was an emotional upset; so, my attention then went towards Gill. The other thing that was happening is that Sir Isaac Newton's name keeps popping up in my head, and I don't know why. I did have a previous connection with someone who told me that Sir Isaac Newton was trying to make contact with me before. That person said I had to get involved with Spirit writing; so, I don't know and we talked about pens and things like that and, him being what he was, I wondered if there could be some sort of link there – but that's me thinking cognitively about it.'

Jim: 'It's maybe something we want to consider for the agenda for the Circle - automatic writing. Mairi?'

Mairi: 'I didn't have as much as all that, I just had a little fox at the beginning, quite thin and slow and he was just watching all the way around, and then I got a little bit of the feeling I got last week – a little bit panic, a little bit restlessness, and a little bit, didn't know whether to move or not move and then I just seemed to, not go to sleep, but just sort of space out and then I became aware of what was happening with Gill and you (Jim) brought us back quite quickly.'

Gill: 'I don't know. I can't really tell you anything except that I felt unsettled.'

Jim to Gill: 'Were you aware of your position?'

Gill had bent right over in her seat so that her head was on her lap and her arms were wrapped around her legs just below her knees.

Gill: 'Yes, I was aware of my position and of not feeling comfortable, of wanting to move but not wanting to move.'
Jim: 'Were you resisting?'
Gill: 'To a certain extent.'
Jim: 'Do you feel that was right?'
Gill: 'I don't know Jim. I was aware of the influences and I didn't feel safe.'
Gordon: 'Was there an emotional aspect to how you were feeling?'
Gill: 'I can't say I felt emotion. I wanted to 'sink' if that's the right word.'
Jim: 'Did you feel you were being forced into that position.'
Gill: 'I wasn't being forced, the choice was mine and then I chose to go with it to a certain extent, but then I chose not to go any further with it.'
Ann: 'Were you not comfortable with the energy coming in, or was it the atmosphere in the room?'
Gill: 'No, that was why I was...., part of me was listening to what was going on outside the room and the words that kept coming to me was that I wasn't safe.'

Once again the Group had become aware of someone outside our room, but this time, they were physical people. We could hear them talking as they climbed the stairs to the top floor.

> Jim: 'The position that I think you may have been trying to adopt was a foetal position, was that right?'
> Gill: 'It may have been but I was trying to form protection, it was protection that I was going for.'
> Ann: 'I was saying that before we started tonight, before you arrived, Gill, that I felt that there was a need for protection in this room. And that was the same as last week – I wouldn't get up and disturb a Circle, I've never ever done that before, but I knew I had to get up for all our sakes and get the candles over there and in that corner, and I felt it was to do with protection. I felt also that the energy was saying that we can't build in that room without it and so I felt it was giving them (Spirit) protection as well, and you (Gordon) and your Buffalo as well, I do feel that there's an element of protection needed in here, for whatever reason, I don't know why, but there is.'
> Gill: 'I know this sounds so contradictory, but I wanted to swap with you tonight (Ann), because I wanted to block that door.... *(Ann was sitting with her back to the door).*
> Ann: 'Well you should have said; we could have done that.'
> Gill: 'I wanted to block that door behind you. I don't know if it's psychological, that I have this view that someone's going to come in and break it (the energy/concentration/contemplation), not intentionally, but they're just going to walk in maybe by mistake, but I think that's maybe just my mind kicking in that I was concerned that I need this protection thing as there was too much going on out there for me to settle.'

We had heard a number of people climb the stairs to go to the tearoom along the corridor. It is interesting to note here that Spirit gave us the intuition that we were going to be disturbed, in their communications weeks before. Indeed, perhaps in an effort to get their point across, they actually disturbed us themselves by walking through the centre of our circle – petticoats and all.

> Gordon referring to the people outside: 'Do you think we should draw their attention to the fact that we're in here, would that help?'
> Ann: 'I think they're being quiet, or trying to be quiet.'
> Gill: 'It's just the fact that they are going around and about and I know how people are, and I just....'
> Ann: 'It reinforces the fact that we need a place to ourselves where we are not going to be disturbed.'
> Gill: 'What about you Jim, what were you observing?'

Jim: 'I felt very comfortable actually, and I felt I could go very deep here, but I thought no, one of us is going to remain fully aware in order to take care of the Group, and then I became aware of you (Gill) and your position all doubled up and from a purely physical point of view, in the position you were in, I thought it would have been difficult to breath.'
Gill: 'My breathing was fine.'
Jim: 'My own feeling as to the absence of the candles - Spirit will be aware that it's not an oversight on our part; it's just that we didn't have a match and I can't imagine Spirit would say well we're going away because you didn't have a match.'
Gill: 'No, I know that they're here, and protecting us, ...'
Jim: 'Anytime I've sat anywhere you don't have to worry about someone walking in, as there's usually a period of quietness for an hour or so, but that just can't happen in this building now and it's unlikely unless we'll get premises on our own....'

Something had changed with arrangements in the building. Up until that point we had had the top floor to ourselves at least for our first hour when we would be sitting in silence. Now for whatever reason we were aware that people were climbing the stairs to get cups of coffee from the tearoom whilst we were sitting in silence. Perhaps this is what Spirit was warning us about – this change in arrangements to someone else's meeting times.

The table was moved nearer to the wall, but a wee bit away from it, as, Jim says, 'last week it was almost knocking the wall down'.
All placed their hands on the table.
Gill: 'It's going now.' *The table begins to move.*
Mayumi: 'Yes.'
Jim: 'I would like to establish who we have working with us, but first, can you show us your signal for 'yes' this evening, is it the same as in previous evenings?' *The table began to rock.*
Gordon: 'There's sponginess this evening.'
Mairi: 'Yes, there is.'
Jim: 'Yes, I can understand you taking time to build up.'
The table begins rocking quite decisively now.
Jim: 'And, 'no'?' *The table falls still.*
Jim: 'I would also like to know, are we working with the same Group on the other side as we were working with last week?' *Table rocks, 'yes'.*
Mairi: 'I think there could be something physically on the table, there's a really sticky, oily feel to it and it wasn't there to start with.'
The table rocks excitedly.
(The substance to which Mairi refers can be clearly seen and Ann remarks that it's similar to what happened to the tape recorder the week before).
Gordon: 'Was anyone thinking of something there just now, because the table's responding?' *The table becomes very animated.*

Ann: 'It's away already.'
Gordon commentating: 'The table is balancing on one leg and moving from leg to leg going around in a clockwise manner.'
Jim: 'We are sitting in partial light, is that acceptable for what you would have us do this evening?' *Yes.*
Jim: 'Could it be that we could perhaps open the shutters completely?' *Yes.*

The shutters had been partially closed to reduce the glare from the August sunshine, which had been streaming in through our top floor window.

Jim: 'Thank you, that's much appreciated. Now, Gill has just gone to the window to open it up. We discussed earlier that we would experience these phenomena in full daylight – this is a good test; would you agree with that?' *Yes.*
The table spins around, knocks Mayumi's knee and tilts in towards Mayumi's lap.
Ann: 'I get the impression that we should just forget the questions and just go with the flow, is that right table – are you away walking?'
The table is rocking from leg to leg and the Group let out a gasp as it responds by spinning on one leg and then lowers itself down on to the floor.
Gill commentating: 'The table is now lying on its side with its legs towards the wall.'
Mairi: 'Come on you've got to get up again, you know like you did last week.' *The table rises to an upright position again.*
Mairi: 'Yes, well done, well done.'
Gill commentating: 'And it's now on four legs - now on two legs bending down.'
The Group let out another gasp of amazement as it shoots along the carpet and comes to rest under the window, some 12 feet or so from the Group members.
Gordon: 'That's what it did last week – that's exactly what it did last week.'
Gill to Jim: 'Now wait, Jim, wait, it's going to do something else.'
The table is upright again and has moved towards the wall and has two legs propped up on the wall so that it is lying at almost 45-degree angle.
Gordon: 'It looks like it's going to climb the wall here.'
Gill: 'No, wait.'
Mairi: 'Wow!'
The table again lowers itself to the floor and slides along the floor at speed and comes to rest with all four legs underneath one of the old, heavy wooden chairs. So only the table top lying on its side is protruding from under the chair.
Gordon commentating: 'From a position on its side, it shot off.'
Ann: 'I can't keep up with it, it's going too fast.'

> Gill to table: 'Come on then, you've got to get yourself out of that predicament.'
> *The table seems to reverse at this point, another movement which is inexplicable given the placement of fingers on the table top. It removes itself from under the heavy chair and rights itself again.*
> Mairi: 'It's trying to do something else.'
> Gill: 'Are you going to go up on the chair?'
> Mairi: 'You're going to do something else; I know you are.'
> *The table then moves towards the chair at the window again, lowers itself to the floor again and on its side slides its legs under the heavy wooden chair. Then as the table attempts to move its legs up it is actually moving the heavy chair under which it is trapped.*

This was a solid wood chair with a padded seat. The legs were sturdy, made of lathe-turned oak. It would have taken two people to move it comfortably, yet our flimsy, wee spindly table which we were always in fear of falling apart was now lifting the heavy chair.

> Gill: 'Oh, you're so good, yes. Come on up.'
> Gill to the Group: 'You've got to build the rods on the ends of the legs to allow it to go up the way.'

Gill is referring here to Spirit Rods. This was a theory from early Spiritualists that Spirit built these invisible rods of energy to move inanimate objects and sometimes people.

> Gill to the table: 'Right come on then, you've got to come back out of that predicament.'
> Ann: 'There's a face on the table. Do you see it? It's building there?'
> Gill: 'There's someone building, it's changing.'
> Gill: 'Now the table top is moving, it's vibrating, so you're now going to have to build yourselves up and push yourself out.'
> Gill: 'It's building now, it's softening, on you go.'
> Mairi: 'I can't hold this position much longer, it's my knees.' *(As the Group is bending over the table lying on its side on the floor under the chair).*
> Mayumi: 'Put your arms down towards the end.'
> Mairi: 'This is a cross between Twister and....'

Mairi is referring to the children's game where participants must place their hands and feet on certain colour-coded areas of a floor mat to win the game – this usually ends up in a tangle of bodies – she was right, there were certain similarities here as three of the Group are on the floor trying to keep their fingers on the upturned table.

Gordon: 'It's wanting space. It wants more space than I can give it at the moment.'
The Group let out a gasp as the table lifts and rights itself and gives a spin of 360 degrees and then steadies itself.
Gill: 'Aye, right.'
Gordon: 'Ops that was a quick whirl to say the least.'
Mairi: 'I can do this with no aches and pains now!'

Mairi had chronic knee problems that caused her to wear a knee brace and heavy walking boots to give her ankles some support. From earlier complaining that she couldn't keep this position for any length of time, now it appeared that her pain had gone.

Gill: 'Thank you, you're a star. The energy has built up so much, it's really quite hot in here, would you agree with that please – it's either that or I'm having a hot flush.'
The table rocks in response.
Jim: 'Now, that's an interesting question because that would appear as if you are diagnosing someone's problem. Are you able to diagnose other medical problems?' *Table rocks 'yes' in response.*
Gill: 'Right, okay.'
Jim: 'I'm happy to ask some questions relating to some of my medical problems and there's quite a few.'
Ann joking to Jim: 'Haemorrhoids again?'
Jim: 'Haemorrhoids for example?'
The Group all laugh and the table rocks in response.
Gill: 'You're not alone.'
Jim (jokingly): 'So there are two of us in this room with it – or are there more?'
The Group all laugh and the table rocks its appreciation.
Gill: 'Excuse me, Ann. Please do not type that!'
Mairi (jokingly): 'That's all right, she'll not know how to spell it.'
Ann: 'That's right; I'd have to use the spell-check.'
Jim: 'Right, I'm going to ask some questions and I want a yes or a no. Some of the questions I will ask about, I will not have those problems, and the others in the room do not know about these, does anyone have any objections?'
The Group asks Jim to proceed.
Jim: 'Do I have problems with my bones?' *No.*
Jim: 'That's the right answer. Do I have problems with my urinary system?' *No response.*
Jim: 'Have I recently had problems with my urinary system?' *Yes.* 'That's correct.'
Gill (jokingly): 'Well, you're getting older.'
Jim: 'Well, that leads me to the next question. Do I have or have I had recently, prostate problems?' *No.*

Jim: 'Have I had urinary problems?' *Yes.*
Jim: 'That is correct. Do I have problems with my pancreas?' *No.*
Jim: 'Do I have problems with my thyroid?'
The table rocks indecisively.
Gill: 'That's yes and no.'
Jim: 'That's because it's being treated. Is there anybody else in this room that has problems with their thyroid gland and is receiving treatment?' *Yes.*
Jim: 'That is correct. Can you move towards the other person in the room that has thyroid problems?'
The table moves towards Gill.
Jim: 'Would the person to whom you've moved agree that this is the case?'
Gill: 'That is correct. I'm receiving treatment for my thyroid.'
Jim: 'Thank you. You're very clever. Excuse my sense of humour; I'm not menopausal, am I?' *No.*
Gill: 'Am I menopausal?' *No.*
Jim: 'I find that particularly of value tonight because it has taken us a step forward in realising that you can identify accurately the known conditions for which some of us have been treated and examined. And in terms of healing, I think that does take me a step forward, Gill would you agree?'
Gill: 'Yes, I would agree with that.'
Jim: 'That's not to say that we diagnose, but it is helpful. Any other questions in that regard?'
Gill: 'Listen, I've got a lot of problems, it would take a lot of time for that table....'
Gordon to Jim: 'You could maybe ask a couple of things around the questions that you started with to see if anyone else has it.'
Jim: 'Right....'
Gill: 'Can I just state for the record that I do not have my hand on the table.'
Jim: 'Right, the other five members of the Group have.'
Jim: 'Are there other people in the Group – now I hope no-one is going to feel embarrassed about it – does anyone else in the Group have a known, treatable, thyroid problem?' *No response.*
Jim: 'Right, I'll re-phrase that. Does anyone else in the Group think they may have a thyroid problem but is not receiving treatment?' *No response.*
Jim: 'Right, I think now what Gordon is indicating is that he wants me to continue through other systems of the body.'
Gill: 'Does somebody else here feel that they have thyroid problems?' *No.*
Jim: 'Right I've got.... no, I'm not going to tell you what I've got, you're going to tell me what I've got...'
Gill: 'Does the night last this long.'

The Group laugh, the table responds.
Jim: 'Have I got a limp?' *No*
Mairi: 'We can arrange it though! Would you like to give him a limp?'
Ann: 'A limp what?'
The Group are laughing and the table responds positively.
Jim: 'Right, I think Ann is referring to the reproductive system. Do I have a problem with my reproductive system?'
The table is rocking and walking.
Jim: 'I do? Well, that's interesting.'
Gill: 'No. It's wanting to try something else. Do you want to try something else?'
The table continues rocking and walking.
Ann: 'Just let it do its own thing and it'll show us what it wants to do?'
The table is steadily rocking on the spot, as if working up energy.
Gordon: 'It's thinking.'
Gill: 'You know what you did last week?'
Jim: 'Gill has changed into her gymnastic gear – so she's ready to go. Could you repeat some of the events that you did using Gill last week, could you?'
Table rocks a decisive 'yes'.

Gill continued to instruct the table so that it repeated many of the moves of last week. The Group did exclaim at one point that some of the moves were even more impressive than the previous week particularly when the table elevated itself up to above head-height and moved across the room at speed. It also revolved in a complete summersault again at a higher level than the previous week.

In addition, once it had reproduced the moves from the previous week, it was as if it had decided to add in some extras just to impress us – which it surely did as it moved towards the wall and proceeded to walk/spin along the wall so that the table was at 90 degrees from the wall, at about shoulder height.

The table moved itself out of awkward positions on four separate occasions when it wedged itself underneath some of the heavy wooden chairs in the room. It appeared as if it was doing this for a reason and to demonstrate some other capability. What was noted on these occasions was that using just the energy of the Group with no-one touching the legs and with only fingers on the table top it was able to move in such a way so that is was moving the heavy chair.

I feel this was a demonstration of the strength of the energy that was being built up. At one point Gordon very sensibly suggested that there should be a period where the table is not given instruction so that any sceptics who may later read or hear about this will realise that the table was moving of its own accord without any possible influence from the Group as they were unaware which way it was going to move. (It is only fair to report that this really didn't happen, and so is therefore something that perhaps should take place in future exercises).

Almost as a finale, the table turned upside down, raised itself to about one or two feet above the floor and it then revolved in a circle; then it rose higher and higher until it was well above head height. At this time, Gordon and Jim's hand were off the table as it moved to about a foot from the ceiling light. After the table had completed its acrobatics the Group settled down again.

Gordon then asked about the Isaac Newton connection and whether there was an influence on the Group. The answer was that there was some slight influence on the Group but only from a distance and through Gordon. Gordon made an amusing observation that given the happenings this evening and the defiance of gravity, it may have been apt for his presence to be here.

During Gordon's questioning, the sound of a loud crack was heard and all assumed that the tape had come to its end and the machine had switched itself off of the play/record setting – this is what it sounded like - as if the buttons had suddenly been released. However, on checking the tape it was continuing to record quite happily and indeed on replaying the tape this noise can be heard.

> Gordon then asked if this noise had been created by Spirit for the Group to hear. The table rocked a resounding 'yes'.
> It should be pointed out at this stage that in transcribing this tape, the author heard another noise on the tape at a much earlier stage – interestingly enough, this was also whilst Gordon was speaking.
> The earlier sound appears to be electronic, similar to a mobile phone bleep or ringtone. This doesn't seem to be of any particular consequence, but it has been noted here as the author has learnt that sometimes these things are explained further down the line. As far as the author is concerned neither she, nor any other member of the Group heard this sound whilst the Group was sitting.

This phenomenon of sounds being recorded on the tape whilst no-one in the room heard them would continue in more dramatic format in future weeks, but for now I was following protocol and recording their presence.

16 THE GLEN

Despite the fact that we had had our summer break in July we learned we were to have an enforced break when the Theosophical Society told us that their building was being used as one of the venues for the Edinburgh Festival Fringe. The Fringe was to run for roughly a month from mid-August, so we found that we would be unable to use our room again until mid-September. For this reason Gill kindly invited us to meet at her house at least for one week during this imposed break so that we didn't lose the momentum that had been built up with our friends in the Spirit World.

On 10th August 2006 the Group met at Gill's house in the West End of Edinburgh. Gill had a beautiful flat with large rooms which looked out on to a very well-tended garden. Despite the beauty of the house and the warmth of Gill's welcome we wondered whether anything would happen in this new location for the Group. None of us had been to Gill's house before so we were unfamiliar with it and so too would be our Spirit Friends.

Whenever anyone enters a place for the first time they tend to feel they are in unfamiliar territory. Humans tend to act a bit like cats – we need to check things out before we can feel totally settled there. This applies even more so when sitting in Circle so we went with low expectations of Spirit when going to visit Gill's house. But we need not have worried, our Spirit Friends were there in surprising force. Perhaps this was because of the location of Gill's house in Palmerston Place. Little did we know that just a few doors along the street we were to find the elusive venue that our Spirit Team had been directing us towards – though it was not to materialize for another four years.

> The Group convened in the usual Circle. I could feel Spirit with me very closely. I then felt as if a very, very strong influence was coming in straight through the top of my head and I felt my heart give a few jumps

as if quickening. I was asking who this was but was not getting any answers. My face started feeling strange as it had done the week before, but it was much more pronounced this time. All the molecules of my face seemed to be jumping around and vibrating. It made me want to rub or scratch my face to get it off or to stop it – but I knew not to do this. I got a fleeting vision at this point of someone with leprosy, but nothing more than that. As I tried to ignore it and maintain the deep meditative state I was then aware of someone whispering my name. My immediate thought was that Mayumi had called out to me as the sound had come from her direction but I then realised that this sound was not on the physical plane. I had only ever experienced clairaudience once before and I now realised this was what it was.
After the review of the meditation, Jim asked if the Group wanted to try the table that Gill had laid out for us and we agreed. After several stunning demonstrations by the table of its ability to maneuver itself around the room the Group decided to ask some more questions of it. We asked questions about the room and whether those in Spirit were happy with our temporary location this evening – this was confirmed. I asked for confirmation that the Blue Goldstone Beads that I had purchased to make the bracelets that Spirit had asked us all to wear were indeed the correct ones. I also asked if the influence that I had received to lay the beads out to absorb energy from both the sun and the moon was correct – this was all confirmed, but when I asked how long I should leave them in this position the answer received through Jim's careful questioning was that I would know when the time was right. And only then would I string them and hand them out to the Group.

I used to hate getting these ambiguous answers but at least it showed that they were not coming from anyone in the Group. The six of us were most anxious to have the bracelets now that we were all aware of their relevance, so if any of us had been influencing it we would have been much more likely to give the definitive answer we preferred.

The Group then asked for confirmation of who was with us from the Spirit World. Our answer was that Mary Duffy[22], Joseph Bell and Giilfeather were all present but that Arthur Conan Doyle, Gordon Higginson and Oliver Lodge[23] were not present. Again from Jim's questioning we got confirmation of a new member of the Spirit Team being present, Arthur Findlay[24], whom we welcomed warmly. At one point during this questioning I got the notion that I wanted to connect with Gordon in some way and I felt that I wanted to put my hand on his back. I had resisted this thought a little earlier but again the influence was there and so I asked Gordon if I could put my hand on his back, which I duly did. At this point the table became even more animated and Mairi referred to this by saying that the table liked it. As the questions continued I kept seeing in my head a vision of Roslin Glen – I had had this thought before a few weeks ago and had felt so impressed with it that I actually jumped in my car one evening, drove to the Glen and walked into the woods. Now it was back again, but it was nothing more than the picture that I was very familiar with, so I tried to listen to the questions that the others were putting to our Spirit Friends via the table. Mairi asked about whether we should go to Rosewell where she'd done sweat lodges. Jim asked about Pluscarden Abbey and Gill asked about a spiritual retreat that she was aware of in Fife. So, it seemed that they too were getting similar information about a location in nature that we should go to. At one point the table came over to me and seemed to almost jam me into my seat by tipping itself into my lap. Jim asked if it was acknowledging the person who had brought the Group together and Gill asked it if it wanted me to speak to it, but I was getting the impression that it knew what was going on in my head and that Spirit wanted me to voice it. This was something that was regularly demonstrated – the ability of our Spirit Team to know the question that a member of the Group was going to ask before it had been voiced, so that as soon as that person began to talk, the table would begin rocking the answer before hearing the question.

In this particular case I deduced that the reason Spirit knew what was going on in my head was that they had put the thought there. I've also learnt that no matter how ridiculous an idea or a notion or a vision seems it should be voiced as it is often found to be of significance later on, or we learn that another member of the Group has a corresponding piece of information which can come together to make some sort of sense. So, in for a penny, I asked:

'Does Roslin Glen hold some significance for this Group?'
The answer came immediately – 'yes'.

Now at that point that was all the information I had, but this new subject sparked off a whole series of questions from the Group. The mere mention of 'Roslin' these days sparks an immediate connection with The Chapel made famous by *The Di Vinci Code* – Dan Brown's book and the subsequent film - so several questions were asked about whether we should visit the Chapel , whether we'd find something of interest there, whether it was a place of significance and so on. To all of these questions we received an affirmative answer; I even asked if there was a memory from my childhood that a visit to the Chapel would trigger which would be of use to the Group (since I used to play in and around Roslin Chapel and the Castle when I was a child going to school in Roslin and there were many stories of myths and legends of the area). But I felt that we were heading down the wrong track with this line of questioning and that we were detracting from the initial influence which was very much of the Glen and in particular a clearing in the Glen – again which I knew well from my childhood and could take the Group directly to – this was what I had seen in my head, not the chapel.

The Spirit Team were asked to confirm whether the main significance was to be found in the clearing in the Glen, and whether a visit to the Chapel, though interesting, would yield less than the Glen which was, after all, the place they were drawing us to. This was confirmed. I also got the impression that I needed the skills of others in the Group to be with me when I visited – it was no good going myself as I had done previously – and in particular I needed Gordon to be there. I felt that his skills with a pendulum would be required (and perhaps his dowsing rods, but the pendulum in particular would be needed). Now in asking our Spirit Team to confirm this for us, the table responded by moving towards Gordon and sort of tipping and turning as it went. I think it was Mairi that remarked that this movement reminded her of the way a dog would move. This in turn prompted Jim to recount an incident when he was out with his dog; they came to a statue in a park and stopped before it but the dog took a wide berth around it as if sensing that something was not quite right about it. Jim said he had learned a lot from observing how the dog behaved and suggested to Gordon that he take his own dog with him to the Glen. Gordon then asked the table if this would be appropriate and again got a positive response.

After this line of questioning the session was brought to a close and the Group thanked spirit for being with us and for communicating through this new table of Gill's and gained confirmation that the Spirit Team would be with us wherever we ended up and that they would communicate with us through whatever means was available to them. Jim brought the evening to a close and we all enjoyed Gill's hospitality. She then confided in us that the table had belonged to her father and that he had made it himself. She thought that he might have come through to us, though this didn't happen. The Group agreed that Jim, Gordon, Mayumi and Ann would meet and visit Roslin Glen one afternoon during the following week.

Footnote: I was glad we had decided that four members of the Group would be visiting Roslin Glen as I felt this was going to need our collective thinking skills and input to decipher what was going on in this area and what the connection or significance was to the Group. Whilst the influence in my head was connecting me to Gordon, this may have been to signal that we needed a pendulum with us when we visited and also someone with the skills to use it. I may have been prompted towards Gordon as he happened to be sitting next to me and I knew of his skills with a pendulum. But Mayumi is equally skilled in her use of a pendulum and it maybe that if she had been sitting next to me I would have been directed towards her. As it was, we had the best of both worlds. Jim, is an excellent Trance Medium who is able to sense energy around him readily and slips into trance with the greatest of ease and I got the impression that this skill may well be needed too to help us get to the bottom of things. And, they were all experienced healers. We needed everyone's input, all working together as a team to sort out this puzzle.

On Wednesday 16th August, 2006 we visited Roslin Glen. I led Mayumi, Gordon, Jim and Gordon's dog, Chip to the clearing in the Glen that was so familiar to me in my childhood. Here are Jim's personal notes of the visit:

> 'As we walked from the car park I became aware of an initial change in energy not long after leaving the tarmac road. Another 50-100 yards further and on a short left-hand bend the energy gradually intensified until the party passed through a quite distinct energy change which Ann described as a 'gate'. This immediately led into a large natural circle of trees approximately 50yards in diameter. The ground was of natural woodland mulch and the surrounding trees were of Sycamore, Beech, Horse Chestnut and worthy of note there were six Yew Trees.
> Gordon dowsed and established the outer energy fields of the circle. Dowsing Rods and Pendulums were used by both Mayumi and Gordon to track the energy across the circle. These lines of energy seemed to be running in towards the centre of the circle similar in format to the spokes of a wheel. Interestingly I and others noted the centre of the circle seemed to be marked by a large stone which was only partly visible as most of it was under the ground level. It was certainly charged with energy. Gordon was intrigued to know why he was not given permission to dowse at a specific area under a certain tree – this apparently was rare for him.
> At Ann's instigation she took us to a specific area where she and Mayumi 'saw' someone from the Spirit World. The Group congregated beside a large stump of an old tree for a short silent meditation. For me, personally this trip will go down as one of life's experiences and I hope to return to this site to further enhance my understanding of such phenomena. The weather for this field trip was around 20degrees and sunny. On this occasion because of the time constraints and the sheer number of visitors we did not go to the chapel.'

From my own point of view I had not visited this site since childhood, apart from a short unplanned and ill-advised attempt to walk down the Glen one evening a week or so earlier. I was not sure what I would experience at this location this time, I was just aware that it had been shown to me in my 'vision' and I recognized it immediately from my childhood memories. But whenever we walked into the circle of trees the energy was amazing and we all felt it. Both Mayumi and I were drawn to look at a certain area just on the outside edge of the circle and it was as if the surrounding vegetation had formed a natural sort of 'frame' that we could look through. We both 'saw' spirit people around but by looking through this large natural picture frame I could see the Glen as it was in medieval times. I could see it busy with people living in makeshift tents as if an encampment had been set up in the Glen. There were camp fires with spits and cleeks for cooking. Urchins and dogs were running around and somehow I was aware that the men were hunting wild boar and badgers for food. The place was surprisingly noisy when compared with the serenity of the circle of trees in which I stood to look at this sight. I was also aware of the road which was the approach road to the castle. It looked very much as if it was in daily use as it was very clearly defined by a dry-stone wall to one side with an avenue of Yew Trees standing just behind the wall. Today this road was almost indiscernible being overgrown and consumed by the vegetation. I was aware that this large encampment of people were living in the shadow of the castle. Although they lived outside its walls, they gained a certain security from living in this area. By comparison the landed gentry would pass along this road in horse-drawn carriages with servants and footmen. The difference in living conditions could not have been starker as I was made aware that at times the outside temperatures could drop to 16° below. I was then aware of an arranged marriage; the bride being brought to the castle in one such carriage – she didn't want to go. As I looked at this scene I was aware that the man with the leprosy would have come from this scene and I wondered what it was all about and why for some reason I was able to look through this 'window to the past'. One thing was sure, just as Jim had referred to in his notes, we would have to come back again.

The Glen would be a recurring theme in the Group with regular visions and confirmations that for some reason this location was of some significance and importance to us. This was further reinforced when Mayumi and I returned to the Glen one evening and sat in that same clearing together in deep meditation. I felt that I had suddenly become enlarged and very heavy. I felt that I had become a very bulky man sitting in a chair. I then felt that I had a heavy weight on my head and when I put my hand up to find out what it was I realised it was a crown, hammered out of metal with some stones crudely set into it. At the same time Mayumi got an impression of King Arthur and saw a knight in armour and a coat of arms. Strangely enough she also saw a building in a field near the chapel and so these visions we both had connected this scene to Roslin Glen but we could not explain why. (When Arthur Conan Doyle was originally trying to impress upon me his presence, he used the vision of King Arthur and the Knights of the Round Table to convey his name to me – was Arthur somehow trying to tell me that he was in the Glen? A few years later I was to discover that Arthur Conan Doyle was actually named after King Arthur[25], but for now the clues and puzzle remained).

When I got back home that day following our first visit to the Glen in 2006, I sat in silence in the evening to ask for some signal from our Spirit Team that we were on the right track and that I was correct in my vision and in bringing the Group here to investigate. I was shown a symbol and told that when I found it I would know that the time was right to take action. I got the impression I would have to work towards the achievement of something at that time and whatever that initiative was, it would be revealed for the benefit of humanity. Despite regular visits to the Glen, the Chapel and the Castle to search for this symbol I have only just discovered it in February 2019. I am aware that the completion of this book forms part of the plan; as for the rest of it – watch this space!

17 THE SOUND OF SILENCE

On 21st September, we returned to the Theosophical Society after our enforced long break. Just as we had been worried about the energy when we convened at Gill's house, we were now concerned that the impetus we had built up with our Spirit Team might have been diminished. This time we weren't thinking about different surroundings since we were back on familiar territory; it had more to do with the time gap and the fact that others had been using our room during that period. More than a month had elapsed since we last met there and in that intervening time the building had been used as an entertainment venue for the Festival. Who knows who had been in our room and how they would have affected the energy that we had carefully built up during the previous eight months?

These feelings come from the theory that we are all energy. Every person, place or thing is made up of energy molecules vibrating at different frequencies. You may remember this from school science class. And energy does not die, it just changes direction or frequency when there is some intervention that induces that reaction. So given that our room would be vibrating at a certain frequency and those who entered that room would have their own energy fields – sometimes called auras – some of the energy from the people will remain in the room and interact with the room's energy. The longer the person is in the room the more of their energy is deposited there and the more it will become mingled with that of the room and gradually change the energy there. It is this mixture of energies which allows sensitive people to pick up on what we call the 'residual energy' in rooms and buildings, especially where someone has lived in that building for many years. Sometimes the energy is so strong it will feel as if the person is still there. This is often misinterpreted as ghostly activity in the house but in fact it is simply the residual energy of a previous occupant.

Our room in the Theosophical Society was already subject to the energy of others who had used the room in our absence although we hoped that the Theosophical Society would attract people with the same approach as ourselves to the business of working with energies, or at least of good intention like the Buddhists. This time though our room had been used by performers from the entertainment field for over a month hence our concern about the impact on the energy we had built up in the room since the beginning of the year. Perhaps this was another reason our Spirit Friends were so keen for us to move.

These thoughts were on my mind on the run up to our meeting as I wondered what would happen next – if anything. We had had such amazing phenomena before our break that the fear that it might end was always present. It was with this thought that I again picked up Arthur Conan Doyle's *History of Spiritualism* in the hope of receiving some idea of what we might do. My inspiration usually came to me spontaneously and not from reading a book; I usually found the inspiration came first and I would then implement it in the Group, and only *then* would I read about it afterwards. But this time I thought we might be in need of some input.

I was only about half-way through Volume One when I read about Mrs Hayden the American Medium who had come to the UK in 1852. She too used the rapping sounds to spell out letters of the alphabet which formed messages for those sitting in séance with her. By all accounts these messages were extremely accurate even when Mrs Hayden had no sight of the letters being pointed to by her sitters. Despite this she was cruelly vilified in the press although the journalists responsible were criticised for not recognising one of their own: Hayden was the wife of a former Editor of a journal in Boston. She was also investigated by some of the scientists of the day as this excerpt from the book attests:

> 'Among the investigators was the celebrated mathematician and philosopher, Professor De Morgan. He gives some account of his experiences and conclusions in his long and masterly preface to his wife's book, "From Matter to Spirit" 1863, as follows:
>> Ten years ago Mrs Hayden, the well-known American medium, came to my house alone. The sitting began immediately after her arrival...................The raps began in the usual way. They were to my ear clean, clear, faint sounds such as would be said to ring, had they lasted. I likened them at the time to the noise which the ends of knitting-needles would make, if dropped from a small distance upon a marble slab, and instantly checked by a damper of some kind; and subsequent trial showed that my description was tolerably accurate.....'

Source: p155 The History of Spiritualism, Volume one by Sir Arthur

Conan Doyle.

Whilst we had already encountered independent sounds of raps and cracks manifesting themselves in our wee room at the Theosophical Society this sound of knitting needles on marble intrigued me and was described in such detail that I could almost 'hear' this ringing myself. I wondered if we might yet get to hear this distinctive sound. Armed with this information I headed off to the Theosophical Society with my 'fall-back' information to hand – if no one had any ideas of what we should do we could try this.

Gordon had followed up his prompt to approach the venue at Holy Corner in Edinburgh during our break but they were unable to accommodate us on a Thursday evening so in the absence of any alternatives we were back at the Theosophical Society. When we entered the room we noticed that the small wooden occasional table that had been used previously as an instrument for Spirit responses was missing from the room. I had brought the candles so I lit them and placed them on the oblong coffee table which was in the centre of the Circle and one was placed on the fireplace. I had also brought the piece of turquoise with me.

Jim welcomed everyone back to the Group, gave the invocation and the Group then sat in silence. As we sat I realised I had not needed to worry about the energy of the room as our Group was very powerful and very connected with one another and with Spirit. Whatever had happened in our absence was already forgotten. I got the usual 'flash' of Arthur's face, which let me know he was with me, as usual. This was by now a very comforting feeling. I could feel his presence around me and it was nice. I knew he supported me and loved me – like a father would, a daughter. As I basked in the presence of Arthur Conan Doyle and enjoyed the peaceful calmness of the Groups' conjoined energy I was startled back into full consciousness by realising that the floor was moving under my feet. There it was again… The floor-boards were actually moving under my feet as if tilting and rising and falling back against one another; it seemed that some heavy force was pushing them upwards and then releasing them again as if something was trying to get through the floor from below. I looked round the room at each of my colleagues but they were just sitting most serenely – was it just me who was experiencing this? I wondered if my intention to look for the 'ring' of the knitting needle had already been picked up by the Spirit World who might be trying to create a vibration. However when Jim brought us back from our silent meditation and asked for feedback I was more than a little relieved to hear:

> Mairi: 'What was the vibration on the floor? Could it have come from those who were walking around in the room next door?'
> Ann: 'Yes, I think so.'

Mairi: 'It was extraordinary wasn't it?'

Yes it was. With my Psychic Investigator's hat on I accepted Mairi's suggestion of the vibration coming from next door even although we had never encountered anything like this before – she had forwarded a reasonable explanation and the rule was always 'eliminate the possible before looking for the paranormal'.

Jim: 'How are you Gill?'
Gill: 'Fine thank you. Were you aware of anything over here?' (She pointed to the corner of the room). 'I thought I heard a slight cracking noise?'
Jim: 'No, I didn't hear it.'
Mairi: 'I did think I heard something in that direction, (Mairi pointed to the same corner) but I was trying to distinguish between all the outside noises and with what was travelling along the floor – as the vibration along that floor was quite strong – I never noticed that before, it's really quite marked, it was lifting my feet.'
Ann: 'Yes, mine too.'
Jim: 'Did you have anything else Ann?'
Ann: 'I felt initially that something was happening to my face and particularly along my jaw and I thought to myself, what is this strange condition – lockjaw? It was either that or back to these helmets with the hinged face-plate – these keep cropping up.' (Ann refers to a previous vision of a Roman Soldier which had happened in The Glen).
Jim: 'The Roman type?'
Ann: 'Yes, but I must admit I was getting distracted with the noise outside.'

Once again we had heard the people coming up the stairs outside of our room and heading along the corridor to the tearoom. They were noisy.

Jim: 'Does anyone have any thoughts about what they'd like to do now?'
Gill: 'Oh, I'm open to suggestions.'
Mairi: 'I don't know, that was going through my mind as well, I was thinking what are we going to do?'
Gill: 'I think it's because it's the first time we're back here after the break.'
Mairi: 'Yes, and it's different because there are different noises and because the table's not here - we're not so sure about how we're going to start.'
Ann: 'We've got that table there.' (She points to the brass-topped table). 'I know we can't use it for the same thing, but....'

The brass-topped table was a small, low, circular table. The sort composed of a folding stand with a detachable brass top which could be lifted off to form a tray.

Jim: 'We could sit for a period of time for each other. I don't know how people would feel about that?'
Gill: 'What does everyone else think – would you like to be sat for (Mairi)?'
Jim jokingly: 'Would you like to be subject of our power?'
Mairi jokingly: 'Sounds a bit scary!'
Jim: 'Would you like it, Ann?'
Ann: 'Well yes, I'd give it a try I suppose.'
Jim: 'Right well we'll do that.'
Ann: 'I've got this notion, ...'
Mairi: 'I could tell you've got a notion; I was waiting to see what you were going to say – tell us what your notion is? It's the only notion in the room, so....'
Ann: 'Well it's not inspiration; it's an idea from a book so this could be boring as hell, but I'm reading the Arthur Conan Doyle book, and because each chapter deals with a different medium or the next stage in development or whatever, I tend to read a bit and then dodge back and forwards. Remember I got it wrong with the lettering and it wasn't like moving the tumbler on the Ouija board at all, it was knocks that were signalling the letters, and that's how it began as everybody knows with the Fox Sisters and raps on the walls. And as I read through the early chapters, some of the scientists such as Crookes[26], start investigating various Mediums and one of them describes what the noise sounded like when they go into trance or an altered state of consciousness. He describes it as if a knitting needle was dropping from a height on to a piece of marble – now I think that's not very loud. It doesn't clatter down, he then goes on to say it's the first drop, it is then held before it drops down – it's the sound of the first hit by the point of the needle.'
Jim: 'And, it would be a metal knitting needle?'
Ann: 'Yes, so I think a metal knitting needle dropping its point on to a slab of marble wouldn't be very noisy? I don't think? He talks about it being like a ping or a zing – he says it sort of sings but it is faint.'
Mairi: 'That would be the sound vibration.'
Ann: 'And I was just thinking that might work – and that table might be used to create a sound - we could try that?' *(She again refers to the small brass-topped table).*
Gill: 'Have you got a knitting needle with you?'
Ann: 'No. But they didn't use a knitting needle. It just *sounds* like a knitting needle.'
Mairi: 'Just as well you didn't say it sounded like an elephant!' *(The Group laugh).* 'Gill would be asking you if you had an elephant with you... Imagine dropping that on to the table.'
Ann: 'I know, but I'm used to her – you see how I just took that in my

stride!' *(The Group laugh).* 'Anyway, *they* didn't have a knitting needle either, he just described the sound. When the sounds were happening – they were just happening in the room for no apparent reason.'
Gill: 'They didn't have anything there for them to use?'
Ann: 'No, and they said, it was like....'
Jim: 'He was clearly indicating a sound that would not normally be in the normal range of our hearing?'

Strange that Jim came up with this explanation. Little did we know at this time that he would be absolutely correct. For now I told him he was wrong.

Ann: 'No, they could hear it.'
Gill: 'So it must be the vibration?'
Ann: 'That's how he described it therefore it couldn't have been happening with anything in the room, but he says it was in various places in the room, it was happening throughout the room.'
Gill: 'I have to say now, that it's very cold now on my left-hand side. It has just got very cold[27].'
Mairi: 'Yes it has. I like the idea of the sound for this evening. That resonates in some way.'
Ann: 'I don't know what we do to make it work!'
Mairi: 'No, but we could just try it and see if we get any sounds - just by sitting waiting, then we could maybe try to visualise something?'
Jim: 'I think that's right Mairi, because I think if we don't try it... I think if it were left to us, you and me, we would never have tackled some of this stuff that Ann's got us doing because it was a non-starter as far as I was concerned - it's just too incredible, yet we've got so much out of it and it has just brought so much information. So, shall we just slide this over then? And bring in this table?' *(He refers to sliding the oblong coffee table out of the way and replacing it with the brass-topped round table.)*
Ann: 'And, the other thing is, thinking about that table – (the brass-topped table) I thought it might make a ping.'
Mairi: 'Yes, when you mentioned the table, that's what I thought.'
Ann: 'I've no idea of whether this will work or not, because the theory was that the sound was just within the room not necessarily on the table.'
Jim: 'But let's just lift it over and put it in the centre of the circle and see what happens.' *(The brass-topped table was moved into the centre of the circle and the oblong coffee table was moved to the side – with the candles still upon it. Ann then placed the round silver top from a candle jar on the table top together with an ordinary biro pen, as tools that may be used to create a sound).*
Jim: 'Well I have no more skill than anybody else. I've certainly got past the stage of feeling stupid about talking to tables because I'm absolutely convinced that it's not the table but Spirit that is making these things happen. So, maybe we just treat it the same way as we did

before?'
Ann: 'I think we should maybe just – can I just go for it?'
Jim: 'Sure.'
Ann: 'Great Spirit, if you are with us and we believe we know that you are, we are sitting for you here this evening once again and asking this time tonight to please make your presence known to us by making a sound – any sound at all – make a sound in the room, please, to let us know of your presence here with us tonight. We will all extend our energy, both to one another around the Circle and to fill the room so that you may use it to assist in this purpose. If this be your purpose then please let it be and please help us in our Spiritual development and our understanding of how these things happen.'

The Group then sat in silence but this time with our eyes open as we all focused our energies on the small brass-topped table in the centre of our Circle, willing it to make this distinctive ding, ring or sing that we were looking for but alas, nothing. There was a slight crack quite quickly but Jim thought it may have been his chair, although he could not repeat the sound when he tried afterwards but this was not what I was looking for. It is interesting that earlier on in our development we would have been delighted to have heard that crack in the room but now we all expected much more.

No-one was within touching distance of the table. I didn't want anyone to lay their hands on it anyway as I thought that this would create a damper to any vibration that might possibly be created on the table top. I had already placed the top of the candle jar and the pen on the table in the hope that Spirit might be able to use either of these to make the zing or ring. I reminded the Group:

> Ann: 'Remember these things apparently are not that loud, although they should be clearly audible to us, so listen up.'

But still nothing. Indeed strangely enough despite the earlier outside noise I noted how we now seemed to be sitting in absolute silence. I wondered if Spirit had engineered this situation to enable us to hear what was going to be this 'faint but clear' sing or ring. Still nothing happened so I tried again:

> Ann: 'Just to repeat, we ask those that are here with us tonight from the Spirit World to communicate with us tonight using sound. We would love to communicate with you tonight. Are you with us?'
> Mairi: 'The energy seems sort of circular to me.'

Then Jim tried again:

> Jim: 'Are you agreeable to the suggestion? One knock for yes, two for no? Or, one sound for yes, two sounds for no?'

> Jim to the Group: 'Would it be useful for us to place our hands on the table and try to get it to communicate yes or no and from that point ask it to communicate using sounds, do you know what I mean?'
> Gill: 'Yes.'

I wasn't entirely happy with this suggestion since I couldn't see how a brass table-top could vibrate and sing/ring when everyone had their hands on it. But in the absence of anything at all we decided to give it a try.

> The Group then gently placed their hands on the edge of the table top.
> Jim: 'You may begin to use the table, Friend, by getting it to rotate, ever so gently, even just marginally and then we can try to communicate with you in that way.'

A further period of silence and still nothing. Jim tries again:

> Jim: 'Can we establish, Friends from Spirit, that there are energies with us who want to work with us in this manner this evening?'

Nothing.

> Ann: 'Come on Spirit, put in an extra effort and let us hear sound tonight. We are eager to hear from you tonight, we are all sitting in eager anticipation here.'

Still nothing.

> Gill: 'It's changing.'
> Mairi: 'I can feel the vibration round the edge of the table.'
> Gill: 'It's as if they can't quite get it together yet.'
> Mairi: 'It's maybe just a matter of time; we maybe just have to be patient and confident.'
> Gill: 'Yes, you see it's changed again. Good.'
> Ann: 'Are you with us? Are you there? Come on come and tell us? Who's there? Who wants to speak to us tonight? Is there any of our friends there? Come on, come and speak to us tonight?'

The table refused to budge and the silence was deafening.

> Jim: 'I'd just like to know if there is someone with us, who has been here before just to confirm that we're on the right road. My dilemma is, that if we don't get a response from you, then we must interpret it that we really must get out of this building So, we're wanting some confirmation that those who were with us before, are still with us tonight. The hardest part maybe getting it to move initially. Because if

we do get it to move we can then help you by questioning you in a specific manner, which has been very successful in the past.'

The table remained stubbornly stationary but strangely enough the candle top began to move.

> Jim commentating: 'It's moving now.' *(As the silver candle-top begins to shake and rock like a pendulum.*
> Ann: 'Come on, come one.'
> Jim: 'Yes, that's it.'
> Ann: 'Come on, roll it, roll it. You're getting a response – keep talking Jim.'

What we were witnessing was very small movements of the candle top beginning to rock slightly as it sat on the tabletop but the table remained still and silent. The fear that Spirit had left us was rising once again.

> Jim: 'We are really wanting to find out where to go from here. We already got your advice, that was very sound advice. You must be pleased that some of us in the Circle have made earnest efforts to try to get other accommodation for the Group, but it just hasn't been possible. At this moment, I cannot believe that you would not be here simply because we cannot find alternative accommodation.'

Nothing.

> Ann: 'So, please, please, let us know that you're there. We've tried ever so hard to follow your advice and guidance and learn from what you've had to tell us, from what you've shown us and from our own idea of experimentation, but really from Sir Arthur Conan Doyle's book – and I know he is with us tonight again. So hopefully, this is going to work?'

Nothing and Jim was now grasping at straws:

> Jim: 'Yes, and one of the questions I'd have to ask is, are you really as disappointed as we are, that our original table is not with us? That is totally out of our control. We will try to get it back, because you may have needed it tonight for such a specific purpose? Because if you would try to let us have some idea if there's someone there with us tonight......
> We set out with the intention of trying to hear sound this evening, that was one of our main objectives?'
> Ann: 'What was that?' *There was a sudden vibration on the table – like a gentle thump, but no sound.*
> Mairi: 'It was a bit of a bump. Just don't know.'
> Ann: 'Did you feel that Jim?'

> Jim: 'No.'
> Gill: 'It's over here (she gestures to her side of the table). Would you try to do that again, please? Perhaps they're trying to make a sound.'

Despite Gill's pleading nothing further happened whilst Jim grasped more straws:

> Jim: 'Now perhaps we owe you an apology. Perhaps the people who worked this table are a bit upset that we abandoned it and moved over to the other table and now that we've not got the other table, we've moved back to this one again, so that may have been seen as an offence. That certainly was not our intention and there was nothing further from our minds, but if that's the case, then we certainly do apologise.'

I had felt another very slight vibration following Jim's garbled apology but still no sound and no movement. He makes another appeal this time to the Group:

> Jim to the Group: 'Do you think we should take our hands off the table again for a few minutes and just sit back and see what happens.'
> Gill: 'Yes.'
> Ann: 'Yes, because you see these table vibrations that are happening........'
> Gill: 'Yes.'
> Ann: 'Well if these were happening when our hands were off the table, they may make a sound. I think our hands are dulling any possible sound from the vibrations. Just an idea?'
> Gill: 'Yes.'
> Jim: 'Just give us a sound, if you can manage it, Friends.'

After this last desperate plea, and a further period of silence, still nothing happened.

> Jim: 'The energy is very strong and I'm getting a very strong feeling of closeness with Spirit.'
> Ann: 'Go on then, they're maybe coming through you for a purpose, just go for it.'

Jim's face changes into the now recognisable image of one of his Spirit Communicators and his voice changes accordingly:

> Jim[in a voice other than his own]: 'The energy which emanates through me is not the same energy that is required to move the table but I do wonder if talking seems to in some way generate energy that Spirit can use if they wish to manipulate things on the table or otherwise.'

Gill: 'Do you think it's the vibration of sound?'
Jim: 'Friends could you try and give us some sound from the table.'

Still nothing, as Jim returns to his normal self:

Jim to Group: 'I think for the rest of you, if you have a similar or different explanation, don't be frightened to talk.'
Gill: 'Yes, it's very dense.'
Ann: 'Yes, my hands have heated up as well, as in healing, or wanting to heal.'
Mairi: 'Yes, it's just got very cold.'
Gill: 'I can certainly feel the trembles.'
Ann: 'Is there anybody there? Are you with us? Please make a sound to indicate that you are there, or move the table?'
After a long period of silence, the Candle-top begins to rock again.
Jim: 'That's it, very good, keep it going that's what we're waiting to see, very good. That's great, keep moving if you can. If it's possible to try to roll it a little bit more, but it's good that you've been able to move it. So, you are there, is that correct? Yes. Yes, they're there. Lovely. When you are moving it like that, are you saying 'yes'?'
Gill: 'Nothing. Try again.'
Jim: 'So, really what we're saying now is, I'm assuming when you are moving the top of that candle thing like that........are those who normally work with us from Spirit, working with us tonight? I'll be more specific. Is Giilfeather with us tonight? Are you there, Giilfeather? Are you there Sir Arthur?'
Ann: 'There's a huge vibration going through the table.'
Gill: 'Yes. It's a bit weird.'
Ann: 'Just move that lid, just move it, it's nearly there, give us a roll. Go on.'

The candle top was still producing only slight movements but as I focused on it I suddenly saw it from a different perspective:

Ann: 'You know I can see some faces in that lid. And I see one that's almost like Santa Claus, just with a thinner face, an old man with a white beard and a white moustache – is that right, is there someone over there that looks like that? O, I think you're new to us – mind you, I don't know, because I don't know what anyone else looks like. Well, it's nice to see you and to see such a smiley face – you look like the Birdseye Man, Captain Birdseye[28].
Oh, I thought that table lifted just now, on the right side?
Come on People, we'd love to hear from you, we'd love to communicate with you tonight, just give us a sound to let us know that you're here and that we're on the right path and moving in the right direction?'
Gill: 'The candle flame went still and then started flickering – there's

your sign. Are you using the candle, this evening?'

Now it was Gill's turn to grasp the straws – and in desperation I followed her lead:

> Ann: 'If that's correct, we'll take a flicker for yes and steady for no – would that be okay?'

Nothing happened and there was no corresponding flickering. Dejectedly Jim and Gill say:

> Jim: 'I think we'll carry on looking at the table.'
> Gill: 'Are you going to move for us this evening, please?'

Realising how dejected everyone felt I picked up the pen and tapped it on the table a few times to see if they could use the vibration of the sound.

> Ann: 'You do it. Please.'
> Jim: 'Did you hear the sounds that were made there, Friends? Did you hear the sounds? Unless you roll it, I have to say, that's a no. It's too vague for me, I'm afraid.'
> Ann: 'Yes, I agree. Nothing is happening, let's close the circle.'

Gill and Jim give a desperate last plea:

> Gill: 'We would like you to move for us this evening, please? Just to show that you're there.'
> Jim: 'Come on give us a sound, any sound.'

Suddenly as if responding to their appeal I'm aware of spirit energy at my back:

> Ann: 'I'm getting pushed, like I was before. I'm getting pushed from the back.'
> Jim: 'Just go with it.' *(Ann starts to rock back and forth in her chair).*
> Ann: 'I've forgotten what this was the last time?'
> Gill: 'Just allow them to use the energy through you.'
> Jim: 'Can I remove the things from the table, as you carry on?'
> *Jim removes the Candle top and pen from the table and the Group replace their hands on the table.*
> Jim: 'If you are there my Friend as well, just carry on.'
> Ann: 'I feel my face is funny; they've done something to my face.'
> Jim: 'Creak in the corner?'
> Ann: 'Yes. Was that you? Was the creak in the corner, you? If so, move the table, or do it again?'

Ann: 'My hands and face are absolutely roasting.'
Mairi: 'There's a lot of energy under the table even although it's not moving.'
Ann: 'You are trying really hard, but there's something not quite right.'
Jim: 'I wonder if they're teaching……. we are always taking it for granted that this will always work, so perhaps this as a lesson for us?'
Gill: 'Did you hear something there just now?'
Mairi: 'Yes, I thought I heard something, over nearer you, but I wasn't sure what it was. It was a sort of scraping noise?'
Ann: 'Yes, that's right.'
Gill: 'If that was you, can you do it again, please?'

Another period of silence elapsed until we realised that we had experienced all that we were going to that night. There appeared to have been a final effort from our Spirit friends to let us know they were there – either through creating a crack in the corner, a scratching noise and perhaps some slight movement of the candle top as well as pushing me forward but the elusive ping or ring that we had hoped for was not to be.

Jim addressing spirit: 'Okay, we'll accept that nothing's happening. But just may I express my thanks for being with us and bearing with us, when obviously we were trying to get you to do something which you weren't in agreement with on the other side; we acknowledge that, and are grateful that eventually we were able to come to this understanding, please accept our apologies for that.'
Gill: 'Thank you.'

As our Circle closed the Group sat back in their chairs dejectedly and began consoling ourselves about a night where nothing happened:

Gill: 'They *were* here.'
Ann: 'Yes.'
Gill: 'But they didn't want to use that.' (she points to the brass-topped table).
Ann: 'But it was as if it was….'
Jim: 'A spin?'
Mairi: 'Yes, a torque on it. Wasn't there?'
Jim: 'Absolutely, torque's the right word. I was going to say a vortex, but you felt it was just trying to sustain that, wasn't it?'
Mairi: 'And it sustained that for a very long time actually, so it wasn't as if nothing happened, it just….'
Gill: 'So, they were just letting us know through… through what we were feeling? Do you think perhaps in respect of what was happening next door, they didn't wish to make a noise?'
Ann: 'That's a good point. Because, they don't really want us to be here

do they? We've had the message loud and clear about going to other premises and that coupled by the fact that there were people next door and making it obvious that they were around, means they were maybe making the point that....'

Gill: 'And perhaps in our subconscious minds we weren't maybe as relaxed as we could have been? It being our first week back after the break?'

Ann: 'We know from some of the messages we got earlier on that they couldn't take us further until....'

Jim: 'Advance us?'

Ann: 'Yes, until we had a secure space, so, maybe we were asking a step too far?'

The mood of seeking explanation and excuses as to why nothing had happened then changed to more frustration with those in the Spirit World:

Mairi: 'In that case, the space should have materialised already, if they really wanted us to be somewhere else and not to do anything until that space.... I would have thought that space would have materialised by now, so it's a little bit confusing.'

Jim: 'Yes it is. Until I can have.... I really feel we require an explanation of why this is not suitable, but obviously wherever we go we have no control over ....'

Mairi: 'Over who else is there.'

Ann: 'But, if they're going to demonstrate the things that they're going to demonstrate they're not going to do it when there's a chance of being disturbed, or someone walking in. It's got to be absolutely private. I think it's that more than anything.'

Jim: 'Right so if we accept that...'

Mairi: 'But what would be so awful about somebody walking in? I mean it would be a bit of a shock maybe for them but is it so important to them that....'

Jim: 'Well I think it really depends on what they want us to do. If for example they chose one of us to be a Physical Medium and knocked us out (in deep trance), and whilst this was happening someone walked through the door, that would be bad news.'

Ann: 'That's right.'

Jim: 'But I accept that's a serious situation and is that what they're really saying?'

Mairi: 'Isn't that just if you're using ectoplasm[29]?'

Jim: 'Yes, that's right.'

Mairi: 'If we're not, if we're developing a different kind of physical phenomenon, which I thought was part of what we were trying to do, then that shouldn't be so much of a concern.'

Gill: 'Would you not feel vulnerable, even if you were just going down into an altered state and someone just came through the door....'

Ann: 'Even just hearing that conversation outside the door tonight was putting me off.'
Gill: 'I was able to just shut that out.'
Mairi: 'No it doesn't really bother me too much as long as it doesn't hurt anybody.'
Jim: 'It doesn't bother me.'
Gill: 'Because you know you're protected?'
Jim: 'Yes, I feel that, but that's with me....as long as I'm aware that there's someone coming in the door, but if I wasn't and I was right out of it, I don't know how...or what would happen, because I've heard Gordon Higginson, he's been badly burned by that, he's told us, so .....'
Mairi: 'Again, that's the ectoplasm.'
Jim: 'Yes, that's right.'
Mairi: 'I don't know but I think this is different.'
Ann: 'We actually don't know what they've got planned for us.'
Jim: 'We're here to give them the opportunity.'
Ann: 'So, we just have to go with what sense we have.'
Jim: 'Right, but in the meantime, there's two options for us: abandon our sittings until we find a place, and I cannot believe Spirit would want us to do that, or the alternative is to be here until we find suitable accommodation.'
Ann: 'Yes.'
Jim: 'So, how do we use this time?'
Gill: 'I think we sit.'
Mairi: 'I had the feeling tonight... I didn't feel that it was a failure; I felt that they were building the energy and working with it, but just very slowly. And I didn't feel that we had made the wrong choice, I just felt that it hadn't taken off in the way that it has before, but I don't feel disappointed and I don't feel it didn't work or anything.'
Jim: 'No.'
Mairi: 'Whatever happened was okay.'
Ann: 'I get that feeling as well, in fact I feel there's something still to come.'
Mairi: 'Yes.'
Ann: 'Even maybe.... I don't know, I just feel that wasn't it, there's a bit more?'
Gill: 'Yes.'
Jim: 'It's amazing that they were able to communicate with us ultimately, in a manner that we understood, but what is it that they're trying to do that we're not understanding?'
Mairi: 'I didn't feel that we chose to do the wrong thing, like you were wrong with your inspiration, Ann, or we were wrong to follow it, that seemed and that still feels right but there was an awful strong feeling of patience with it, just to take your time and just build it up.'
Gill: 'Yes, I agree with you Mairi, it was as if, something is going to happen, but it was taking so much longer, I just wondered, are they trying

to teach us patience?'
Mairi: 'I think we were getting a bit impatient.'

The Group closed and I drove home still with this feeling that Mairi and I had voiced that somehow *'there's still something to come'* that we had missed something, that *'that wasn't it, there's a bit more'*. I can't explain these feelings and I didn't have an answer to them, I just knew that something wasn't quite right and things weren't all that they seemed. I consoled myself with the thought that maybe patience was the lesson and if I waited until next week, I'd get the answer in our next session. I didn't have to wait that long.

When I got home I settled down at my computer desk to start typing the transcripts of the meeting. I always typed them immediately after the meeting, so that if I had difficulty hearing any of the tape I could usually remember what was said. This job usually took me two or three hours to complete so by the time I got home, set up the tape recorder and started typing, I usually found it wasn't finished until the wee small hours. This didn't faze me at all I've always been a night owl - indeed my husband always says 'Ann doesn't go to bed the same day she gets up'. In any case I preferred to get it over and done with than have something hanging over me still waiting to be done.

This was a laborious process. I was continually playing the tape, typing a bit then stopping the tape and rewinding halfway back then playing and typing again. Although I'm a good and fairly fast typist I couldn't keep up with the speed of the conversation. I had completed nine pages and was just starting the tenth and wondering how much more there was when this thought was dropped into my head. *'Stop typing and listen to the tape'*. I was immediately aware that I was being directed – it wasn't my own thought – I wanted to finish this as soon as possible, I wasn't going to stop. Along with the thought was a feeling that I was going to hear something important on the tape. I lifted my hands from the keyboard and leaned towards the tape-recorder and pressed the play button. After a short silence there were three separate taps or cracks heard on the tape but this had not been mentioned by anyone in the room. It was clear that no-one had heard this and I got the distinct impression that this was something quite different that I was being allowed to hear. So much so that I actually typed a note to myself at this point in the transcript: *'Note to yourself, Ann – try to find out how to get this tape analysed for EVP[30]. There may be something on it'*. I typed that sentence in blue to prompt my attention when it was printed off and meanwhile I continued typing. I knew I was nearing the end of the transcript as I was typing about the Group agreeing that nothing was happening that evening and were about to close the Circle. As I began typing about the Group discussing possible reasons and excuses as to why nothing had happened the thought returned, *'stop typing and listen – you're going to hear something'*. Once again I lifted my hands from the keyboard and leaned towards the tape-recorder. The earlier sound had not been very loud although loud enough for me to wonder why no-one in the room had heard it so I wanted to make sure I didn't miss anything as I once again pressed 'play'.

This time the sound was undoubted and utterly amazing. It was a metallic sound and much louder than the earlier sound and it repeated several times on the tape. It could only be coming from the brass-topped table, either that or someone was rapping on water pipes. I was amazed. How could sounds like this appear on the tape when no-one in the room heard them. I sat there in the dark in the quiet of the wee small hours staggered at the sounds I had heard on the tape.

The irony of the situation hadn't escaped my attention. At the time the Group were discussing why nothing had happened and possible reasons for this, these loud repeated metallic sounds were appearing on the tape. I immediately took to my email and sent out urgent messages to the Group asking *'is anyone there', 'is anyone still up, still awake'*. I couldn't wait to tell them that something *had* actually happen just as Mairi and I had suspected. I waited in hope but got no response from my emails, so with my excitement raised I continued typing knowing that I had been allowed to hear a new phenomenon – not the one we had expected but a very real acknowledgement that Spirit were answering our request to make a sound. As I marvelled at these thoughts there it was again - that thought, *'stop and listen'* - there were two further loud dongs on the tape and although I suspected that Spirit had somehow used the brass-topped table to create these sounds they actually bore a much stronger resemblance to the sound made by the man with the gong at the start of Rank Organisation films!

18 PENNIES FROM HEAVEN AND KEYS TO THE CASTLE

By the time we returned to the Theosophical Society the following week (28th September, 2006), I had already had excited telephone calls from each member of the Group as one by one they had checked their emails and realised that I had made frantic attempts to contact them in the early hours of the morning after our session the week before when strange and loud 'gong-sounds' were heard on the tape.

'What does it sound like?' 'Can you describe it?', 'Can you hear it clearly?' and of course, 'Can we hear it too?' they said. Yes, of course they would want to hear it – and I wanted them to hear it too. I wanted them to experience the same sense of wonder that had stuck me when I realised that Spirit were indeed creating sound - just as we had asked - but not the sound we had expected. Instead, just as Jim had inadvertently said the week before, 'sound that was not within our normal hearing range', at least not whilst we were sitting in that room - yet here it was as loud as could be on the tape. So, I told the Group that I would bring last week's tape recording into the Theosophical Society with me and we would play it back so that everyone could hear it and I could document their reactions.

And so it was with this sense of excitement that everyone reconvened in our top floor room in the society's building. Jim was already in the room when I arrived and as he and I waited for the others he asked me if we could use the letters with the upturned tumbler – Ouija-Board fashion - as he had some questions he wanted to put to Spirit via this method. It was a surprise to me that he wanted to return to this method especially since we had had some not too favourable episodes with it previously. But he said he had some ideas about what had happened the week before and he didn't want to divulge this information in advance as he didn't want anyone to know of the situation beforehand so in this way there could be no possibility of anyone influencing the results. He seemed quite ardent in his request and so when he asked me if I had the letters (letters of the alphabet) with me I reluctantly agreed and started delving into the bottom of my bag to find the envelope which held them. As I did this the others were arriving and so I told them of Jim's request to use the Ouija-Board method so he could ask some questions. I could see the puzzled look on their faces – they had come to hear the tape - but as usual they accepted what had been said as I produced the envelope from the depth of my bag. As I spilled the contents of the envelope out on to the table there were the little paper squares each sporting a letter of the alphabet that had been made some several weeks earlier together with some money. This was the remains of the kitty from the pub from the last time we were there. As I sorted the paper money and coins from the letters I spotted a foreign coin and joked with the others that someone had put a foreign coin in the kitty and in jest I asked which one of them was responsible. The others laughed and suggested that I had probably got it in the change from the pub. With my banking background I could spot a foreign coin a mile away – I had been trained to do it – so I disagreed with them; it was highly unlikely that anyone could pass a foreign coin into my hand unnoticed but I accepted this retort. It wasn't really important anyway as we had much more interesting things on our agenda for this evening, but we had a laugh about it. The letters were arranged on the circular brass table top and the Group convened. We sat in silence for some time as usual and then Jim brought everyone's attention back to the room. He explained that he wanted to try to establish just what had taken place last week because he thought that we were all slightly confused about the whole thing. He mentioned that he had had a sleepless night on Thursday evening thinking about things and how we could try to get some answers to what had happened – so he decided on the Ouija Board.

> Jim: 'I'm aware this is maybe slightly different to what we had planned but if you could maybe just bear with me?'

The Group agreed although I could tell they were itching to hear the tape. But Jim continued by directing us all to place our fingers on the upturned glass – except his – so he could ask his questions.

> Jim to Spirit: 'Right. Were there events which happened here last week which we were unaware of?' *(No response).*
> Jim to the Group: 'Did that question seem strange to you or did you understand it?'
> Ann: 'I think it was too ambiguous.'
> Mairi: 'You'll need to be more specific, are you asking about sounds or……'

> Jim: 'Right. We had intended last week - it was our purpose to try to work with sound, were you aware of that? Were you aware that we were trying to work with sound?' *Yes.*
> Jim: 'Right. Were there sounds made manifest which we were unable to detect?' *Yes*
> Jim: 'Thank you. It is our intention later on this evening to play back a tape I think, and could there be sounds on that?' *Yes.*
> Ann following up: 'Created by you?'
> Jim: 'Yes, were the sounds created by you?' *Yes.*
> Jim: 'We were unaware of them, is that correct?' *Yes.*
> Jim: 'What were the sounds? Did they emanate from the brass table that we were using?' *Yes.*
> Jim: 'Did you use the two objects that were placed upon the table to make the sounds, was that correct?' *No.*
> Jim: 'Right, so the sounds that you made that were emanating from the table were not made with physical implements, is that correct?' *Yes.*
> Jim: 'Right. I think at this stage, unless my friends round the table have other questions relating to this, I'd like to move on to other things. Do any of you have other questions relating to this?'

I was surprised that Jim's questions seemed to be over so quickly since he had seemed so ardent earlier about the need to use the table in this way. I had another question just to further clarify the origin of that sound:

> Ann: 'The sound that you created last Thursday for us – did you use the vibration of our voices to create that sound?' *Yes.*

Gill and I had discussed this in the intervening time as we had been aware that the energy of our voices was being utilised in some way. Now it was being confirmed.

> Jim: 'Right. Thank you. Anybody got anything else?
> Well friends we may come back to this later but I've been wondering about this situation. Could I just draw this matter out just a little? Were there other things which happened in this room, which we were unaware of which you....' *Yes.*
> Jim: 'Yes, thank you.'

Jim had not even finished asking his question yet he got a 'yes' from the upturned glass – remembering of course that he did not have his finger on the glass. So as it moved to the affirmative the members of the Group were beginning to look to me with questioning expressions on their faces – I had no idea what Jim was referring to – this was news to me and everyone else here as far as I could tell.

Jim: 'I think I may know what happened. I've given this much thought in my mind. Do you think I may know also, is that correct?' *Yes.*
Jim: 'Was that awareness meant for me very shortly after a dream last Thursday night, is that correct?' *Yes.*
Jim: 'Thank you. I am not trying to be secretive or anything else but it seems to me that you know and I know what happened. If what happened involved anything else in this room, could you perhaps spell it out for us, is that possible?' *Yes.*
Jim: 'Lovely, thanks very much.'
Mairi: 'You're going to have to ask it to spell it out.'
Jim: 'Right, let's return to the question I asked you, what I think happened involved something else in this room, can you try to spell it out for us please? Is that possible?' *Yes.*
Jim: 'I am going to ask another question; can you spell out what we understand took place – I'm the only one who is aware of it – I wonder if you can spell out what we call it in Spiritual/Mediumistic terms please? Could you do that?' *Yes.*
Jim: 'Right, thank you friends that's good, but let me make it clear to you, something happened here and there is a word we use in the paranormal to describe that, can you spell that word to me now.'
The glass moved to P, H, Y, S, I, C
Gill: 'Yes, psychic.'
Ann: 'Yes, spelt wrongly that's all. Is the word Psychic?' *Yes.*

Of course looking back at this transcript now our spirit team could have been right first time – it could have been physics.

Jim: 'Well Friends you're going to have to be a little smarter than that. Right, can you say, what happened here, was it something to do with an object, was that correct? Was there an object in this room, moved, unbeknown to us?' *Yes.*
Jim: 'Right. What was that object, can you spell it out please?'

The glass started moving around the table with everyone except Jim's fingers on it as the Group continued to look to one another wondering what this was all about.

Gill: 'Where are you going? What are you looking for?'
Jim: 'You're probably unsure of my question. Is that correct, are you unsure of what I'm after?' *Yes.*
Gill: 'What object did you use, can you spell it out please?'
The glass moved to B, O, O, K).
Jim: 'That's not what I'm aware of, but perhaps we can bear that in mind and perhaps come back to it.'
Ann: 'Okay, well let's just confirm. Did you use a book to create a sound whilst we were here last Thursday?' *No.*

Gill: 'Was it referred to in a book?' *Yes*
Ann: 'You were reproducing the sound last week; that was referred to in the book?' *Yes*
Gill: 'But we didn't hear it physically at the time?' *Yes.*
Gill: 'Okay, you are agreeing with us?' *Yes.*
Gill: 'Right. Would I be correct in saying that it was only audible on our tape machine as proof?' *Yes.*
Gill: 'Will we hear other sounds from your side with our physical ears in future?' *Yes.*
Gill: 'Good, I'll look forward to that. What was also mentioned last week was patience, is this relevant?' *Yes.*
Gill: 'Okay, thank you. We are anxious to know how best to proceed; can you help us with this?' *Yes.*
Gill: 'Is it a question of asking the right questions?' *Yes.*

I was aware that this retort about asking the right questions was gently aimed at Jim as I realised his line of questioning had been hi-jacked. So I asked him if he had more questions and he answered with some frustration:

Jim: 'Yes. I'll try to be more blunt. Has this Group experienced an apport?' *Yes.*
Mairi: 'Ohhhhhh!'

The surprised looks circled the room – this was not what we were expecting at all.
(An apport is where an object is transferred from one place to another allegedly by Spirit or where an item suddenly appears from an unknown source. This is an extremely rare but recognised phenomenon in physical séances.)

Jim: 'Did it occur last week?' *Yes.*
Jim: 'Had it anything to do with a metal object? Was that which was apported made of metal?' *Yes.*
Ann to Jim: 'What was it?'
Jim: 'I know what it was.'
Ann: 'Well ask them – what was it.'
Jim: 'Can you tell us what it was?' *Yes.*
Jim: 'Could you now do so please?' *Yes.*
Jim: 'And the first letter would be....' *The glass moved to C, O, I, N.*
Gill: 'Ah, yes.'

Gill appeared to be the only one who seemed to understand this response whilst the rest of us including Jim were looking puzzled.

Jim: 'Well that's not what I had in mind.'
Ann: 'Are you saying that there was a coin apported here, last

Thursday?' *Yes.*

The Group are all puzzled. Then I remembered the kitty.

> Ann: 'Can I just ask, is it the one that we referred to, earlier tonight?' *Yes.*
> Mairi: 'Oh, you beauty – the Bermuda one!'
> Ann: 'The one from the Caribbean that's in our kitty money!'
> *The Group are all amazed and there is some stunned laughter.*
> Jim: 'Well we're absolutely delighted to hear that friends, but that's not what I was thinking of.'

As once again the bemused looks flashed around the faces of everyone – surely there couldn't be two apports?

> Jim: 'Were the keys of this building apported last week?' *Yes.*
> Jim: 'Were they apported out of this room?' *Yes.*
> Gill to Jim: 'Were they?'
> Jim: 'Were they laid on the floor outside the door, is that correct?' *Yes.*
> Mairi and Gill: 'Ahhha.'
> Jim to the Group: 'Do you recall the incident?'
> Gill: 'Yes.'
> Mairi: 'I do.'

The previous week Jim had opened the door with the keys and handed them back to me. At the end of our session when Gill and Mairi had opened the door the keys were lying on the floor in the hallway immediately behind the door. They picked them up and handed them back to Jim who once again handed them to me. I hadn't seen this interchange or thought anything of this when Jim handed me the keys. I suppose I had presumed that Jim had just taken them back somehow. Jim however had clearly put some more thought into this and was now telling us that he had had a dream about it. In the dream he had been made aware that the keys had been taken and apported through the door to the other side. All of this was subsequently confirmed by asking questions via the Ouija Board.

To look at this more critically, I suppose some of those who are reading this will just dismiss the coin as having been included in the change from the pub as the Group had originally suggested. However one must bear in mind that when asking for answers via the board none of us had the least notion that the answers that Jim was looking for were in relation to an apport. As you can see from the transcripts above, his line of questioning was actually hi-jacked as everyone was focused on hearing the tape with the sounds from the previous week. When 'coin' was spelt out no one was expecting this - including Jim.

Next the Group examined the question of the keys. I had not seen Gill and Mairi pick up the keys from outside the door. When Jim handed them back to me I just assumed he had taken them back again for some purpose. It was Jim who was puzzled as he knew he had opened the door with the keys and that he had handed them back to me. I had laid them on a side table next to my coat. Therefore they were on the inside of the room throughout the time we were sitting in Circle. If he had actually dropped the keys whilst he was opening the door and they had inadvertently fallen to the floor all of us would have had to step over them as we arrived and as most of us had subsequently visited the toilet further along the corridor after we had arrived but before our session had begun then surely one of us would have seen them.

Jim summed it up:

> Jim: 'I woke up from my dream last Thursday Night about 1.30 or 2 o clock in the morning. I had rather a nice dream actually, but I was almost compelled to go downstairs and write down that those keys were apported.'
> Jim to Spirit: 'Did you influence me to get out of bed and write that?' *Yes.*
> Jim: 'Well I'm going to use a legal term, 'I rest my case', and I simply cannot believe how privileged we have been to experience that. I just want to ask now if any of my colleagues want to say anything in that regard, is that all right?' *Yes.*
> Ann: 'Can I check something. I just want to clarify please? Are you telling us that there were two apports last week?' *Yes.*
> Ann: 'One of the keys and one of the coin?' *Yes.*
> Ann: 'Or, just for clarity, did the coin apport happen at another time?' *No.*
> Ann: 'No, they both happened last week. It's just that I've never opened that envelope since we were in the pub, months ago.'
> Gill: 'Yes.'

Once the Group had got over the revelation that we had indeed experienced not one but two apports in the previous week we returned to the question of the sounds on the tape. I inserted the tape from last week into the tape recorder whilst I asked Gill to read through the transcript to help me find the location on the tape where the first sound was experienced. The tape was played and the first 'crack' was heard. The Group were listening intently as they hear the sound of the first 'crack'.

> 'I don't know what that could be' says Mairi, 'but I don't know the noise the mic would make if it did get jolted.'

I told Mairi that when the mic is moved it makes a sound like interference on a radio.

'Well you don't get that do you', she says. 'That sound is very strong'.

I played the tape again and whilst I was looking for the second sound on the tape I came across an example of the mic being moved and played it so that the Group could distinguish the difference in the sounds. Then the second sound is heard on the tape.

'Sounds like Pipes?' says Mairi, 'It's like knock three times....'

Mairi was referring to a popular song with the words, 'Knock three times on the ceiling – twice on the pipes..' and when those words are sung in that song the percussion follows up with two loud metallic bongs which sounds just like someone banging on metal water pipes. This was a very accurate summation of what the sound on the tape was like. I played the next part of the tape with the louder metallic-type gong sound. The Group were all leaning forward to hear the sound and when it was played they all jumped back from the recorder because the sound was so loud. Some nervous laughter broke out as they couldn't believe the sound they had just heard.

> Mairi (laughs): 'Oh, my goodness! It sounds like somebody picked up the tray and went...' (she motions as if to bang the tray over her knee).
> Ann: 'Exactly. You're all hearing this? Right? It is there?'
> Gill: 'It's there. Can you play that bit again?'
> *The tape is played again.*
> Ann: 'Now no-one said anything like, 'Oh sorry that was me', or anything like that. Because if someone had let's say kicked the tray - it would have had to be something as loud as that - it would have interrupted our conversation. If that had happened you would have expected someone to say something or to apologise.'
> Mayumi: 'But that sound is not an accidental knock against the table. It would have to be a very deliberate action to be as loud as that. As Mairi says you'd have to pick it up and hit it against something solid to make as loud a 'gong' as that. Or hit it with a hammer, but it would need to be wielded with some force.'
> Jim: 'Is that it finished or is there any more on the tape?'

I forwarded the tape to the last sound and both Mairi and Mayumi laughed at yet another indisputably loud sound on the tape that was not present on the night.

Gill: 'Well I think that's phenomenal; incredible!'

Ann: 'Good. I'm glad. Because I was typing away and hearing the noises and firing out emails, and thinking, 'Oh, no, there's nobody on-line'.' *(The Group laugh).*

As an experiment Jim then decides that for the purposes of the tape and to provide further evidence that this was not created by us – he decides to try to recreate the sound. He hits the table with his hand to try to simulate the sound but it was nothing like what was heard on the tape. The Group made various suggestions of how he might recreate the sound including kicking the table with his feet but that didn't work. It was not the same. It lacked the vibrational sound that was heard so clearly on the tape. After a few other failed experiments, the nearest we could get to what was heard on the tape was when we stood the brass table-top on its side so that it had the least point of contact with any other surface and in this way we tried to increase the reverberations. (It was at this point that I realised that what we were doing was creating a vibrational sound – much like the sound described by Professor De Morgan as like the elusive knitting needle hitting the marble). When the table top was hit hard like this by Jim using his knuckles in a sort of punching movement the sound was beginning to resemble what was heard on the tape. The problem was that Jim couldn't do this more than once as it was taking so much effort to strike the blow it was hurting his knuckles.

Ann: 'That's better. Sounds a bit more like it.'
Gill: 'He was doing it with his knuckles at that point.'
Ann: 'Yes.'
Jim: 'Well I'm not doing it again because it hurts.'
Ann: 'Well, I'm overwhelmed.'
Gill: 'Yes. Because there's no way that it was any of us that did that.'
Jim: 'It does really indicate how fussy we're going to have to be.'
Gill: 'Yes, we're going to have to really pay attention.'
Ann: 'But we weren't hearing that on the night. And Gill, you hit it on the head, you said you thought they were using the vibration of our voices and you were right because whilst we were all sitting in silence nothing happened and then when we all sit back and start chatting and nobody's got their hands on the table, that's when it happened.'
Gill: 'That's right, nobody had their hands on the table.'
Ann: 'That's right.'
Mairi: 'The problem with them doing things like this is, that unless they have a way of communicating that they've done it, then you're not really going to know.'
Ann: 'But they did find a way of communicating it – they let me know when I was typing the transcript from the tape that I was going to hear something. And they told Jim about the apports through his dream.'
Mairi: 'Yes. And, we've had corroboration here tonight. The problem is, yes, we were paying a lot of attention; we were being very patient; we

knew something was happening; we knew we were missing stuff, but we had no way of knowing what it was, we were missing, we did our best.'
Gill: 'But the difference is, we got it later.'
Ann: 'Which makes it more evidential.'
Jim: 'Absolutely.'

I was right in saying that it was more evidential since no-one in the Group the week before had heard the sounds which subsequently appeared on the tape. And this is evidenced by the tape as the recording proves that we didn't hear anything; indeed you can hear us consoling each other over the fact that we experienced nothing that night. Equally, Jim was very careful in not revealing the information that had been imparted to him via his dream – the information that we had received an apport. He did this so that it could be established via the table (acting as an Ouija Board) which of course it was. But almost in a further corroboratory move a second apport was established – one which even Jim did not know of.

I went home that evening even more amazed at what had happened that night. I had gone with the tape to let the others hear the recorded sounds from the week before – and I had come back having experienced two apports. It constantly amazed me how Spirit continued to manifest different phenomena in our Circle. It was unbelievable - but I was aware that's exactly what the sceptics would think – that it was unbelievable. I needed more. I needed further proof that these really were apports. I needed the objects apported to be something other than everyday things like keys, and albeit it was a foreign coin – it was still a coin. I needed an apport of something different, something unusual – so I asked Arthur for it.

And a few weeks later, on 16th November 2006 my request was granted – again when I least expected it and had forgotten all about my request. On that particular evening Gordon had actually brought along furniture polish and a cloth and he set about polishing up the Formica-topped coffee table as we had had instances before where a sticky substance seemed to manifest on the table top and had the effect of stopping or slowing the upturned glass when it was used Ouija-Board fashion. That night I had brought along the bracelets which I had been carrying in my bag for several weeks as I wanted everyone to be present before distributing them – and tonight we were all here.

And so it was that the newly polished wood-effect Formica-topped coffee table stood in the centre of our Circle as we sat in silence. Gill had suggested that as a final empowering of the bracelets a circle of candles be arranged on the table top and lit so that the bracelets could sit in the middle of this circle whilst we sat in silence. I had also arranged a circle of candles on the floor to encircle the Group before we sat.

During the silence it was noted how one by one most members of the

Group coughed – this is not a usual occurrence for them. Also Gill whispered about how cold it had become in the room as I lifted the bracelets from the table and stood in the centre of the Circle:

> Ann: 'Dear God, Great Spirit, Master of all that is. Please hear me now because I have before me these bracelets – the ones you requested, the ones that you asked us to get so that each member of this Group here present tonight should wear them. They are here now. I have them before me in my hand. They have been made with Blue Goldstone – you requested Blue Goldstone. Goldstone has its origins in the ancient city of Venice. It is said to have been discovered by a closed order of Monks in that city. It may well have been discovered in their search for alchemy. It is also said to have some healing properties. But no matter what properties it has it has been sought and found and used in these bracelets for this Group as you directed. These bracelets also hold an emblem – the Caduceus. This is another ancient symbol. This is the symbol of the serpent and the staff and signifies powerful spiritual healing energy and is carried by the messenger of the gods. It has been adopted in modern times by the majority of the healing agencies. And again no matter what its power it has been sought and found and incorporated into these bracelets as directed by you. These bracelets have been put together by me as directed by you. These bracelets have been empowered by the energy of sun and the moon – again as directed by you. These bracelets have been empowered still further here tonight by being encircled in a circle of light. That suggestion came tonight from a member of this Group and has been utilised as I'm sure that it may have come from you too. As you empower these bracelets still further and as they are distributed here now to each member of this Group let them signify our unity our commitment our love our loyalty and determination to one another and also to the Spirit World. As they are distributed let each member of this Group feel the power that comes from these bracelets and let each person in this Group wear them with pride and as a symbol of our commitment, love, support and loyalty to each and every one of us – each to the other – each member of this Group. And also, as a symbol and a signal of our commitment to you and our loyalty to the Spirit World. Let them feel that power now as they are distributed.'

I slowly walked toward each member of the Group allowing them to pick a bracelet for themselves and as each person placed the bracelet on their wrist I brought my ritual to a conclusion – 'So let it be'.

> Jim: 'Thank you Ann, for those lovely words. I'm sure people will cherish them and be aware of their purpose. It is to be hoped that when we gather here we will wear them on our wrists. Do cherish them and at times when you may feel in need of the love of Spirit yourselves perhaps you may wish to use them and be aware that when you touch them Spirit

is with you each and every one.'

Jim then asks the Group to come back from their meditative state. During the period of meditation some of the candles had gone out. But as we looked at the table we found it was totally covered in short lengths of cotton thread. These threads were not fine; indeed they were sort of frayed and they were only about one centimetre in length but there were lots of them covering the whole surface of the table.

Mayumi to Ann: 'What are they?' *(Mayumi points to the little fibres of string all over the table top).*
Ann: 'I don't know.'
Mayumi: 'It was not here when we put the candles on it.'
Ann: 'No, no. What is it? Like little bits of thread. No they weren't there when we put the candles on it. Will I put the light up so we can have a look at it?'
Mayumi: 'It's like cotton thread, isn't it?'
Ann: 'Yes, it's like the wick from a candle but it's not that because those candles all have much thicker wicks.'
Jim: 'Ann, was there anything on that table when you put the candles there?'
Ann: 'No.'
Gordon: 'And the wicks from the candles are black - they have all been used before.'
Ann: 'Hmm, interesting.'
Jim: 'It's as if they send us things to intrigue us.'
Ann: 'Is this another big thing? They couldn't have been here when I put the candles down as we all would have seen them. We were all looking at the bracelets in the centre of the table – we would have seen this.'
Gill: 'Yes, because you would have taken them off.'
Ann: 'Yes, but remember Gordon polished the table before we started. Just for the benefit of the tape the table has been sprinkled with what appears to be thread – pieces of string or candlewick that hasn't been used and we don't know where it has come from. It hasn't come from any of the candles on the table anyway because they're not the same and they had all been previously used.'
Ann: 'Did anybody feel when they were doing the meditation - did you feel the energy in your throat?'
Mayumi: 'Yes, and I started coughing.'
Mairi: 'And, I did too, so did Gill. That's the sort of thing you get, just before you speak. It's a sort of peculiar sensation.'
Ann: 'Well, that's just exactly what I thought – everyone's going to speak tonight!'
Gill: 'Can I say that during the meditation I asked if they could... if it was at all possible to show us something in the centre, either by making

something move or giving us something. And, I don't know what I was expecting, but it wasn't that.'
Ann: 'It doesn't matter, you've got it.'

I felt that it didn't matter that I had asked for an apport too; if Gill had also asked for something - here it was answering both our appeals.

Gill: 'I was surprised when I looked and saw this.'
Ann: 'Yes. These little bits of whatever it is weren't there before because when all the candles were lit you would have seen them quite clearly because everyone was saying how nice it was with the bracelets in the centre of the table with the candles around them and the table was clear then.'
Mairi: 'Yes, that wasn't there before we began.'
Mayumi: 'No, it wasn't.'
Jim: 'Where could that have come from?'
Gordon: 'It's as if snow has dropped from the ceiling whilst we were sitting.' *(He checked his hair to see if anything had dropped on his head).* 'It's only on the table, there's none on the floor or anywhere else – that's strange.'
Jim: 'Could it be an apport?'

The Group looked at each other and those strange smiles of surprise and disbelief played over their faces.

Gill: 'Well if this is an apport it has to have come from somewhere – where could this have come from?'
Mairi: 'Well not from this room. There's nothing in here that would produce that stuff.'
Ann: 'Well let's just check. Firstly is anybody wearing anything that these fibres could have come from?'
Gordon: 'No, they are not. Can I suggest, just for purposes of recording this that everyone turns out their pockets? Just to prove that no one has put it there.' *(As he said this he stood and pulled the linings of his pockets out from his jeans.)*
Mairi: 'No one except you and Jim have pockets.' *(Jim reluctantly stands and pulls the lining of his pockets from his trousers, catching a handkerchief as he does so).*
Gordon (still recording events for the benefit of the tape): 'And none of the bags are within reach. So we have another apport then. Does everyone agree?'

As the Group all recorded their confirmation I smiled to myself. Here was another lesson from Arthur. This time showing us that objects could be moved by Spirit and those physical barriers like doors and walls presented no obstacle. This apport was just as I had asked, something different something unusual. Indeed no-one knew what it was or where it had come from. And I wondered if Spirit had influenced Gordon to suddenly bring along some polish and a duster – and Gill to suggest the circle of candles on the table - each action demonstrating that the table was clear and clean beforehand and that this phenomenon manifested not only in the light of the room but in the bright light of the candles. I had asked for an apport that was different and something that was less controversial. Here it was. This was far harder to explain away by the sceptics - especially since we couldn't explain it ourselves.

(In parapsychology and spiritualism, an apport is the alleged paranormal transference of an article from one place to another, or an appearance of an article from an unknown source that is often associated with poltergeist activity or séances. Source: Wikipedia).

If you think about Captain James Kirk from the Star Ship Enterprise when he utters the immortal words, 'Beam me up, Scottie', you'll have a fairly good impression of what an apport is.

If we return to my school science class where I reminded you that everything is made up of energy molecules just vibrating at different frequencies then the apport theory is that molecules from a chosen article are dematerialised and transported to another location where they are re-materialised.

This may be a stretch too far for some but research in the field of parapsychology has already discovered the poltergeist phenomenon whereby ghosts or some form of non-physical force are able to move objects and in some cases throw objects, and these objects can be very heavy. One such famous case took place in a lawnmower business in Cardiff, Wales. This involved various articles being thrown in the workshop and this was witnessed by various third parties including Professor David Fontana from The Society for Psychical Research. He found the case to be genuine and wrote a report confirming the presence of a poltergeist which he stated was 'demonstrably intelligent' and possessed a willingness to interact with the human's present.

Further if we look at the evidence of some of the feats of Daniel Dunglas Home one of the most celebrated Mediums of all time (and referred to earlier in this book – See Chapter 14), testimonies state that he would levitate at will and so too would heavy wooden tables that would float around up to the ceiling until he would gently bring them back down to the floor. If he could levitate out of a third-floor window and float along the outside of the building to re-emerge back into the building via another window then how much further would he need to go to move those objects or indeed himself into another room or place or time? And no tele-transporter required – eat your heart out Scottie.

19 HIT AND RUN

Gordon had been absent for the previous couple of weeks and was eager to catch up on what had been happening in his absence. In particular he had read all the transcripts and like the others was keen to hear the sounds on the tape from the week of 21st September. He asked if I could bring the tape back into the Theosophical Society so he could hear it first-hand. Because of a number of other engagements there were only three of us available to meet on Thursday 5th October 2006 so we decided to use this week to bring Gordon up to date with the events of the last two weeks and to play the tape and get his comments and reaction – he was the only person in the Group not to have heard the tape.

And so Jim, Gordon and I sat down with the transcript of the meeting of the 21st September together with the tape of that night – pretty much as we had already done the week before - and allow Gordon to hear the recorded sounds. He listened to the loud crack and then the series of noises which I have described as either like the sound of someone banging water pipes or the sound of someone drumming on the brass-topped table.

We then proceeded to play the series of rumbling or drumming noises that got increasingly louder with each excerpt played. He too thought it sounded like water pipes except as he said there were no water pipes in this part of the building as the plumbing runs down at the back of the building. He then tested out the sound the small brass-topped table made when it was knocked (with his knuckles) just as Jim had done – the sound was very similar to that recorded on the tape.

He deduced that although no-one could explain how it happened the only thing in the room that could have been responsible for such a sound was indeed that small brass-topped table. Gordon also agreed with our view that it was clear that no-one who was present in the room at the time could have heard those sounds as no mention of them whatever is made on the tape and he like the others had no memory of such a sound either on the night in question or indeed any other night.

After our lengthy discussion and analysis of the tape we realised the time was around ten past eight – we usually finished at 9pm - so we decided we would just sit for a little while to see if we would get anything. Jim said an opening prayer and then asked Gordon to talk us into an altered state to help raise the energy. As Gordon was talking we heard a couple of knocks inside the room towards the direction of the door but not quite as far as the door. Shortly after that another knock was heard in the same area. Gordon and Jim confirmed that they too heard the sound from the same area. I asked Spirit if they had made the sound that they repeat it. There was again a little quieter single knock from the direction of the door.

The energy in the room was very, very strong even although there were just the three of us there. It was as if Spirit had been using the energy of our voices just as before to create sound (the knocks). Or perhaps they were encouraged by what we had been saying about having worked out that we were getting even greater phenomena than we had anticipated.

As we sat in silence I was aware that I was being heavily influenced by Spirit but I opened my eyes to see what was happening with the others and I could see that Jim had gone into his trance-like state and so I invited him to speak. I wished at this point I had had the tape-recorder on, but it still had the tape from the 21st Sept in the machine. This new communicator coming through Jim seemed to be almost preaching to us; from my own psychic observations I could tell that he was a very large man from Spirit that was communicating. He had long wild hair and a beard and I felt he was some sort of Lay Preacher or Missionary – something that Jim himself noted was completely alien and at odds with his own views of religion.

Gordon also confirmed that he was aware of the Spirit man with Jim. He was aware of his size and hair but wasn't sure if it was a beard he had or a double-chin but he was aware of his bulkiness and of the Preacher-like status.

As Jim was talking I was able to ask questions of the Spirit Being with him. I asked if he was a Preacher of some sort and he said he thought he was but felt that he wasn't an ordained minister; he was doing it on more of a voluntary basis. I described the place I could see him preaching in. A sort of wooden hut like a Missionary Hall and it was out in the countryside amongst the fields. Jim could not feel this but our visitor asked me if I thought he was wearing a hat. To which I replied, "not in church, but there's one at your feet and its black with a wide brim". Jim agreed and wondered therefore if he could be a Rabbi? The Spirit Entity joked at this point that this would be amusing as Jim wouldn't know what a Rabbi did. Just at this point I had a sudden inspiration that I knew that he wasn't Jewish but Amish – and I told him so.

This Spirit Preacher through Jim's Mediumship gave us a lengthy, deep and meaningful sermon on the values of the world and of what was important. He remarked that he was a very spiritual person rather than one holding to a religious persuasion and indeed mentioned the fact that many religions were fighting with one another.

I then deduced a change in personality and realised someone else was coming through Jim. This new communicator seemed to congratulate us on our work and for working out what we had actually been receiving these last couple of weeks. This second Spirit Being with Jim then thanked us for being present and interested and mentioned that Gordon had remained quiet for most of the interchange. Gordon replied that he had at first been aware of the vibrations in the building coming through the floor at the same time as a car alarm was set off outside. (We had experienced these strange feelings before; it was as if the floor was actually rising under our feet. I didn't experience it this time as I think I was more focused on the Spirit Communicators but I knew exactly what Gordon was talking about and strangely, just as before, there was a car alarm going off outside at the same time.) To travel across the floor in this manner and perhaps even reverberate outside to such an extent that it sets off a car alarm would suggest that the energy is vibrational – this is certainly how it felt.

Gordon continued explaining to Spirit why he had remained quiet. He was telling us that he was drawn to observing the candle flames that became much more animated as soon as the Spirit Person came forward to speak through Jim. Gordon explained he meant no disrespect as he was still listening intently but was simultaneously intrigued by what appeared to be a possible elevation of the candle-jar slightly above the table. He explained that he had contemplated searching for a piece of paper in his jacket pocket and trying to slide it under the glass jar to prove it had risen off the table. As he started to rummage in his pocket the glass appeared to come back down to rest on the table and the opportunity was lost.

Unfortunately I hadn't seen this latest phenomenon and so was not in a position to corroborate it. I was focused on Jim and his communicator, so clearly Jim was not in a position himself to be able to confirm what Gordon had seen either but nevertheless I was pleased Gordon, who had missed out on some of the phenomenal events of the last couple of weeks, now had his own small miracle to enjoy.

Jim then slowly came out of his trance and asked if I had got anything whilst in the silence; it was at this point that I started to tell of the vision that I had been getting. I had been very heavily influenced earlier whilst in the silence and I told Jim so and then I told the Group what had happened.

I had become aware of a street scene in Edinburgh and a small boy of around ten years old who had been hit by a car. I was able to see that the boy had pressed the button to cross at a pedestrian crossing when the car hit him. I think the boy had been going to the shops which I could see nearby. I got the impression that the boy had just walked through a large grassed area which would be used for dog-walking and by kids playing about with footballs. When he reached the main road he pressed the button on the box of the pedestrian crossing and had crossed with 'the green man'[31]. This is where the car had hit him – and the car hadn't stopped. I didn't know why I was seeing this scene or receiving this information as it didn't seem to have any connection to any of us in the Circle. And just as I had dismissed Arthur Conan Doyle much earlier in the Group's formation I now told Gordon and Jim that I thought this was some sort of random information that I had picked up somehow.

It was then that Gordon mentioned that there had been a report on the radio to say that a child had been knocked down in Edinburgh and that the police had taken the unusual step of issuing a description of the car. I hadn't been aware of this but now the information became much more meaningful and Gordon started on a quest to see if I could ascertain where this scene was that I was seeing in my vision. I thought the area looked as if it was around the Broomhall area (a suburb of Edinburgh) and I described it as being like the road that comes from PC World (a well-known computer store in Corstorphine, another suburb) heading towards Sighthill (another surburb). I could see the road end of a housing scheme which came to a main road where the pedestrian crossing was and a parade of shops. I was aware that there was a green space like a sort of park area nearby and I thought the boy may have come from that direction towards the crossing. This was the scene I could see in my head. Jim (who lives in Corstorphine) mentioned that he passed a junction that had been cordoned off by police as he drove in towards the Theosophical Society that evening but it wasn't where I was describing and he too didn't know anything about a child being knocked down.

I couldn't get any more information than this and Gordon didn't know from the radio report whether it had been a boy or a girl who was knocked down and wasn't sure where the accident had occurred; he only thought that it was not in the city centre but a little further out of town. The meeting closed and we agreed to meet again next week. I forwarded my apologies in advance as I knew I couldn't make it.

The next day Friday 6th Oct 2006, the day after our meeting, Jim called me. He was the first to break the news to me that a boy had indeed been knocked down and killed by a hit and run driver in Edinburgh the day before. He had just seen it on the TV news and asked if I had seen it. I rarely watch daytime TV so he asked me to watch the evening news which I did, and there the story was, on the 10 o'clock news. Sadly a 10-year-old boy had been knocked down and killed on a pedestrian crossing on his way home from school, and there was the road, the parade of shops and the pedestrian crossing just as I had seen them in my head. The police were looking for three suspects in the hit and run vehicle which had been dumped shortly afterwards as they made their escape.

I felt so sorry for the boy and his family when I realised that the information I had received the previous evening was correct. As had been the case with the Dunblane Disaster I felt the heavy responsibility of possessing information like this. There is a dilemma over what you should do with it. On the one hand you desperately want to bring some comfort to the family, but on the other hand you know this will not bring back the lives of the children that have been lost. Unlike the Dunblane case, this time I apparently had received the information just after the incident had occurred rather than beforehand so there was no opportunity unfortunately of being able to prevent such a tragedy. I was glad in a way that I wasn't going to the meeting the next week. I needed a break. The impact of information such as this is like an emotional blow. Psychic Investigators are like the majority of people: humanitarian and wanting to help and make things better, but they are often unable to do so and can be left with feelings of sadness and guilt. I would take the next week to come to terms with these thoughts.

Gordon too was unable to attend the next meeting but Jim, Gill, Mairi and Mayumi met as usual in the Theosophical Society Building. Here is an excerpt of the transcript of their meeting:

> Jim: 'I was aware this evening I think... I feel there was somebody with me who was connected with the little boy who was knocked down last week, ... Ann was not aware of the events which had occurred approximately 2 hours prior to our meeting last week - the incident with the wee boy and the car - and it may well have occurred roughly at the same time because at that time I was coming down from Slateford Road and as I approached the traffic lights at Broomhouse Road, North Saughton Road, you know where I am? And there were a couple of Police Cars and I had assumed that that's where the accident had occurred. So, in my wisdom last week I was trying to say to Ann, when we were discussing the events here, I was saying, 'but Ann, that doesn't seem right because the accident actually happened at the traffic lights', but Ann was quite adamant that it had happened at a pedestrian crossing and there was a parade of shops and it was in fact exactly as Ann had described it. So I phoned her up the next night about 6 o'clock when I saw it on the BBC News and when I saw exactly what the situation was and I asked Ann if she could look at it when it was repeated on the 10p.m. news ... sure in the knowledge that if Ann said that those things happened then that gives us confirmation that that was the way of it – that the little boy had pressed the button, the red light for the traffic had come on, the wee boy had crossed the road; that was how Ann was seeing it and that's what she told us last week and then we subsequent heard that that's exactly what had happened; the guy in the car had gone crashing through the red light. So it was really, I thought, quite

evidential.'
Mayumi: 'Yes.'
Gill: 'Yes.'

While it was nice to receive the confirmation from my fellow group members, particularly in my absence when there was no need for politeness and they were free to say whatever they wanted, I was always looking for something much more meaningful to come from such a tragedy and I wanted to help in some way. And it is strange how Spirit picks up your intentions even when you don't know them or haven't quite formulated them yourself. And so it was when we met again the following week Thursday, 18th October, 2006. (Gordon was absent. He was self-employed and had to earn income when he could and sometimes that meant he didn't get finished in time to attend our meetings at 6.30pm.) We sat in silence, the five of us and afterwards Jim asked everyone as usual what they had received.

> Ann: 'I'm going to tell you what I've been getting. It might be nothing, but I know to say it and to record it in case someone else can make something of it. I knew there was somebody (a Spirit Person) trying to influence me and not really coming very close to me, and I kept seeing jewellery. We've been dealing with jewellery all day today, Mayumi and I, and I kept seeing all this jewellery flashing in front of my face, and I was trying to get that out of my head but I knew there was somebody around. I was trying to get them to come closer and find out what it's about and then I got, 'Strawberry Fields Forever', the song from the sixties, and the Beatles. And I thought, okay, what has 'Strawberry Fields' got to do with anything? Is it something to do with, 'I'll take you there', and I thought, 'where'? I was asking all these questions and I wasn't really getting a lot of information and then they showed a picture of a wave. And I thought, okay, a wave - the sea?'

This was how our Group usually worked. Invariably it would start with me getting something, something I didn't understand the relevance of usually but I would have absolute faith and knowledge that I had got it for a purpose. The challenge was to find out why and what that purpose was. For this I knew to use the collective input of the Group and together we could normally work it out. And so it was Mairi who spoke next:

> Mairi: 'I got a flash of something too and I didn't really attach much meaning to it until you started speaking about the sixties and I felt just at the beginning there as if I was looking down on myself but it wasn't me and I was dressed in purple Pan velvet, very sixties, with silver buttons. It's quite like, I think it's an album cover with John Lennon I think wearing a big coat in this velvet colour with silver buttons down them. And again, I saw it and I could see it quite clearly, but it didn't

> seem to be going anywhere but I just thought I'd register it in case anyone else got anything, but again, it was Strawberry Fields, which is the Beatles. But I didn't get anything much after that, but it was the silver buttons I was drawn to, as they are a bit like jewellery, this big row of silver buttons down the coat.
> Gill: 'Strawberry Fields, was that not the Orphanage? Or where he was brought up?' *(She refers to John Lennon).*
> Ann: 'It was a Street in Liverpool.'
> Gill: 'It was either where he was brought up or there was an Orphanage there.'
> Ann: 'Well when I got Strawberry Fields, and I thought, what's the next bit? And it's 'let me take you there' and I thought, okay, take me, if it's wanting to show me, and that's when I saw this wave from the sea. So, don't know how these things are connected?'
> Gill: 'At least you have the information now on tape, ……..it will probably happen at a later date.'

Gill didn't know what would happen at a later date nor did anyone else but we had all become familiar with accepting that information like this usually had meaning and if we couldn't figure it out at the time invariably its relevance would become clear at some point in the future. It was for this purpose that we recognised the need to record what on the face of it would seem like random information so that it would become evidential in the future. For now however we moved on.

> Mayumi: 'Can I just make one comment that's totally different from what you've been saying? I had this flash of a picture, you know when you drive somewhere and there's a lay-by by the side of the road, but this is just a small square one at the side of the road, but there's a car, it's small and it's a dark colour, either black or dark blue, which is probably older. A small car, sort of boxy, so it's an older model, it's more like a Fiat or something I can see the back of the car and there's three guys. I can see clearly one guy has a white and black or navy stripped top and jeans and he has quite shortish hair, I think he's in his twenties, and kind of rough sort of people. There's another guy and he was in the front of the car – the other one was in the side, this one was in the front – and I can see his face and he is slightly chubbier and short, spiky-type of hair. And the other guy is already down into the field and I can see him going down there.'
> Ann: 'Do you think this is linking to the incident with the wee boy? They left the car at Saughton Prison, didn't they? In the car park?'

A fortnight had passed since the incident when the boy was knocked down and during that time a manhunt had been going on. The suspects had not been caught and there were appeals to the public for information. It was known that there were three men in the car and that it had been dumped shortly after the hit and run incident at a nearby prison from where the three had made their escape. Descriptions of the men had appeared in the newspapers at this time although the police did not know who they were or where they might be in hiding.

Ann to Mayumi: 'So, why are they there, what are they doing?'
Mayumi: 'You know when you're on the Western Approach Road *(she describes a semi-rural road in Edinburgh),* and there's a lay-by on the side of the road? Sometimes the bus is in there, it's something like that, but a lot shorter, because only a car can park there. And, on the other side of the road I can see plants and bushes, it is woodier, bushy and that's all I saw. It's not a busy road.'
Ann: 'So, it's not the Western Approach Road?'
Mayumi: 'No, it's not. It's somewhere like that type of road. I feel it could be just outside of town.'
Jim: 'What about you, Gill, what did you get?'
Mairi: 'It's quite cold.'
Jim: 'Yes it is, and it is about knee level. I'm aware of several presences but I can't determine who they are at all.'
Gill: 'The other word that came to mind, was like a 'collective', does that make sense?'
Mairi: 'I thought I heard a noise inside the room that sounded like somebody speaking in a low voice but it was really hard to distinguish.'
Gill: 'I heard something too.'
Mayumi: 'I heard that as well.'
Mairi: 'It sounded like a woman's voice and it was as if she said something just about one sentence long, just low enough that I could hear there was something but not well enough to hear the words. Because what I heard from inside the room had a sort of echoey quality to it as if it was bouncing round the room.'
Gill: 'I was conscious of that as well ……….'
Jim: 'Does anyone have any thoughts as to what we want to do?'
Ann: 'Here's a thought… I'm just wondering if it's possible for us all to tune into what Mayumi's picking up, as I'm wondering, if this has to do with the little boy incident and these three guys that the police are looking for – and tell me if it doesn't seem like that, and I'll just stop – but if it is that Mayumi has linked into the Universal Consciousness[32] and they're trying to say, this is a second car that they've all jumped into, or whatever……I've just got really, really frozen.'

I had to stop at this point as the room became suddenly icy cold as if you had just walked into a deep-freeze. The others agreed that there was a sudden and dramatic drop in temperature (this often is an indication that Spirit is present) and at the same time a car horn is sounding outside as if a car alarm that has just gone off at the very moment when I referred to a 'second car'. The horn sounds extremely close as if it is in the room. From recent events we had almost grown to accept this as an indication that something was going on in the room that required our attention and here it was again.

> Ann: 'I'm just wondering if we can all tune into that energy and try to get some information, given the current police investigation that's ongoing, but just.... *(Ann realises the Group have all immediately started to tune in)* .... It was only a suggestion not a directive.'
> Jim: 'No, no, let's do it.'
> Mairi: 'Yes, I've just suddenly got a wave of extreme cold.'
> Jim: 'If anybody feels anything, gets anything, just speak up.'
> *The Group sit in silence for a few minutes.*

The following excerpts from the transcript of the meeting gives a feel of how we work together to make sense of the information that each of us receives:

> Ann: 'I see an old car, it's pretty dilapidated and there's something inside the car maybe in the back seat, or over the back of one of the chairs and it's like a cushion cover[33] or something like that, cotton with a light background and a multi-coloured print on it.'
> Gill: 'What I am getting is a flashback of something that I saw from the train when I was going to Glasgow on Friday and it was like a travelling people's encampment. I'm linking with Mayumi's description of him. The people, the travelling people all have a certain look.'
> Ann: 'Is he wearing an earring, Mayumi?'
> Mayumi: 'I didn't see that. I can see the car, inside the car and .... I'm looking at the front seat on the passengers' side, and it's like, you know how an older car has, not leather but looks like vinyl .... it's an old-style interior.'
> Ann: 'My description is not of the car, but something that's inside the car that's been left lying around.'
> Gill: 'Is it like a blanket?'
> Ann: 'Something like that. It's either a blanket or – it's fairly flat so it could be a cushion cover ...'
> Mayumi: 'Is it sort of beige colour?'
> Ann: 'Yes, it has a light background but it has a coloured pattern on it and it's in the car.'
> Ann: 'Do you see the surface of the road that the car is sitting on, Mayumi, is it actually asphalt or is it concrete? Is it a piece of concrete? Or a concrete road?'
> Mayumi: 'It's more like that I think. It's not the same as the road, it's a slightly rougher surface.'
> Ann: 'That's right, is it pale coloured?'
> Mayumi: 'Yes.'

Gill: 'It's an old road.'
Ann: 'I feel that the railway's nearby as well. There's a railway embankment not too far away.'
Gill: 'This is what you call, 'lying low'.'
Ann: 'I feel somebody hitched a lift from a lorry.'
Mayumi: 'Probably from where they hid the car.'
Ann: 'Yes. It's like they all split up and one of them thumbed a lift from a passing lorry.'
Mairi: 'As you said that, I saw the A71 *(the A71 is a rural road that links Edinburgh with Kilmarnock on the West coast, crossing the A74 the major trunk road to the South en route).*
Ann: 'Right. Good. I was actually getting that road as well.'
Gill: 'Which is the A71?'
Mairi: 'The A71 goes out towards Kilmarnock. Kilmarnock eventually but it goes out towards Livingston and West Lothian, and funnily enough earlier on I got Straven, which is on the A71, just further along.'
Ann: 'You got the A71, I was going to say the A74. But in my head, I was thinking that's too far away.'
Mairi: 'But you could go on the A71 out to the A74.'
Ann: 'Fire Station. I've got a Fire Station.'
Jim: 'Sighthill?'
Mairi: 'That's on the way out to the A71.'
Mayumi: 'I got Wester Hailes.'
Ann: 'Right, that's on the A71 as well.'
Mayumi: 'And I think the three of them, they took off to different areas.'
Ann: 'Someone's heading South, hitching a lift from a lorry heading South, and I would have said Southwards on the A74.'
Gill: 'Right, one is going further south than that. I'm being shown Liverpool. Can you go to Ireland from Liverpool?'
Mairi: 'Yes.'
Ann: 'Funny, I've just got 'green' and I was to go to the West, but I was thinking that's Glasgow and it's something to do with Celtic. *(Celtic is one of the two main football teams in Glasgow, the 'green' Catholic one).*
Mairi: 'Celtic. Yes, football. That's a sectarian football song, 'We're off to Ireland in the Green'. The Celtic supporters sing that, it's a Republican Song.'
Ann: 'Oh, is it? Right. I've just been shown somebody losing a button off of something. In their haste to get away out of the car, they pulled a button off a shirt or a jacket or something. I think if they find this second car, they'll find a button lying that came off of the guy that was sitting in the back seat.'
Mairi: 'This is an objective question, as I don't know much about it really, but were they running away from a robbery or something?'
Ann: 'The police were chasing them, not when they hit the boy, but they had been chasing them and I think they lost them, but there was a

suspicion that they were doing the bogus workman routine somewhere.'

Mairi: 'I just got the feeling they were trying to get rid of something, they were in a hurry to get rid of something, but it wouldn't tie in with that, because ....'

Gill: 'I keep being shown this encampment from the train because I remember sitting in the train and actually looking back at it because I thought it strange, and there were no dogs, which is unusual.'

Mayumi: 'I've seen one of the other faces and I think it's the older man, which I didn't see earlier and I think the two I saw are slightly younger, quite young, I think. But I asked what this other person looked like and he has an earring and the closest I can pin point to what his face looks like is, you know the youngest member of the Bee Gees, the one with the glasses?'

Gill: 'Maurice Gibb? The one that was married to Lulu?'

Mayumi: 'The youngest one. He had a face similar to that.'

Gill: 'Gaunt, quite gaunt?'

Mayumi: 'But he looked rougher though... thin face with an earring.'

Gill: 'Jim, what are you wanting to say?'

Jim: 'I've got nothing to say, I'm not getting anything at all.'

Mairi: 'There's another bit of that song that will fit in with travelling, as it's 'I've always been a wanderer from the day I was born', this would tie in with somebody that travelled.'

Ann: 'Did you feel they torched that second car? I just had a sort of impression that they were talking about torching it.'

Mairi: 'I think they talked about it but they didn't get time to do it.'

Ann: 'That's right Mairi.'

Mairi: 'I think they had to run or something or move very quickly and they didn't get time to do it.'

Ann: 'That's right, Mairi, and also it would have drawn more attention to them. So they talked about it but they didn't do it, so it's lying somewhere to be found.'

Mairi: 'I also felt earlier on and I felt it coming in again... there's an older woman, who knows what happened who's protecting them. An older woman perhaps in her 70's or something like that, who's trying to justify it by saying, 'well it won't bring the boy back'.'

Ann: 'She's a Granny.'

Mairi: 'She's a Granny. But I feel she's struggling with her conscience. Quite protective towards her family, but she's pretty tough, but she's trying to justify it to herself and her conscience is really bothering her, because she knows it's not right, but she's saying would them being in jail bring the boy back and she feels it wouldn't do any good.'

Ann: 'I'm trying to concentrate as to where that car is because there are clues in it as to who these guys are.'

Gill: 'There's an embankment on the left-hand side of it.'

Ann: 'There's a railway embankment but I feel it's further away.'

Mairi: 'I keep getting place names form Ayrshire but I don't know if it's just my logical mind. Johnston, Kilwinning.'
Ann: 'I had Johnston earlier actually.'
Mairi: 'I'm going down there this weekend, so I'll keep my eyes open, because I'm going down by train so I'll be going through a lot of these areas.'
Ann: 'It was actually when you said, Tommy Thomas or something, I got Johnston then, as a name.'
Mairi: 'I got Johnston ages ago and didn't say it and I'm not sure about that, because I'm not sure if it's a name or if it's the place, because I feel it's in an area where it's not that unusual for cars to be dumped, which is why they're hoping that it will not be picked up because it will just be thought of as another car that's been dumped. I don't mean its beside other cars that have been dumped, I just mean it's in an area where it's not that unusual.'
Ann: 'Ratho came into my head as well.'
Mairi: 'Do you go through Ratho on the A71?'
Ann: 'Well you bypass the end of the road.'
Mairi: 'And the end of the A71 ends up in Johnston and Kilwinning.'
Gill: 'Mayumi, you do dowsing, would you be able to dowse a map?'
Mayumi: 'Well I've practised, so I don't know if it'll work or not.'
Gill: 'It's cold.'
Mairi: 'Yes, I'm freezing as well.'
Ann: 'They definitely want us to do this, don't they?'
Mairi: 'I had a feeling earlier on that it was a relative of the young boys in Spirit that was wanting to find answers, and I don't know if he's a Grandfather....'
Ann: 'Oooph, *(as a rush of freezing cold air passes)*. I think you're right.'
Mairi. 'Ask him to tell you where the second car is then.'
Mairi: 'Foxbar. There is a place in Ayrshire called Foxbar. It's such a long time ago since I've heard it, I'd need to look it up but it's near Kilbirnie, Dalry – it's near Johnston, it's on the road to Johnston. It's between Kilbirnie and Johnston. I've never heard of Foxbar for 30 years.'
Ann: 'Can I just say to the Spirit who's with us tonight. If you give us enough information, clearly enough, accurately enough, so that we're convinced of it, we'll go to the police with it, if that's what you'll have us do, so please draw forward and give us the information and we'll try and help. *(Another strong wave of cold air penetrates the room).*
Gill: 'Does that feel like the destination or was that a place that they passed.'
Ann: 'I'm en route, I haven't come to a destination.'
Mayumi: 'Can we try to get the number plate?'
Ann: 'I feel the car's grey. You said black or blue.'
Mairi: 'I saw it as a sort of Grey/blue.'

Ann: 'That's right, that's what I'm seeing. One of them was sick. One of them was physically sick.'
Mairi: 'Well, they'd get the DNA from that.'
Mayumi: 'It's funny that Mairi mentioned DNA, but I was getting that they don't have DNA on record, but in a few years' time, they will do something and then they'll be able to match the DNA.'
Gill: 'It's the younger one of the three that's going to Ireland. He's going to Ireland. I've got a feeling that the older one can look after himself but the younger one is being looked after by the family.'
Ann: 'And he's the one that was sick.'
Mairi: 'I feel he's got family over there.'
Gill: 'Yes, and he'll just blend in there. I feel like they're like the Dingles *(this is a reference to a TV programme that portrays a family of ruffians).*
Mairi: 'I've got, 'it's just spinning a yarn to make a buck'.'
Gill: 'This older guy, he's been in trouble before. He's on record, he's got form.'
Ann: 'Gill, can you do me a favour, can you come across here and stand behind me, because I know you're awfully good at linking in, as I know he's here and he's really, really, strong, but I'm not getting the information can you help please.'
(Gill moves over to stand behind Ann).
Gill: 'I'll just come into your energy. Just go with it.'
Ann: 'Oh, yes, he got on a boat. Can you feel him, Gill?'
Gill: 'I feel a presence but I'm not consciously picking him up.'
Gill: 'He's very, very, close.'
Ann: 'I know, he's been like that for a while now.'
Gill: 'He's showing you something – it's the road.'
Ann: 'Good, you've got the road too.'
Gill: 'Yes.'
Ann: 'Well describe it, what does it look like?'
Gill: 'Well I've got no sense of direction.'
Ann to spirit: 'Come on, where's the car. I think Mayumi's right with her 'Fiat'. A grey Fiat.'
Gill: 'You know what, they've pushed it down that banking. It's not in the lay-by, it's been pushed down. It's down that country road. Oh come on. What's that one that goes diagonally from Edinburgh. It's quite moory.'
Ann: 'Well that's the A701.'
Jim: 'Abington.'
Ann: 'Which is on the A74.'
Mayumi: 'Coming back there's Abington then Biggar.'
Ann: 'I think I'm losing him.'
Gill: 'Right one last.... Right, Rosewell.'
Jim to Gill: 'Penicuik, Roslin way, Bonnyrigg.'
Gill: 'Is that on the A71?'

Ann: No. Heather, there's a lot of heather around.'
Gill: 'Yes, I can see the heather. You know what they did, they showed me they did a lot of communication by mobile phone and arrangements were made for him to…..they were picked up and that's when they split, and one was taken right and one was taken left and one was taken South, right?'
Ann: Yes, that's right.'
Gill: 'They met at this point and that's where they were all …..they knew where they were going because it had all been arranged by mobile phone, but it's like a network, it's like a spider's web, and it's like Mairi said, there's a Matriarch and she was involved.'
Mairi: 'I think she organised everything.'
Gill: 'Yes, she knew just where to put everybody. I tell you something, she's not fussy about the older one getting caught as long as the bairn doesn't get caught.'
Mairi: 'Just cold again.'
Ann: 'Is there anything else we can do to make one last effort – has anybody got anything else? We could dowse for the letters and numbers on the number plate.'
Gill and Mayumi: 'Yes.'
Ann to Mayumi: 'Have you got your pendulum with you, because you are the dowser.'
Mayumi: 'Gordon is the dowser. *(Mayumi gets her pendulum from her bag; Ann gets a pen and paper from her bag to take notes).*
Ann: 'They're still around, aren't they, you can still feel them.'
Mayumi: 'Yes, somebody's there.'
Gill to Mayumi: 'Somebody's working with you. Good.'
Mairi: 'It's still freezing.'

At the close of the meeting we dowsed for further information and as a further check I then sent a list of the same questions to Gordon and asked him to dowse for the answers too so we could compare the results. I sent my email to Gordon on Sunday, 22nd October, 2006 and he replied to me on Monday, 23rd, however by the following Thursday, 26th October the first of the three fugitives had been caught and was charged in court with culpable homicide. So, if there was a matriarch and she was concerned about the younger 'bairn' – he was the one who got caught first. And, he was caught in Glasgow, which was part of the information received in our session. Our information also suggested that these two were brothers – which proved correct. We were correct that they were travelling people, there were two younger men – very young, only 19, so that information was also correct and they had been involved in a robbery (as well as the bogus workmen routine), so as Mairi had said she thought they were trying to get rid of something. This would be something incriminating and I suspect it was jewellery.

At the time of writing I do not know if there was a second car involved or not and if so if it was ever found or if it is still at large. However, from the information that was subsequently released we can deduce the following: There were three men involved and they all went their separate ways as Spirit told us. Our descriptions were accurate including the description of one as 'gaunt' and the other having a fuller face and wearing an earring. We were correct that there would be no DNA held on record for the younger two but that the older one did have a criminal record. A mobile communications expert was used in court to pinpoint their positions following their use of mobile phones to organise their escape – just as we had been told. I have not been able to ascertain the details of how they all made their escape or whether indeed there was a second car. But what we do know is that the main culprit made his way to Liverpool and the roads mentioned in our session – the A71 and A74 - are the routes that would take you from Edinburgh southwards to Liverpool.

The Court transcript details the route that the driver took before hitting the boy. He drove along the main road in Corstorphine to PC World the store I had referred to. He then turned into Corstorphine High Street and on towards Saughton Road North where the accident took place just at Broomhall Avenue – just the area that was first highlighted to me on the actual night of the accident. Finally the last fugitive went on the run and strangely enough finally gave himself in to the police. He had fled to Liverpool and was living between there and Newry in Ireland to evade capture – just as our Spirit friends told us, indeed a song had been used to get the message to us – 'We're off to Ireland in the Green'. But, if we had listened to Spirit even before we had started our psychic detective work, we would have realised that they were giving us the answers even before we had asked them: Strawberry Fields – let me take you there – where? Liverpool, and then showed a picture of a wave to convey the fact that the fugitive had gone over the sea from Liverpool to Ireland. Complete with the jewellery!

Footnote: There is an ancient theory that the mind is universal and not part of the physical brain. The theory follows that individuals can 'download' information from the Universal Consciousness or the Universal Mind which is a central source of knowledge and information. This concept works rather like a laptop connected to the web or a cloud which stores the information. In this analogy the human brain is represented by the laptop which connects and downloads from the web and/or the cloud. This suggests that all information is available to us if we can just connect to it.

If we follow Professor Archie Roy's theory of the early warning signal of pending doom and disaster, then in this case that signal would appear to be that of a tragedy that had just *happened*. But if, as he says, some people are sensitive enough to pick it up, I like to think that my Group showed that those same people can access it for positive reasons and perhaps in the future to assist the police in cases like this. (Indeed, I did have the opportunity to work with the police on a cold case – a murder case – some years later).

Arthur Conan Doyle not only invented the famous detective but he was something of a detective himself, overturning a couple of unjust convictions – one of which was murder. He was a stickler for fairness and justice. It was hardly surprising that he would bring me this crime-scene to help solve together with my team.

The final point in this case is that the main culprit who had been on the run for 5 months since the tragedy, eventually gave himself up after writing a letter of confession to the parents of the young boy who he killed. The fugitive said his conscious was bothering him. I wonder if Spirit had a hand in this too!

20 WHAT HAPPENS WHEN WE DIE?

I referred earlier to the emotional blow that occurs when you receive information that someone has died – even when it is someone whom you do not know. That emotion is heightened when the death is sudden and unexpected and even more so when it is that of a child. I referred in the last chapter to this emotional blow when I realised that the information I had received on 5th October about a child being knocked down concerned an event that had occurred just a couple of hours before we sat in silence that night.

When I returned to the circle a couple of weeks later not only had Arthur answered my silent appeal to help the family involved in this case by providing clues as to where these fugitives could be found but he also provided some comfort to me and I believe it is my role to pass it on to the wider public to help people understand something more of life after death and about what happens when we die. Arthur Conan Doyle made this his life's mission – to get the message over to people - to give them some hope, some comfort that they will meet their loved ones again. I believe he is still doing so and by any means at his disposal – including me and this book.

Here is some of the philosophy that was communicated from the Spirit World via the Mediumship of firstly Jim and then Mairi. I start by quoting a question that Mairi posed to our Spirit Team during our session.

> Mairi: 'I am very interested in what you have to say, because it ties in with the work I was doing last week in Stansted. *(Mairi had been attending a training course at The Arthur Findlay College, Stansted, for Mediumship Development).* The tutors were discussing the personality and what happens after death. My own thinking since I came back is that the personality only survives in the Spirit World as long as there are people coming into the Spirit World who will be looking for it in that

form. And I feel that once we are in the Spirit World and we move a little beyond that... what I'm trying to say is that the personality really attaches to the human being when we live as a human being and then when we pass into Spirit we only retain enough of that to be recognised. Could you say anything about that?'

Jim (channeling Spirit.): 'Yes I can try to add to this discussion. What you may find difficult (because I'm aware that the Medium finds it difficult) is the wording; he's satisfied as indeed you all are that there's life after death, but he's not satisfied with how that is talked about. There is no proof of life after death they say. But there is proof absolutely of the continuation of knowledge once the human body has deceased. Undoubtedly the knowledge that that body or mind contained continues beyond death as we know it, does that prove life after death? I don't think so. It proves that there is a continuation of thought but the real answer to your question I would guess is this: if after a personality has passed to the other side and that personality with its knowledge can return to a member of the same family in this life and say to them 'after I passed over I became aware of such and such a thing happening and that occurred after my passing over', that I would suggest does prove that there is life beyond death. But be prepared. As you must have heard, as my Medium has heard on many, many occasions, 'but nobody has come back to tell us'. But, my friends, I would 100% disagree with that statement because I know that proof of survival in that regard can be given and has been given on numerous occasions. It is ironic that in your Christian religion and within your funeral service the ordained minister will say, 'in the sure and certain knowledge that life continues after death' he says something to that effect does he not? And then they have the audacity to say, 'but never speak of it'. It is the very essence of life that you are 'in the sure and certain knowledge that life goes on and you will meet up with your loved ones again' – they say that do they not? - but yet they will deny that it can happen. They will say to you; you should not contact the dead. What nonsense. My friends, if the dead wish to contact you is that not a wonderful experience, in order that the individual who is bereaved can see that yes, my loved one has passed on and in the passage of time I shall join them? There is another question and I'm sharing my Medium's thoughts with you here, things he may have thought aloud with you before, he is, as he says, convinced of life after death, but you know what he thinks, that in the event of his pre-deceasing his wife, or more importantly in the event of his wife pre-deceasing him, she may not be there to meet him, because she may - her personality, on coming to your earth - may have had a specific purpose and having achieved that, may pass on to the other side of life and having fulfilled it, she may not wait for her husband – is that not a thought? He hopes that's not the case, but then, why did he come? He's not aware in his life as to why he came to earth but he is aware that everyone comes with a purpose. Some realise that purpose quickly and having achieved it quickly pass on to the Spirit World – they return home. They are the lucky ones, the highly evolved spiritual beings - some would call them angels. They have little to learn from this physical earthly existence but have much to give and usually their light shines the brightest, even if it is only for a short time here on earth. They will leave in their wake a message, a hope for those that are left behind, and they will lead the way for those who follow and be there when those whose hearts they have touched on earth come to join them in the Spirit World. It has been a joy to speak with you and perhaps from time to time this may be the function of your Group, and it is not confined to any individual person in this Group to act as the Medium in this case, there will be other purposes for you each and every one of you to work for the Spirit that chose you before you came here and that Spirit agreed with you that that was your function. So, my friends nothing is left to chance. Each of you has a furrow to plough. Make sure you sow good seed in it, which will come to fruition. With that, I bid you farewell my friends, thank you for listening to me and may your God be with you.'

And now Mairi is channeling a woman communicator from the Spirit World with a strong religious faith who had died in her 80's:

Mairi: 'I'm picking up the impression of what it is like when you're in the Spirit World and you have just been present at your own funeral service and the pull of the emotion makes the picture a little confused because although you are in the Spirit World and you know that and the people who are around you are very happy... there is a strong pull to those who are left but also to the memories and the memories of *(Mairi becomes overcome with emotion)*......it's not unpleasant it's just very powerful.....it's the memories of the people and the memories in your mind which were just moved over but also the memories in the place, because of the connections with the church and the memories of the births and deaths that have taken place in that building and in those buildings where you have lived your life and where others have lived their lives and you have been together. It's as if when you watch the service you are in two worlds at once and whilst you are safe and secure in your new surroundings part of your mind wanders around in the building with the people and when they leave you continue to explore the building and to what it has meant and there is a little bit of reluctance to leave. But it's just memories. I know I'm in my eighties, but I can see right back to all the years right back to baptism and through my childhood. I want to help not just to make the emotional connection with this Group but more importantly to contribute to the discussion that you were having and the questions that were raised about the personality and the survival and the transition to the Spirit World and how that is experienced and how that links to joint memories and communication.
Jim: 'Were you aware of your funeral?'

Mairi: 'Yes.' *(Once again Mairi becomes overwhelmed by the emotion and is crying).* 'It is not unpleasant - it's part of the transitional process because in addition to the human emotion you immediately have more awareness of your soul connections - the power of the connections Spirit-to-Spirit is very emotional in a different way, it's just very, very strong in a more acute way especially if we have been in the habit and been taught not to express emotion. It is very powerful and not to be avoided but a more difficult experience to handle.
Jim: 'Does the joy of returning home overcome the sadness you experienced of leaving your loved ones on earth?'
Mairi: 'Yes. Yes.'
Jim: 'Is that return, what you would have expected – what you thought it would be like?'
Mairi: 'It's difficult to express because I want to smile wider than my face can possibly smile, but the emotion is so intense... but the peace that comes with it makes it much easier to handle the joy, handle the separation and the change of role because you have to hand over the responsibility back to the people for their own lives because you no longer have an influence on earth in the same way and you have to trust them to make the right decisions. There is that process of stepping back and allowing people to carry on without you.'
Gill: 'You are coming home to Spirit and you must be experiencing a change in the vibration of energy and that must be quite difficult to deal with, or maybe not, I could be wrong?'
Mairi: 'For me - because my faith is so important to me and the experiences I have had in life through prayer and contemplation - it was very akin to that, very similar feeling of communion, and all that that means to me. It is very similar in feeling and in vibration to the first experiences of the Spirit World, very peaceful, very deep, very connected.'
Gill: 'When you are in true communion with your God?'
Mairi: 'Yes, and the angels and the saints.'
Gill: 'Yes.'
Mairi: 'And all those that have gone before.'
Jim: 'Those whom you expected would be there to greet you, did that materialise for you?'
Mairi: 'Yes. I didn't have any disappointments, just a big party!'
Jim: 'Can you understand the grief for those who you have left behind?'
Mairi: 'Yes, but it was harder for me to leave than for them to let go, because it is easier to let go when someone is ill and is suffering. Life is created in such a way that the decision is made easy. No-one wants to hold on to someone who's life is finished and is ready to go, but it is actually much harder to close the door behind you. Walking through it is really easy, but turning and seeing the door close behind you is really hard.'
Gill: 'Yes, it must be, but you will be able to take some strength from the

knowledge that as time progresses, you will be able to make that contact with them, and view them, if you like? Observe their lives?'

Mairi: 'Yes, for me it will be straightforward but not for them, they are not of this system of belief that you have. It is not of their faith and their faith allows communication of a kind but not as directly as I am experiencing here.'

Jim: 'Do you have any desire to, or have you indeed visited those who were very dear to you, just at your passing with close family members, have you been able to be there, or try to be there?'

Mairi: 'They are always in my thoughts and I find that the thought takes you there, it works in a different way, it is a very quick process, the thought takes you to where they are. The thought of love, on either side, takes you immediately to their side.'

Jim: 'Is it frustrating for you that they don't seem to acknowledge your presence?'

Mairi: 'No, because you can communicate the feelings. There has been some awareness but it's just not as direct as what we are attempting now. They have... I think they have met me in the dream-state.'

Jim: 'Subsequent to your death?'

Mairi: 'Yes. And I think that there has been awareness. If I could try to explain something, I'm not sure I have the words, this is complicated, it's as if two things are happening at once. You try to make your presence felt against the physical, but actually your main means of communicating is through thought, so you expend more energy trying to impinge your thought into their minds. So, you're concentrating very hard sending the thought, and it's almost like you are playing games and you're trying to put a word into somebody's mind to guess it, so it's that type of feeling. At the same time there's also my Spirit being, my presence close which creates a sort of ripple in the energetic body in the physical person you are trying to communicate with so it touches the aura, it impinges, there's a vibration of impinging and that can often be felt as heat or cold or as a shiver or also sometimes people detect something out the corner of the eye, but it's not actually to do with the eye it's to do with the energy. So when you're trying to communicate like the process of going to the person and linking with them it's almost instantaneous as it follows the thought on either side and then you get this, trying to put the thought into the mind, so they can understand, because you can see their thoughts, reasonably clearly, but it's harder to get them to be aware of yours.'

Jim: 'And if those who are nearest to you on this side of life as you passed over, if they had an understanding similar to Mairi's, would this make it easier for you to communicate with them or to comfort them, as they would know what it's all about?'

Mairi: 'I don't think for me it makes any difference because they understand it in a different way, because their faith is of a different type but it's just as meaningful and the quality of the experiences that they experience during mass or during contemplation is very similar to Spirit Communication, so it will be, for example, when they attend mass, they will be very conscious of my presence, because I will be with them and they will feel it, so again, there's a link there.'

Gill: 'Because they have a very deep belief that you have God and that you are being looked after and their prayers that they say are for you and that must be very comforting to both you and to them. If they are unswerving in their belief, then they'll know you are there.'

Mairi: 'Oh yes, they do. The young people have their own version of their faith, they have their own way of worshiping they have their own beliefs and customs, they do not have the same dogmatic faith that we were brought up in, but on the other hand they love their God.'

Jim: 'It's nice to know that there is no difference between religions.'

Mairi: 'Well, from this side, anyway, because it is based on love. And that's what pulls people together whether here, there, between the two worlds - the theologians can all get together and debate the Bible and the word of God and all the other holy scriptures and it doesn't really mean anything, it just all comes down to the love that we have between us and nothing else really. It makes no difference at all.'

Gill: 'No matter your religion... it is that that you have a belief in a Being of Power of light and ultimately of love and if all believe in that power of love it would transcend all the other feelings of inadequacy that can happen between religions.'

Mairi: 'Yes. I feel sympathy for those who are misguided and commit acts in the name of religion and in the afterlife, they must have to work out the consequences and they must realise how mistaken....'

Jim: 'Or misled?'

Mairi: 'Misled they have been... and how simple things are in reality. But I'm sure God forgives them.'

Gill: 'And as long as they forgive themselves.'

Mairi: 'That's the difficult bit. The coming to terms with the lessons of life.'

Gill: 'I'm conscious now that the energy is changing, are there any last words you would want to say to us before you continue on your journey?'

Mairi: 'No. Thank you for allowing me to be present. It is a very interesting life....'

Gill: 'Yes, we thank you for making your presence known to us, take care, good night and God bless.'

Mairi: 'God bless.'

Jim *(gives closing prayer):* 'Can we just thank the Great Spirit for all that has taken place here this evening. Once again, it has been an evening with a difference. It is always a joy for us to sit in the presence of Spirit. To those who have worked with us this evening, we express our sincere thanks to those who have tried to get through to us, and to convey whatever message they have for us and for others, just be aware that we send our love to you and hope that you have the opportunity to work with

us once again. To all those who have passed recently may they have a pleasant journey and may their loved ones, wherever they may be, feel supported. And to all those who are ill this evening, particularly those very close to us, may they be aware that our healing thoughts are always with them and our love and the great Spirit will comfort them as they comfort everyone else. Amen.
End of transcript.

21 SPONTANEOUS PHENOMENA

During the last six meetings of the year held during November and early December of 2006 the Group continued to experience what the investigators call spontaneous phenomena. On 8th November just as the Group were about to sit in silence there was a knock on the door.

>Jim: 'There's someone at the door.'
>Mayumi: 'That'll be the lady to collect the money.' *(Mayumi was also our treasurer and she used to collect a subscription from each of us and then pay the Theosophical Society for the room hire. As this payment was paid in blocks of 8 weeks it was only collected every couple of months).* "I'll go, I've got the money".

Mayumi went to the door but when she opened it there was no one there. The Group all laughed with surprise as Mayumi went out into the corridor and looked down the spiral staircase to see if anyone was on the stairs but no – there was no one there. Later that same evening when the Group were actually giving their feedback after sitting in the silence we became aware of a strange noise, something we hadn't heard before. As one by one each of us focused our attention in the direction of the sound we realised that the Dictaphone[34] recorder which had been placed on the table in the centre of our Circle was hopping from corner to corner of its casing as if it was walking.

'Look at the Dictaphone. It's moving' Gill exclaimed. On seeing what she was pointing at I quickly checked the table legs to see that no-one was touching them either with their hands or feet. Gordon's feet were nearest simply because he had such long legs but even they could not reach the table.

'They're probably using the vibration of our voices again so if we just keep on talking let's see what happens'. At Gill's instruction the Group continued with their feedback session whilst the Dictaphone continued to dance on the table top. 'It's moving back and forward so much you would think it would fall over'. But it didn't, it just kept on hopping in this strange movement until someone suggested that we put our hands on the table so we could feel the vibrational energy too, which we did. The energy was amazing but of course this stopped the Dictaphone doing its dance. Later that same evening Mayumi declared that a portal would be opening for us. She had got that information before from Spirit and so it was recorded in the transcript once again but it wouldn't be until we found our elusive new premises that we would eventually find our portal.

Meanwhile during the next couple of weeks when I was sitting in silence myself at home I got the fright of my life as my telly suddenly burst into life loudly and noisily. The first time this happened I looked around for the remote control wondering if I had inadvertently sat on it. But there it was lying on the TV table as usual. I just put it down to a fluke but when it happened for the third time I realised Spirit was trying to get my attention. When the Group next met and we had the Ouija Board on the table I asked if Spirit had done something in my home to get my attention – I asked what that was (whilst removing my finger from the glass so as not to influence it). The answer came back 'TV'. I confirmed to the other members of the Group that this was indeed the case. On another occasion whilst sitting at home my printer sprang into life and started spitting out page after page of blank pieces of paper. This when neither my laptop nor PC were switched on.

On 23rd November, 2006 the Group were to encounter yet another new sound. This time as well as the candles that were placed around the room there was a single candle set in a glass jar. When Gill was lighting all the candles she lit the candle-jar and then inadvertently dropped the lit match into the jar but just left it there to burn out. When the Group sat in silence we all jumped as we heard a sudden sound which was a sort of popping sound. I didn't open my eyes to check but envisioned that the candle-jar must have burst with a popping explosion as the heat of the dropped match must have heated up the glass too much and it had broken. I was expecting that we would have a mess to clean up off the floor after our session. However, when we came back from our silent meditation the candle jar was still intact and burning away. No reason for the popping sound could be established. That same night I experienced extreme coldness such as I'd never felt before – it was as if I had walked into a deep freeze - and I began to shake uncontrollably and Jim, a trained nurse, said it looked to him like 'rigor'[35]. Further knocks and clicks were heard and that strange vibration on the floor that we had experienced before was again present. Later, when I typed up the transcripts another strange incident occurred, I realised that the recorder had recorded for exactly the same amount of time as the previous week's session – in hours, minutes and seconds.

On 14th December Gordon had his French friend Sam staying with him and he asked if he could bring Sam with him to the Group. No-one objected to a one-off visit on the basis that we would check with Spirit first that there were no objections and that Sam gave his undertaking that everything that happened in the Group would remain confidential. This was agreed and Sam joined us on that evening. His presence proved most useful as we demonstrated the Ouija Board and we were able to test the quality of the evidence received by asking Sam to pose questions which of course no one in the Circle knew the answers to. This testing was taken a step further when Sam was asked to pose his questions in French. We had already ascertained that no-one in the Group could speak or understand French – especially when spoken quickly by a native speaker. Again when we checked with Sam, he confirmed that the answers from Spirit were correct. So a final test was devised as Sam was asked to pose his questions in French and we asked that they be answered in French. This took some time as Spirit spelt out the answers letter by letter in French on the Ouija Board– very appropriately since it has its origins in France. The answers were scribbled down and again checked out with Sam who confirmed the results as correct. Isn't Spirit amazing?

By the following week, 21st December, Sam had returned to Paris and we were enjoying our Christmas Night Out in a local Chinese Restaurant in Edinburgh. We were discussing all the various happenings throughout the year and what a marvellous year it had been for us. Jim summed it up by saying that he had never thought that he would have experienced so many amazing phenomena in his lifetime – let alone in one year. He was very thankful to have been invited to be part of the Group. Everyone agreed that we had achieved a great deal during the past year and looked forward to much more to come, but we were also aware that throughout most of the year Arthur and his team in the Spirit World had been warning of the need to move and there had been continual prompts to find new premises and more recently there was another occasion where once again our Ouija Board was infiltrated by a drop-in communicator and had to be shut down. This we took as further evidence of the need to find somewhere quieter where we would have our own space for our own purpose and no noise to contend with or the danger of someone walking into our room without our permission. When asked what it was that our Spirit Team wanted to show us that could not be achieved in these premises to everyone's surprise we were told 'materialisation'. Materialisation is where a Spirit Being actually materialises to such an extent to be visible to all those present. This materialisation can be as solid as you and I or it can be in various stages of completeness and so sometimes appears etheric or semi-transparent. But however Spirit chose to materialise in future we were looking forward to it. Little did we know that this would come sooner than anticipated and was not at all what we expected.

22 A NEW YEAR

We returned to the Theosophical society for our first meeting of 2007 on 18th January and Jim welcomed everyone back to this the first meeting of the New Year. We discussed what a wonderful year we had enjoyed in 2006 but we also said to each other that we had perhaps been a bit blasé about the use of the table with the letters and glass as we had allowed drop-in communicators to emerge. We had all become very aware of the dangers of Ouija Board when it was first suggested by Spirit but it seemed that our early reluctance and wariness may have become overlooked in our excitement as we were overawed by the information we could obtain with it. We resolved to be more careful in future, a resolve we were to find out was going to be tested sooner than expected. But meanwhile I was compelled by Spirit to give an affirmation on this the first meeting of a new year. Jim was disappointed that no further direction had been forthcoming from Spirit as to what we should be doing since we couldn't find new premises and he asked me if I had had any further inspiration from Arthur Conan Doyle.

> Ann: 'I still feel driven and still feel confident in the knowledge I was given by Spirit at the very beginning as to why the Group was to be brought together and the reason for our development. I feel sure that the plan is to allow us to experience even greater Physical Phenomena than we have witnessed to date, but until we can find a suitable venue the confines of this building will dictate what Spirit can do. I am sure in the knowledge that our Spirit Team, led by Arthur Conan Doyle, will not leave us and we will be able to continue with the tools we've been using up till now, but that they are restricted in what they can show us, here. Spirit did attempt to move us forward a little more towards the end of last year, when they began experimenting with sound recorded on the Dictaphone and I feel they will continue with this – perhaps with actual

audible sound and with Direct Voice[36], but this may need to be in the new venue – once it is found.'

This prompted a discussion about various venues that could be tried and why the present building was not suitable. During this discussion I became overshadowed by a presence that said, *'It's a School'*. This confused us at the time as none of the possible venues that had been suggested were schools. We decided to file this information away for future reference as currently it did not make sense – again. It would take another few years before our current building would emerge as the venue – and to discover it had previously been a school.

Meanwhile we continued with our purpose and we continued to experience different phenomena. The following week, 25th January, when sitting in silence Mayumi and I received a vision of a bombing. Mayumi said she saw quite a disturbing sight. It was that of a concrete block but with the legs of a baby or toddler protruding out from underneath it. She also said she was experiencing a sharp pain across her left shoulder which ran vertically at a 90° angle to the line of the shoulders. At this point I said I felt I knew what Mayumi was experiencing. I felt the Spirit Entity with me was in fact a bomb-blast victim. He was Asian, perhaps Indian, and I felt that this happening was very recent – as if it had just happened today or tonight… or perhaps would happen tomorrow. When Jim asked where I thought it had happened, I said I thought it was "Beirut in Lebanon or maybe Kuwait". In the scene I could see a white/yellow/light-coloured saloon car with the boot and all the doors flung open. The person communicating with me had his shirt torn off and he was standing in his vest. He had also lost his shoes; they too had been blown off. And I had tremendous pain in my ears and realised that the bomb victim had burst eardrums from the blast and couldn't hear anything – everyone appeared to him to be silently moving in slow motion. I felt that this man had died in the blast but not yet realised it. He was worried about his wife and children as they wouldn't know where he was. He lived in a high flat and I felt he was a taxi driver and had been driving his car when the bomb went off. I felt that this man was walking around in a daze not realising he was dead and that he was unlikely to move on as he was determined to see his family again. I could see a bus in the scene – a single decker also bombed out – and thought that the bomb may have been on the bus. It was a busy road junction or intersection in the city. I was also aware of a considerable pain running down my left shoulder in the same place that Mayumi had indicated so I felt that this was probably related to some of the other injuries this Spirit Person had encountered and the scene of the baby under the concrete block I suspected was some of the same information that Mayumi was picking up.

Later that night Jim called me and asked if I had seen the news. I hadn't.

Jim said that there had been a huge bomb blast in Beirut in the Lebanon and a lot of people had been killed. Back in the Group the following week we had a discussion over why it should be that I had received prior information again that was either very current or received almost simultaneously to when the news bulletins were going out. There had been the previous case of the boy who had been knocked down by the speeding car in Edinburgh; then more recently I had received a vision of a young woman being pulled out of a river – this was subsequently reported the following week when the police started to discover the bodies of the first victims of a serial killer who was murdering prostitutes and the first two of his victims were pulled from the same river.

I could only deduce that somehow I was attuned in such a way that I was able to pick up tragic events that were actually happening, about to happen or had just happened. I did not know why this should be but it seemed to correlate to what Professor Archie Roy had told me ten years beforehand that there can be an early-warning signal that goes out which, if you are sensitive enough, you can pick up, or pick up parts of it. This time Mayumi was seeing the bomb site too and there were now two of us on the same wavelength.

These wavelengths or early warning signals took on a different format when on 8th February, 2007 in our feedback session Mayumi said she had heard a sort of clicking noise coming from the corner behind her. She then said that she had seen us all with wings – as if we were all angels. Then Gordon ascended - but only he - and from this vision she saw him rising up and wondered if Gordon had experienced an Out of Body experience at some point.

Gordon said he had felt a lot of energy. He had gone really deep, and so he too could not give much feedback although he had felt he had been quite far away. He was aware of a jerk in his body and then felt hot, cold and clammy all at the one time – as if he had a fever. Gordon then added *(as if he had just regained full consciousness)* that he remembered being in a position from where he was looking down on a figure. He felt he was in a place of nature, but didn't know what it was all about.

Mayumi said that this probably related to what she had seen, as she felt Gordon had ascended to a higher position, and this is why he would feel he was looking down on this person that he had seen.

The Group joked about this feedback and asked Gordon 'are you leaving us so soon?' Of all of us in the Group Gordon was probably the fittest. He was a marathon runner, a munro-bagger and as a healer he was very aware of the needs of his body and looked after his health and nutrition. Jim joked that he was the eldest and he would probably go first but we all agreed that if anyone was going to ascend, it was unlikely to be Gordon.

At the time of writing Gordon is the only member of the Thursday Group who is deceased. Just two years after this early warning signal that Mayumi picked up Gordon would be diagnosed with cancer. Gordon continues to work with us from the Spirit side of life.

Back in 2007 however, our tutelage by Arthur and our Spirit Team continued apace just as promised and as well as the more unusual phenomena we also enjoyed some exceptional examples of Mental Mediumship - cases where a Medium makes contact with a Spirit Person and gives evidence of the encounter so that the recipient can verify the identity of the Spirit Communicator. Generally this happens in private sittings, but sometimes it occurs in public demonstrations of Mediumship too although in public the messages tend to be shorter and don't go into much detail to avoid making private details public.

In our case we would get this type of communication whilst sitting in Circle and so it was on 22nd February 2007 that Mayumi said she was aware she had a gentleman with her from the Spirit World – quite a tall gentleman in Victorian clothes. She asked why he had come here and he showed her one of his sons; she also got the number '84', which she presumed meant 1884. She also got the name 'James Cunningham' of Edinburgh and that he had died of something contagious – perhaps the Black Death or the Plague. She asked him where his wife was and he said that she had died while giving birth to another child – a son. Again Mayumi asked why he was here and he said he had heard about the other world *(the physical world)* and the communication between the two and wanted to see if it was real.

At our next meeting on 1st March Mayumi brought in a page which she had down-loaded from the internet about a James Cunningham of Edinburgh who had been a Nurseryman and involved with the Royal Botanic Gardens at Kew and was florist to the Queen in Scotland in 1837. Interestingly he was born in 1784. All of this ties in directly with what Mayumi had received in her meditation the previous week except of course that she got the century wrong. Her assumption that he was referring to 1884 was wrong – but if she had thought about it, she would have realised he was referring to 1784 as he would not have died of plague in 1884.

And on 10th May 2007 I gave another demonstration of Mental Mediumship when I received a communicator for Mairi. The first image I got was a strange one - it was a baggage carousel such as you would see at an airport and there was a 'ghetto blaster', that is some sort of portable music centre going around on the carousel. Mairi said that this had evoked a memory of when she was travelling in the U.S. and due to storms her flight had been disrupted and this had meant that she had been separated from her luggage and it was being sent on on a different flight. She remembered when she got to the luggage carousel at her destination airport there were her bags circling on the belt along with a ghetto blaster. She remembers it as a very odd image. *(This image was only used in order for me to get to the correct recipient – sometimes Spirit does that as a tool – it had no other relevance).* As the energy built up I asked Mairi if the name of Colin meant anything to her and she agreed it did. I could also see a black and white collie-type dog which connected to Mairi – again Mairi recognised this vision. I also saw images of a train and of the West of Scotland; this made me think of the West Highland Line so I knew I had to look to the West Coast of Scotland to pinpoint where Mairi was born – which proved correct. I also knew that another memory from Mairi's childhood was of a young Minister who would call in to see the family. I received the name Sheila and that there was a local church which was prominent and another name, Richard. I also got the name Rupert – Rupert Blair. There was knowledge of someone who had had some sort of problem with their left arm and I could also see an image of a wooden board with wheels on it on the sand at the beach. I wasn't sure what this was and wondered if it was some sort of sand-racing vehicle; anyway I knew it was something that would have run along the sand on wheels of some description.

Then I could see Mairi taking a rabbit out of a cage and holding it. More names appeared to me: Isa, Timmy, Flopsy and I was aware of Animal Farm. This meaning was two-fold: not only would Mairi have been reading that book – perhaps at school - but there was also a place where there were a lot of animals around, like a sort of menagerie. I felt that there was a local character around when Mairi was growing up, an elderly lady and she would be referred to – at least by the children – as Granny Mack. I speculated as to whether this name might mean that her actual name was MacGregor or Mc Donald or something similar but the colloquial was Granny Mack. I could also see a railway station close by and I got the sentence 'Get me to the Church on time' from the song of that name. But I felt that, unlike in the song, this wasn't to do with a marriage but more to do with a function that Mairi was to attend at a Church where she thought she was going to be late. I was also aware of Uncle Tommy; he was a tall slim man and Mairi had a good relationship with him and he was good fun. All of these Spirit People were coming forward with these various images and a wish that they be conveyed to Mairi as a remembrance of them. I finished by saying there were oodles of them around and as I said that I noted that this was not a term I would normally use and wondered whether oodles of noodles or oodles and noodles was significant.

> Mairi: 'All this information is accurate, with one or two little amendments. Sheila was one of my closest friends at that time and I was nearly late for the service where they brought the body into the church the night before the funeral. One of my dad's closest friends was Richard. My mother-in-law was Isa, but my mum's cousin, who laid her out, was Ina, which is similar. I'd also forgotten that another close friend at the time was Fiona MacGregor and we spent a lot of time with her and called her "Mrs Mac". Flopsy was in fact Floppy and I think Timmy is my

current friend Micki's little dog in Spirit and we talked about him together recently. Uncle Tom wasn't tall or slim but was good fun and I was close to two other uncles who were both tall and slim. All other details are exactly as recorded.'

Mairi responded further after the meeting: 'The information Ann has given was accurate.' Floppy was a favourite toy made of straw. She remembered her Mother taking it from her and putting it in the bucket (the trash) as it was coming apart and leaking straw after which Mairi hid in the cupboard crying for four days. There was a woman at the time whom Mairi remembered later worked in a shop, and there could have been a character around when she was a child but she couldn't remember if that was Granny Mack or not, she'd have to check but she did know the person with the problem with their arm. Ina was her Mother's Cousin; there was a young priest who came to the house at the time of the death and they went to the local church as well as other chapels and churches too. She could accept all the names too, but Rupert Blair was actually Rupert Bear – another favourite toy. And the board with the wheels on the sand was actually one of the 'guiders' that they had made as kids and used to play with on the sand dunes. She remembered the rabbit and Animal Farm, both as the book and as a little farm-type place that had lots of different animals where the children could go to pet them.

Finally I got one last vision of the same church I had referred to earlier and I felt I could see Mairi's Mother's Funeral. I could see the organ and the organ pipes in the Church and outside just across the road from the church I could see a yellow Shell sign, the sign of a Shell petrol station. Mairi confirmed this to be the case. I felt this was the final bit of confirmation that it was indeed Mairi's Mother who was communicating and really wanted Mairi to forgive herself and enjoy her life.

Another example of evidential mediumship had taken place earlier on 12th April 2007 and this time I was the recipient and it came via the planchette[37]. We had purchased a planchette and realised that Gordon and Mayumi were particularly attuned to using it but we also found we could dowse for answers simply by writing 'yes' and 'no' on a piece of paper and allowing the planchette to move to the answer rather than actually writing the answer each time. Before using the planchette that evening I had seen the letter 'M' in my meditation written in fancy script-type writing. It looked as if someone had taken care writing this letter as it had a scroll-type spiral at the start of the letter and I could almost feel the flow of the writer as I observed the style of this letter. When we used the planchette we asked the following questions:

Gordon: 'Are you always here?' *Maybe*
Jim: 'Is Mary here?' *Yes.*
Jim was referring to Mary Duffy one of our Spirit Team.

Mairi: 'Can the person who's communicating write the first letter of their name?' *M.*
Gordon: 'Was the letter *'M'* sent to someone here in this Group when we were sitting earlier?' *Yes.*
Gordon: 'Could you move towards the person that received that contact please?' *The planchette moved across the table to the corner nearest where Ann was sitting. (It should be pointed out at this stage that once again Ann had removed her finger from the planchette in order to take the notes, and therefore could not have been an influence upon the planchette).*
Jim: 'Was that you, Mary?'
There was some hesitation in the planchette and then it moved to indicate, 'maybe'.
Jim: 'Did you go to Ann earlier?' *Maybe.*

At this point Gordon realising the reason for the vague response hit the nail on the head and asked:

'Is there more than one Mary'?
There was immediate and hurried response from the planchette, 'yes'.

I suddenly became flooded with emotion and my tears flowed as I realised who was communicating. Jim tried to continue with the questions but the connection had been established directly with me on a one-to-one basis. Jim asked if I could take over the questioning.

'Is that you, Granny?' *Yes.*

Jim then suggested that if this situation was a personal one that I should ask questions of my Granny in my head and the planchette would signal the answers. This was another good test of the planchette which responded accordingly.

The planchette then wrote, *'Trust'* and something else which was indecipherable.

Ann: 'Did you write, 'Trust', Granny?' *Yes.*
Ann: 'We can't understand the second word; can you write it again?' *Yourself.*

Jim then asked me if I was sure it was my Granny. I could feel the emotion and realised that this was what had made me so tearful earlier, so yes, I was sure it was my Granny. But I also understood that Jim was trying to check the evidence as this is what we had said we would do. So I said I would pose some questions:

Ann: 'Granny, I was away for a run in the car on Sunday, did I go to,

> Granthouse?' *No.*
> Ann: 'Gospel Hall?' *Yes.*
> Ann: 'Gowkshall?' *No.*
> Jim: 'What is the month of Ann's birth? Can you write the number of the month in which Ann's birthday falls?' *The planchette wrote '9'.*
> Jim asked if this was correct, and Ann agreed.

The planchette then began moving again, unprompted. 'What is it?' I said and Jim suggested that it was simply that my Granny wanted to give me a big hug. Before I got a chance to respond to this suggestion the planchette responded, *'yes'*.

> Jim: 'You want to give her a big kiss, don't you?'
> *The planchette then began moving again as all watched to see what was being written. The planchette wrote, 'XXX'.*

My granny was a beautiful writer and she always wrote with a lovely hand. The curly spiral at the beginning of the initial letter was recognisable in her handwriting. She also used to make pursing movements of her mouth – Gordon had got this impression earlier; she had false teeth and she would occasionally move them around in her mouth in the fashion Gordon had described.

I had had a notion to visit Gospel Hall in the weekend before our meeting. This is a farm in the Borders, near Jedburgh owned by Father's Cousin (my second Cousin). We visited them and saw the new lambs that had just been born that day, the calves, cattle and sheep. This was something I used to do as a child when my Granny and Grandpa used to take me to Gospel Hall in the springtime to feed the pet lambs.

> *The reference to 'bondagers' (in the transcript below) refers to my Granny's life story which features in a book called The Bondagers[38]. The first chapter is dedicated to her memory and is entitled 'Mary King', her name.*

I have not revealed here all that was communicated between my Granny and myself for personal reasons, but it appeared from these exercises that our new piece of equipment the planchette was working well. However, as we had been warned, we were about to get an early indication of how careful we had to be with using these forms of communication. This became apparent the following week when we were once again using the planchette and asking questions:

> Gordon: 'Can we establish who we are communicating with?'
> *The planchette began writing what was thought to be 'Gordon'.*
> Jim: 'Is that Gordon Higginson?' *Yes.*

> *It then wrote, 'Mary'.*
> Jim: 'Is that Mary Duffy?' *No.*
> Jim: 'Ann's Granny?' *Yes*
> Jim welcomed Ann's Granny and asked if she was just helping out the team on the other side tonight? *Yes*
> Jim: 'Did you have an interest in this when you were alive?' *Yes*
> Gordon: 'Have you come for a specific purpose?' *No*
> Jim: 'I have knowledge of the Bondagers and was interested to hear Ann refer to this in her notes, was Granny a Bondager?' *Yes.*

At this point I was not convinced that this was my Granny who was communicating. I had been fully convinced last week as I had felt the energy, but I felt something wasn't right this week. I began to ask questions to establish credibility.

> Ann: 'In The Bondagers, you are in one of the chapters. Which chapter is it? Is it the first? *No* The second? *No* The third? *No* The fourth? *Yes*

This was the wrong answer.

> Jim then asked: 'Is it that you appear or are referred to in the 4th chapter?' *Yes.*
> Ann: 'There is a chapter of this book which is dedicated to you. Which chapter is it?'
> *After going through the numbers again, the answer came that is was chapter 3.*

Again this was wrong.

> Jim: 'Is Chapter 3 dedicated to all bondagers?' *Yes.*

I wasn't sure and so Jim asked me to check the book and report back but I was unconvinced and so continued with my questions:

'How many children did you have?'

After going through the numbers the answer came back as six children. This was the wrong answer. Jim I think had been so impressed with the accuracy of the personal information that had been revealed the week before that he seemed convinced that we should continue with this line of questioning and suggested that there may have been miscarriages that I was unaware of. So I asked again:

'How many children did you have that reached adulthood?'

The wrong answer came back 'four'. Jim immediately followed up by asking:

'Did you have 2 miscarriages?' *Yes.*

All of this information was wrong and I certainly did not feel that it was my Granny that was communicating and so I insisted that we shut this down right away – which we did.

Just as there's a feeling of immense joy when you realise that your loved one is communicating from Spirit and can prove it, it's a strange unnerving feeling when you realise that there is another intelligent agency that can communicate in this way and purport to be someone whom they are clearly not.

Footnote: If this was an exercise by our Spirit Tutors to enable us to recognise a drop-in communicator who was trying to infiltrate like this, then perhaps they were preparing us for an even bigger lesson just around the corner.

23 CREEPY CRAWLEY - OR CROWLEY

Having encountered the drop-in communicators during various sessions with the Ouija Board the year before, and more recently during the manipulation of the planchette by another entity pertaining to be someone they weren't, we had made a commitment to be ultra-careful this year and not too blasé when dealing with these tools. Quite separately we had been told by Arthur and the Spirit Team that the building was not conducive to taking our development much further under these circumstances and although we should continue with our circle here for now we were promised much greater things once we found the new place - indeed we were promised materialisation. Little did we expect that these two things would come together in the current building.

On 15th February 2007 as I arrived in the Theosophical Society for our Group session, I noticed how busy the building was as there were a lot of people milling about on the stairs. As I climbed the stairs up to the first floor there was Archie Lawrie my fellow Paranormal Investigator and Vice President of the Scottish Society for Psychical Research. I hadn't seen him for some time since I had redirected my focus more towards my own spiritual development than investigations. 'What are you doing here?' I asked.

'We're trying to drum up more support from Edinburgh so we've hired the hall here to put on a talk' says Archie.

Archie was a good speaker and very popular so if anyone could drum up support he could. 'I didn't know you were going to be here Archie. We could have met up, but I'm going to my own group tonight and we start at 6.30pm so I'm afraid I'll need to catch up with you another time'. I said my goodbyes to Archie and continued climbing the stairs. He was in the big lecture room on the first floor whilst we were in our wee room on the top floor. When Jim arrived he too mentioned that he had seen Archie downstairs and passed pleasantries with him.

Our Group then convened and we sat in silence. After sitting for a few minutes I became aware of a presence in the room. This was not unusual - after all that was what we did; but this time the presence felt uncomfortable as if someone was watching us but with ill intent. Now I can't exactly explain that but there is now recognised scientific experiments that have been run separately by Rupert Sheldrake[39] and Bernard Carr[40] that demonstrate that people are aware when they are being watched. However this was a bit more than that. You know how you feel if someone looks at you with hatred in their eyes? That is how it felt although I still had my eyes closed as we sat in silence.

The feeling grew stronger and stronger as if someone was really staring into my face at close quarters and willing me to open my eyes to see their anger. When I could stand it no longer I slowly opened my eyes and found I was looking downwards towards the floor. As I slowly lifted my gaze I was sitting opposite Gill and when my eyes met hers they were wide open and she was wearing a shocked impression. I was immediately aware that she was picking up the same energy as I was; then she beckoned me with her eyes to look towards the corner of the room, and that's when I saw him, a man partly materialised in the corner of the room with evil oozing from his very being. He was a big man with a big nose and he was leering or even sneering – I really didn't like him. I felt he belonged to the house (the Theosophical Society building) and may have been into magic – black magic - and liked tricks – nasty tricks. I felt that in his day he would have been interested in what we were doing and he would have liked to experiment, and that he would also have liked to play tricks on us. He wore a strange looking pill-box hat and a fancy jacket like a smoking jacket. He reminded me of the comedian Tommy Cooper[41] in facial features – even down to the black version of Tommy's red fez that he wore. But this was an evil man.

He was aware that Gill and I were looking at him but he seemed in no hurry to go. He appeared to revel in our distaste for him and liked the idea that all our instincts were telling us to shout out a warning to our Group but that we were torn by the need to be careful and respectful to the others who were sitting in silence. Gill took the initiative (which normally fell to Jim) and asked quietly if the others would bring themselves back from their meditation. As she said this the man in the corner slowly disappeared like a wispy mist.

As soon as the others returned to their normal consciousness Gill said 'Well what was that?'

'I don't know' I said 'but he was pure evil'. The others began asking what had gone on. Gill and I started explaining what we had just witnessed.

'Maybe that's the reason we've to move?' Gordon suggested 'and maybe that's why we've had so many drop-in communicators in different guises?'

'Yes, you're right Gordon' I said 'it's all beginning to make sense now. If our spirit team were aware of this man who seemed intent on playing tricks on us then no wonder they want us to move.'

Gill said, 'Our spirit team must have been working hard all this time to keep him at bay whilst at the same time trying to foster our development – no wonder they can only go so far in this building. Who would want to open up or even do any deeper trance work if there's someone like that around?'

I had to agree with Gill because I could feel it from him too, this blackness. We were both so shaken by the incident we closed our Circle – we were glad to get out of that room that night. When I got home that night I wondered where that left our Group. Yes, we had been told to find alternative accommodation and that intervention had happened quite early on in our Group's history but since then we hadn't come up with any alternatives and we had been told by our Spirit Team that we should continue there until we found an alternative – who would want to go back now? As I pondered that thought another thought came to my mind – I'd phone Archie and tell him what had happened to us whilst he was rabble-rousing downstairs. When I told Archie of our close encounter of the most evil kind and described the man I had seen and his unusual garb Archie immediately said 'I know who he is'.

'Who is he?' I asked.

'He's Aleister Crowley'.

'Who?'

'Aleister Crowley – haven't you heard of him?' Archie enquired.

'No, I haven't.'

'I'm going to send you something I've just been writing about him for my next book. I'll send you the chapter about Aleister Crowley. I know you'll keep it confidential'.

'Yes of course I will, Archie'.

Archie was a prolific author and he used to send me his manuscripts for comment and input or for proof-reading so he was comfortable offering me his unpublished papers. 'But can I share it with my Group please Archie? They've had this experience too and I can vouch for them they'll keep it confidential too'. Archie agreed and what he sent me was the following excerpts from The Psychic Investigators Casebook Volume 3, Chapter 4, 'The Phantom in the Mirror', by Archibald A. Lawrie. (p142-149)

> The Scottish Society for Psychical Research, while being based in Glasgow in western Scotland had a minor branch of the society in Edinburgh… but alas by the late 1990s so few members attended that it was thought expedient to close it down. By the time the year 2004 came around there was a new and keen mood in the air and the Council of the above Society thought that perhaps the time

had arrived to attempt to re-establish a branch in Edinburgh once more. To whet the psychic appetite of the Edinburgh citizens, the small Theosophical Hall in Great King Street was booked in November and a few speakers brought together to give an afternoon of lectures to the public. I was one of those people. My very good psychic medium friend Francesca had lots of contact with people with an interest in the paranormal and so it was arranged that she and they would come and sit in on the lectures that afternoon. That would help to fill the hall at least.

The hall itself was, in fact, a series of intercommunicating rooms of various sizes which meant that the size of each room could be conveniently matched to the anticipated size of the audience. We had been allocated quite a large L-shaped room where the speaker took up his position at the 'heel' of the L so that both groups could see and hear him and yet each group could see little of the other. While I sat with the group at the 'base' of the L, Francesca and her friends sat with the other group and had the benefit of seeing the lecturers face-on. That fact, you will soon see, was of importance for above the lecturer was a large reflective surface that, in some lights, looked like a darkened mirror but was in fact a large dark painting of Indian Hindu topics of some kind: it was very difficult to make out details. It was to that reflective surface that Francesca's eyes had been drawn during the first lecture although I did not know it until the coffee-break had arrived and in mingling with the others I bumped into my medium friend.

"Glad you could come and bring your friends along," I enthused and then, knowing that Francesca had a habit of mentally and psychically 'sweeping' older premises like these Theosophical Halls for lingering spirit entities I put my mouth close to her ear and whispered,

"Are you feeling anything in this old building?"

"You're going to be surprised!" the lady responded, "But I can't tell you now. We'll meet at the end of the lectures."

I had another chocolate biscuit and pondered over Francesca's cryptic words before taking my place 'on stage' for I was the next speaker. I could scarcely wait to know what Francesca had seen or heard for, while we meet and experience some very strange events together, I could see that this talented medium was either excited or even upset by what she had come across.

At the end of the lectures, the crowd eventually streamed down the stairs and out of the main door but Francesca drew me to one side at the head of the stairs.

"I saw the most evil man you can imagine, Archie, almost as soon as the first lecture began….."

"You mean, a spirit-man?" I interrupted for I did not know where our conversation was heading.

"Yes, he appeared as clear as you are now and he showed himself to me in the centre of the mirror in my part of that room we've all just been in." The lady paused and looked almost flustered.

"It was the evil of the man that quite overcame me. He positively radiated evil. It came out of his eyes and it sort of hung like a dark cloud around his head…it is so hard to explain. I've never come across anything like it before. I just know that this man was into occult practices of a severe and truly demonic nature."

Then Francesca added, "I am absolutely convinced that this individual had made concerted attempts in his own lifetime to meet the Devil or at least attempt to have direct communication with him. While I am sure he belonged to the early 20th century his aims were not to understand the psychic world like other spiritualists of the time but to use the world of spirit for his own ends …to gain power over others in all sorts of ways. That was his main aim, 'power over others' by occult means!"

I admit to being flabbergasted …and puzzled and I remember wondering if some student of philosophy of past years had had such a strong and unpleasant character and nature that his psychic memories had somehow seeped into the very fabric of the building.

"Did he allow you to get a good look at him?" I asked. (I asked that because sometimes spirit beings of an unpleasant nature take steps to conceal their images from people like Francesca who can see them.)

"Oh, yes! He made no attempt to hide from me at all. In fact I'm sure he knew I was looking at him and was angry at that. He was also angry …and amazed, I think… that we were all discussing the topic of the spiritual world in a logical and worthwhile way.

He was quite a tall man and well-built too but besides

his eyes which radiated this evil light he was noticeable for two other things. He had a large and drooping Mexican-style moustache and the strangest hat you ever saw upon his head! It looked exactly like a black up-turned flowerpot!"

I couldn't help but smile a little at that for it seemed so ridiculous.

"Really!" put in Francesca, "And he was wearing some sort of wraparound garment. It wasn't like a cloak…..more like a towelling dressing-gown. He could almost have been taken for a stage magician if he had not been such a powerful and nasty character."

We walked out into the sunlight fascinated but simultaneously puzzled as to who had been spying on us from the spirit world. I said my goodbyes to Francesca and the friends she'd brought along and moved off along the pavement in a different direction and by chance I found myself walking behind two other members of the Society who had been at the lecture. I could overhear the other two talking in front of me about Aleister Crowley* and the fact that he had lived in Edinburgh for a period of his life. It did not strike me then that the conversation had actually been centred on the fact that this devil-worshipping man had actually lived in the building we had just left…the Theosophical Hall! I only discovered that after I got home and made a few phone calls. Only then was I was told that this man had lived in and operated his occult circle from a room on the top floor of the building and that until comparatively recently that room had remained locked because of its previous use. *(*Aleister Crowley was a famous…or rather infamous… demonologist and occultist of the early 20th century who lived at various places in Britain and Europe and had quite a wide following of 'trendy' people keen on devil-worship and power over others through means of magic and the occult. He died in 1947 leaving a trail of mentally and financially broken people behind him. There is much literature upon his life.)*

Armed with the knowledge that Crowley had lived in the property I had no doubt at all that it was his spirit-self who had appeared to Francesca. The evil feeling that overcame this medium said it all. The fact that his image was seen moving out of a mirrored surface on the floor below where he was supposed to have lived makes me think that he may have owned or rented the entire building.

Unfortunately the description of the man with the strange Mexican-style moustache and the black 'flower-pot' hat did not tie up with any photograph I had ever seen of Aleister Crowley. I therefore decided to pass the word around all my friends with an interest in the paranormal to see if they could remember seeing a photograph of Crowley in such a hat.

Eventually my tenacity paid off and none other than my society associate David Melrose sent me a photograph of what I wanted to see. He had actually been one of the two men who had been walking in front of me after the lecture and had been so fascinated with the tale he had heard that, quite independently, he later looked up as much as he could on Crowley. It was then that he had stumbled across the very photograph that I wanted to see. It showed Crowley in a typically arrogant and masterful pose, no doubt lording it over his devotees. It must have been in his later years for he appeared bald under the large black fez hat that he wore. I noticed too that there were no traditional golden tassels attached to the top of the hat and I could not help but notice the unusual Mexican moustache that he sported and which had so taken Francesca. I have seen no other photograph of Crowley with either such a hat or such a moustache and must therefore suppose that that stylish mode was something that may well have been developed by him during his stay in Edinburgh towards the latter part of his life.

Nothing more was either said or done about that short incident until Francesca and I realised that the Scottish Society for Psychical Research had once again hired that room for a further public meeting on Feb. 27th 2005. We decided that we really wanted to be there to see if our angry Mr. Crowley would also be in attendance at this further meeting.... .....

That afternoon's lecture was to be by one person only, the eminent Professor Archie Roy and he was to talk on various ramifications of 'Spiritual Possession'. While I was listening to my fellow Society member, the professor, my eyes kept flashing across to Francesca for I rather thought that sooner or later Crowley would put in an appearance, particularly since the topic being discussed was 'Possession'.....something that Crowley himself must have thought a lot about.

> I was not to be disappointed for about fifteen minutes into the talk I saw Francesca's eyes open wider and stare past the speaker to the wall on his left. She then turned to me and nodded silently: I knew that Aleister Crowley was with us again!
> ....It was the interval time before I could actually talk with her about the re-emergence of Crowley and because of others close around us we were able to exchange only a few words but we talked enough for me to learn that we had an angry man present with us once again but this time he was even more angry than previously.....
> "He's one really angry man, today," Francesca whispered. "He hates the psychic world being explained in any sort of logical and scientific way. He's shouting out that everything is "supernatural" and he is moving to and fro around Professor Roy all the time."
> ....*The meeting finished after the usual 'question and answer session' and we all drifted out of the building*.....
> Normally Francesca would have gone down the road to her own home which is close by but on that occasion we had a case to go to.....
> Naturally, during that car journey we talked about Aleister Crowley and Frances told me that this time he was not wearing his strange hat but he still had his Mexican moustache below his prominent nose and hatred still streamed out from his piercing eyes. The man was dressed in what could only be described as a 'long silky smoking jacket'......
> ......I look forward to our next meeting with this most unusual spirit-person.

Archie finished his chapter by saying he was looking forward to his next meeting with Crowley – which I certainly was not. Nor I suspected was Francesca. And from her we have evidence of the same description of the man, the same evil intent and the same manipulation of people for his own ends. This was not a man to be tackled either when he was alive or now that he was in the Spirit World – and here we were sitting in his room – the one the Theosophical Society had kept locked for the last number of years – until they rented it to us.

Addendum: The excerpt reproduced above with the kind permission of the author, Archie Lawrie, is actually part of an unpublished manuscript dated 22 February, 2007 – this being the date when he sent it to me. It was subsequently published in Archie's book (already referenced above) in May

2007, but when going to print Archie added an addendum:

> Addendum, February 2007 I have been told recently of two changes that have taken place in that building in the past year. Firstly an upper room that had always been kept locked has now been made open to the public for letting purposes and secondly that the reflective Hindu painting has been removed from the wall in that larger lecture room.
> At the time of going to press, the group using that upper room has "felt compelled" to look elsewhere for a suitable alternative let because of "strange influences" that they felt there. I am assured by that group that they knew NOTHING about the possible presence of Aleister Crowley: most had never even heard of him.
> I should imagine that no spiritual/psychic action has been taken by the property owners to remove our Mr Crowley from the premises but if such a thing had been attempted I would imagine that, due to the man's evil nature, it would have failed abysmally! A determined and evil entity of such a nature is a VERY difficult thing to move on. (From The Psychic Investigators Casebook volume three, by Archibald A. Lawrie, p149.)

Just as I had respected Archie's request for confidentiality of his unpublished manuscript, our Group was also operating confidentially, as instructed by Spirit. And as you can see here from this excerpt, Archie referenced my discussions with him at the time about what we had experienced in that room on the top floor but maintained and honoured our need for confidentiality too. Thanks Archie.

Footnote: Do I think Aleister Crowley was continually haunting The Theosophical Society since he died in 1947? No. Apart from anything else, he travelled extensively throughout the world and he did not die in The Theosophical Society building. Throughout his life he experimented with the occult. He was sexually promiscuous, bisexual and sadomasochistic. He experimented with recreational drugs and used these and other hallucinogenic substances to push the boundaries of the esoteric world to frightening new heights —or in his case, depths.

But I do think there are 'triggers' which can help initiate Spirit contact – indeed Crowley experimented with the darker side of this phenomenon through Voodoo, ritualistic magic, etc. and coincidentally he too had an interest in alchemy. Historically there are plenty examples of people in extreme situations where they believe either an angel or some stranger suddenly turns up to save them. This may indeed be Professor Archie Roy's 'early warning signal' working in reverse, but I do believe if we send out a thought it can be picked up. So that being the case, if we, the Thursday Group, started experimenting with the Ouija Board and Planchette whilst sitting in, of all places, his room – this would have been an irresistible invitation to our Mr Crowley – he could experiment and have fun with us from the other side. Just as I believe he did with Archie.

Footnote: Francesca is a pseudonym for Frances Ryan. She too was one of the Mediums selected for the PRISM exercises referred to in Chapter 5.

24 SYNCHRONICITY

The emergence of Aleister Crowley unnerved the Group especially when we looked further into some of his occult activities. The fact that he had materialised in our actual séance room was worrying to say the least. But we re-grouped. We discussed all the positive things that had happened over the past year and the fact that we trusted our Spirit Team to guide us. They had told us that we could use this venue until such times as we found an alternative and so we should do so. However we now had gained more appreciation of the reasons behind the continued push for us to find an alternative venue and understood now why some activities in this venue might be restricted because of the presence of this individual. We trusted that Arthur and our Spirit Team would always endeavour to keep us protected from any intervention of this sort but realised that we had a part to play too in being especially vigilant now we knew we were actually occupying *his* space.

And so we continued. We resolved not to use the tools that might be more easily manipulated by this type of character and strangely enough what we were experiencing was the very thing that I had always warned about right from the very start. I had not heeded my own warnings. I was aware that this form of communication can allow those from the lower realms access to our world. We had also learnt by using the planchette that some entities are able to infiltrate and present themselves in another guise. But when we examined this most recent experience we realised that I identified my grandmother not from the evidence she brought but from my own senses – I could feel it was her even when the only piece of communication we had at that point was the letter 'M'. Equally, I was able to determine on the second occasion that it was not my grandmother again by using my senses – even when Jim was giving our communicator the benefit of the doubt. Therefore if we want to remove the opportunity for Mr Crowley and his associates to play tricks on us we revert to using our senses and Mental Mediumship which is a far more intelligent form of communication than the basic Ouija Board and Planchette.

And so it was that we continued our activities throughout 2007. We soon found that the sounds that we had initially experienced in the room returned and new sounds were added to our portfolio. As well as the loud cracks we had first heard more than a year before we were now hearing clicking sounds popping sounds and a sort of pinging sound which sounded like something was being strummed but instead of making a musical note it made this ping sound — much like 'the elusive knitting' (from Chapter 17). On another occasion (9th August, 2007) there was a sound as if someone was scrunching up cellophane so a bit like 'white noise'[42] but it seemed to emerge from the wall and then run along the length of the wall and shortly after that the door of our room burst open. We assumed that it just hadn't been closed properly but it was strange that that had never happened before in all the time we had been sitting in the building. What was a common occurrence was invariably when we became aware of vibrational energy in the room (like the floor boards rising and falling, etc) it would shortly be followed by a car alarm going off outside — we could almost set our watches by this. But on that night of 9th August after our door burst open (and we carefully closed it again after checking that there was no-one outside) it was the alarm in the Theosophical Building that went off.

We observed other changes in our development throughout the year. Almost as if our Spirit Team were aware our practices were restricted to Meditation and Mental Mediumship and tried to make those experiences more meaningful for us. We found that we all started going very deep in our meditations and there are many reports throughout the year of various members of our Group reporting 'sleep-like' states and feelings of dizziness.

On 14th June, 2007 we welcomed another visitor to our Group who was able to experience the energy being generated. We welcomed Eiric Campbell to the Group for the first time. Eiric was known to a few members of our Group and was mediumistic herself but was very ill suffering from mouth cancer. The Group had been sending distant healing[43] to Eiric throughout her illness but now she had a little respite and was able to join us in person as a one-off to experience this healing first hand. Jim extended a warm welcome to her.

Eiric acknowledged the Group's welcome but stated that she had just realised that she had actually seen this room before probably whilst she was in hospital when the Group had been sending her healing and she had a feeling that she had been in the room before. The Group then arranged themselves into a smaller circle with Eiric in the centre so that healing could be administered. Afterwards Eiric gave feedback:

Eiric: 'Wonderful, absolutely amazing. When I sat down first, I felt that

the chair was disappearing into the floor and then it came back up again.'
This could have been some of the floor vibrations and fluctuations that the Group were accustomed to but which Eiric was experiencing for the first time.
Eiric: 'Jim said something *(Jim didn't say anything)* but I wasn't aware of it then I got this head wobble which is a condition of my illness but it started and it didn't feel the same as it usually does. It was as if I was out of my body and watched what was going on. My head tilted forward and then I sensed as if Ann and Mayumi were talking away to each other *(which they were not)*, but I didn't know what they were saying. There was a letting go, a release. When I did the 'crumble' *(she was overcome by the energy and started to cry)* I became aware of a deep feeling of a real strong energy away inside that made me feel 'wow – this is magic!' It maybe my own higher self or something else I became aware of but it touched my heart and soul and I started to cry as I hadn't been there for so long. But the way I'm feeling now I don't need a train to get home (to Glasgow) I'm going to walk along the motorway!!!'

This was a good accolade from someone who understood energy and had experience of sitting in various other Circles over many years so she was in an excellent position to make a comparison. Her view of the strength of the energy in our Circle was evidential of the intensity that we too were experiencing. Jim too commented:

Jim: 'There was such immense power in the Circle. I had to open my eyes, as just like Mayumi said; I was going to get thrown around too with the vibration. *(Mayumi had mentioned that she couldn't keep her balance because of the vibrational power of the energy)*. When I took your hands, Eiric, I could tell that there was a lot going on. I'm pleased for the Group that we we're able to do that.'
Eiric: 'There's a real purity that I feel here in this Group, a real togetherness. I've been in many Circles but I've never felt the energy like this before.'
Jim: 'I want to just mention, Eiric, this is a Private Circle. Not many people know we sit like this, we keep it confidential.'
Eiric: 'Yes, I understand.'

I think this feeling of 'togetherness' that Eiric reported would have partly been due to the fact that the Group were based on trust and unity one for the other but I think it also stemmed from the fact that we now had a common enemy – nothing unites more than a common enemy – and so Crowley's appearance had done that for us. We were now more secure more bonded together and more protective of each other – nothing was going to come between us.

The feelings of sleepiness and dizziness continued too and members of the Group started reporting that some of the phenomena experienced in the Group were now being felt outside the Group. I had already had the experience or my TV turning itself on of its own volition as well as my printer deciding to spew out blank paper completely unprompted; now Mairi was reporting that her bathroom door would suddenly swing open as if someone had just walked through it and Gordon said that strange lights were appearing on his living-room wall. Both Gill and I had lost jewellery only for it to reappear exactly where it should have been and Mairi had a similar event involving a soft toy that sat on one of her easy chairs – it disappeared and she couldn't find it anywhere only for it to be back sitting in the chair when she returned home from work. Mayumi said that she had experienced a loud crash in her house as if something large and heavy had fallen off the wall to the floor but she could find no cause for this noise. Gordon too reported a crashing sound so much so that his flat mate said it sounded as if something had fallen. Whilst the casual observer I'm sure could explain these away as draughts or shadows these people were all experienced psychic and mediumistic workers – they knew when there was something different going on. As an example on 12th July both Mayumi and I informed the Group of symptoms of strange dizziness that morning so much so that we each had phoned the other at the time this was occurring to record the symptoms. In other words we were both experiencing something that we were concerned enough to phone each other about. For my part I can only describe it as if I was under the influence of drink or drugs – neither of which was present – either that or I was slowly losing consciousness due to some illness of some sort in my own home. This is why I called Mayumi because somehow I realised this was not a physical symptom but a psychic one. She was experiencing exactly the same thing. And now as we reported this to the Group on 12th July there was another member of the team experiencing the same strange physical symptoms. Jim said that he had experienced a strange sensation a few days previously whilst he was sleeping and had to get up during the night – it was a strange swirling sensation, like a swirl of energy.

> At this point, Jim asked if anyone had any ideas of what they would like to do this week, but a strange sort of calm had befallen the Group and whilst all heard what Jim had said, everyone continued to sit in silence as the energy seemed to be very heavy and it was almost as if everyone was about to fall asleep. After a further 15 minutes or so of this calmness Jim again asked if anyone had anything they'd like to share from that experience.

This experience was almost as if everyone had been gassed or intoxicated with some invisible substance. However we pulled ourselves back to a more conscious state to answer Jim's request. And since we had recently purchased a trumpet we thought we would experiment with it. *(A trumpet is a piece of equipment traditionally used in spirit communication in the past. It is not an actual trumpet but a cone-shaped item usually made of light-weight metal or card).*

It was agreed that the Group would then sit around the small square topped table, just sitting in silence with the trumpet standing, end-on on top of it, to see if it would move. After some time, the energy could be felt building up in the table until the table began to vibrate, thus making the trumpet move. As it moved it caused a strange noise and a sort of jumping motion. Eventually it dropped off the edge of the table. Spirit confirmed via mental mediumship to Ann, Mayumi and Gill that the energy was almost trance-like tonight and that was why we were all so quiet. The change of energy was Spirit's intent. This was something they had been preparing us for over the last few weeks which is why we had all felt so tired at each session over the last number of weeks.

We received further information or even reprimand from our Spirit Team for using the trumpet in this way. We were shown how easily it was for us to revert to looking for physical phenomena i.e. looking for the trumpet to move when in actual fact the original purpose of Spirit Trumpets was to amplify sound. In other words if Spirit could communicate with us directly i.e. speak to us rather than produce cracks and bangs on the walls then if we provided an item that could amply that sounds perhaps we would hear them. Spirit directed that the trumpet should be placed on the floor – lying down on the floor – it couldn't amplify sound standing on end – we had just placed it in this position because we wanted to see it move. And here endeth the lesson from Spirit!

There were also some strange synchronicities going on that year of 2007. It seemed to focus around me so I wasn't sure if this was something personal for me or something for the Group so as usual in these circumstances I recorded it in the Group in case it meant anything to anyone else or if anyone had anything to add.

I live in the south suburbs of Edinburgh. And had noticed that a large red van had been parked further along the road in my street for the last couple of weeks. I wondered if it perhaps had broken down or why it hadn't moved from there in this time. Now I should mention here that I'm not usually a very observant person in this way. Usually I wouldn't notice things like this but for whatever reason I felt drawn to this red van – strange as that may seem. I decided to wander along to investigate. There was nothing wrong with the van that I could see but the odd thing was that it had two addresses written on its side and each one was the location of a previous address where I had lived. One of the addresses was Auchtertool, in Fife and the other was Grange Terrace in Edinburgh, and now the van was parked in my street, where I currently lived – I thought this was a remarkable coincidence. However, as I was marking this down into the 'strange but true' category, the situation became even more conspicuous when the next day another van had appeared in my street, this time a large white van with an address in Humbie on it – again where I had lived prior to moving to Edinburgh.

Whilst this can be put down to coincidence and one can accept that in a large city like Edinburgh its perhaps not that unusual to see a van sporting a previous address of yours from the same city, but two of the addresses concerned are tiny little villages – Auchtertool in the county of Fife, which is across the Firth of Forth from Edinburgh; and Humbie which is a little hamlet in the county of East Lothian. Three of my previous addresses were being displayed in the location of my current address - someone was trying to get my attention.

When I reported this back at the meeting there was no further comment from anyone other than they too found it a strange coincidence. We then sat in silence and during my meditation I saw a large rabbit again *(I had seen it before but disregarded it – I usually have to see things three times before I start to pay attention)* and this time I got the impression of Alice in Wonderland and the instruction, 'follow the rabbit'. As it disappeared down a hole!

> Mayumi: 'I know why you're getting that Ann. The next version of 'What the Bleep', is called, 'Down the Rabbit Hole'!' *Note: What the Bleep is a DVD explaining the laws of Synchronicity and Sacred Geometry and how they affect our lives.*

So here it was – synchronicity – and the message: sit up and pay attention there's more going on than you realise – a message for all of us and I hope what I'm conveying to you in this book.

This focus around me seemed to continue. I've always been of the opinion that the Group was brought together to experience every aspect of spirit phenomena so that they could learn from it and then speak about it to the wider community when called upon to do so. I've always felt that this was a Group initiative rather than it falling to one specific individual. Despite the fact that some of the older members of our Group were looking to see who would emerge as the Physical Medium I always felt that the phenomena would manifest with the Group as a whole rather than with one individual – and I said so. However, towards the latter half of 2007 the energy certainly seemed to be focused around me. That was either brought to my attention through a series of synchronicities, some already mentioned or through the powerful energies which would make me shake uncontrollably and for which I did not have an answer. An example of this happened on 19th July 2007. After sitting in silence I just began to talk asking that the Spirit use the energy of the Group for their purpose. I repeated this a few times then both Mayumi and I became aware of a sort of ticking noise – like a clock but there was no clock in the room. This happened on three occasions starting and stopping each time. Gill and Jim who were nearest the source of the sound did not hear it. Then I became aware of a very intense energy I became very cold and I started to shake. I thought I was going to be sick. This shaking became quite pronounced and I was unable to stop it. I remember Gill asking me to relax but I was unable to do so. Mayumi came around behind me and tried to relax my shoulders and then began rubbing my arms and shoulders to warm me up. I too began to rub my legs very briskly to try to warm them up and Gill instructed me to take some deep breaths and eventually the symptoms dissipated. Another occasion was on 9th August and because we were uncertain as to why the energy had built up to such an overwhelming amount previously, we asked permission to use the table again for clarification – this was allowed:

> *The table then became animated again and bounced around the Circle coming to rest again in front of the trumpet.*
> Jim: 'Are we to use the trumpet tonight?' *No.*
> *The table circled again quite aggressively.*
> Ann: 'Are we to learn something new tonight?' *Yes.*
> Ann: 'Is it levitation?' *Yes.*

I'm not sure why I jumped to this conclusion – I must have sensed it.

> Gordon: 'Levitation of the trumpet?' *No.*
> Gordon: 'Levitation of the table?' *No.*
> Jim: 'Levitation of a person?' *Yes.*
> Ann to the Group: 'Well, it'll have to be you, Mayumi, you're the lightest!'
> *The Group laughed and the table became more excited.*
> Jim: 'Go to the person who is to be levitated.'
> *The table moved over to Ann and leaned into her lap.*
> Ann (with surprise): 'Are you sure it's me?' *Yes.*
> There was some discussion in the Group at the surprise of this development – then further questions were asked and from these it was deduced that Ann and the chair she was sitting on were to be levitated. She was to be positioned on the chair in the centre of the Circle and the table moved out of the way to facilitate this. Jim positioned himself to Ann's left, Gordon to her right and Mayumi at the front, near her feet. All went into a meditative state. Quite quickly Jim asked if it was okay to hold Ann's hands. Ann said to him that he should just do whatever felt right for him as none of us knew what to do. Jim came to the front of Ann and swapped places with Mayumi. This session went on for about half an hour during which time the powerful energy and vibration was felt by all. In general discussion afterwards, Jim asked Ann why she had held her hands and arms up in the air, and that this must have been uncomfortable. Ann said that it was because he was pulling her hands up and indeed she felt

compelled to stand up because he was pulling her hands up so high. Jim said that he wasn't and that she was doing this of her own accord. Ann said she could feel hands in hers pulling her up – she could also feel someone stroking her hair and hands on different parts of her body, which after asking those present, was able to deduce that it wasn't theirs. Gordon also said he felt a 'fuzzy' energy. Ann said she felt a strange and powerful energy running through her and she was aware that Spirit had wanted her to be horizontal and had kept pushing her head back and she knew they wanted to lift her at the hips and stretch her legs out, but this wasn't possible from the chair, in the sitting position. She was also aware towards the end of a sort of sporadic pulse, almost like a spasm running through her that made her muscles twitch. As this discussion was going on, Gordon was suggesting that he could bring his treatment table with him next time.

And on 16th August, 2007:

Ann: 'I was very deep – similar to last week, I felt my head getting pulled back again and it felt like I was being prepared. I didn't want to come back, it was a real struggle to come back.'
Jim: 'Well I was asking that you be prepared for this.'
Ann: 'So was I.'
The Group then sat around the table and asked for further clarification via the table of what we were to do tonight. (Gordon had very kindly brought his treatment bed with him, as requested). From the questioning it was eventually deduced that the session tonight was to be some sort of healing exercise but it was to be focused on the room and seemed to be about healing the room, ensuring that there was no negative energy, and increasing or preparing the energy for the next exercise – levitation. It was agreed that Gordon would lead this exercise and the Group sat in Circle and focused their energy in the centre of the room. It was apparent that the energy was currently being utilised to cleanse and build the room. After some time it was suggested that Ann sit in the centre of the Circle for the Group to focus on her again – this was done. Afterwards Ann said that she felt strange, not like last week. This time she felt very, very heavy – like a lead weight and she was being pulled down. Then there was a change and she became lighter, but she had no indication of being lifted off her chair, despite some feelings of her head being pulled back again.
Mairi felt that we were going along the right lines and that Spirit were happy with us, she also suggested that the heaviness that Ann felt was possibly to do with her going into trance and being prepared for what was to come.
Mayumi said that she had tried to lift Ann's pinkies (little fingers) whilst she was sitting to see if Ann would lift her hands, but no. However, she said that Ann had held her pinkies in the same position as Mayumi had left them, i.e. sticking straight upwards.

Jim said he too had tried to lift Ann's hands but the fingers were left where he had left them, but there was no lifting movement.

And on 18th October:

> Ann (conducting mental mediumship): I feel like I have a man with me, and I'm aware of a hospital neck brace, an old-fashioned one with leather straps on it – they fasten at the back. This man is of average height – certainly not small and is big-built in fact, I'd say, fat. He is dressed like Santa Claus, and I think he's been playing Santa Claus at the local Village/Church Hall. I think he fell or slipped or something and now he's in hospital with this brace on his neck. By the look of the hospital and the people visiting and the look of their dress, I think we're in the 1960's. I want to be in Strathclyde – Lanarkshire – Larkhall. I have a wife and kids there. I am a postman and I can see an envelope coming down from the ceiling – for the Group. I can hear the Carpenter's song, 'Mr Postman look and see'. I know this is for the Group and now I can see a parcel, in brown paper, tied up with string – and I now want to say, these words from the 'Sound of Music' song – 'these are a few of my favourite things – tied up with string'. This is also for the Group – a parcel of 'Wonderful Things'.
>
> As Gill questioned Ann as to how this person might link with the Group, Ann said she got the impression that he was being used by the Spirit Team, to deliver this message – and to tell us that it comes from them. At this point, just as Ann said this, she began to change and the Spirit Entity that was with her was replaced by another. At the same time, Ann reported as feeling as if a rod of ice had just been inserted through her from the top of her head, right through her body – she felt freezing and was shaking with the cold. This she took as a sign that her impression was correct. She continued: 'I feel as if I now have one of our Spirit Team with me, I don't know which one, but he is one of the senior, significant members, he's tall and slim-built with grey, receding hair, a gentleman, and he's confirming that this message is indeed from them. I get the feeling that this time, they are telling us beforehand that these gifts come from them – usually we experience some phenomena and then we ask if it was from them. I get the feeling this time, that they are telling us in advance.'

And on 22nd November:

> Gill then noted that Ann had a presence over-shadowing her. Gill asked Ann to speak:
> Ann: 'I'm aware of a strong presence with me and I know he's come to speak to me, but that I'm supposed to speak these words aloud, but I'm embarrassed to say them.'
> Gill asked Ann to proceed:
> Ann *(speaking in a deep, loud, male voice)*: 'I am the leader. I am Arthur. I am speaking to you through your leader.' *(And then speaking*

to Ann): 'I write the books. You write the book. You have been away for some time. When you're away, I'm away. You need to come back. The Group need you. But now you have returned.'

This comment referred to the fact that I was dealing with some personal problems at this time. I was aware that my attention had been focused elsewhere and not on the Group. What I now know is that you can't deal with the Spirit World if your own physical world is not stable. If your own emotions and sense of equilibrium is out of kilter then you can't hope to be able to work with Spirit.

At this point the Group concurred with Arthur's comments and asked Gill to talk Ann down into a deeper meditative state and Gill asked Ann what she was seeing:
Ann: 'Blue. I see a cloak of blue. It's beautiful. It's like an old-fashioned cloak on the edges but the centre of it is moving and has colours of turquoise and white and sparkly and it's all sort of moving and merging together with energy. It signifies firstly protection but also healing – it's for the Group. The Spirit Team are swirling it round all of us. Its purpose is many fold – to keep us protected but also to send us healing – not physical healing but a pool of energy to pull from. It will help us and help us with all those we come into contact with. It may be a challenge to others. It is for the Group as a whole. It will radiate out from each one of us but more so as a Group.'

As the energy of the Spirit Person dissipated I became aware that another Spirit Being was with me and Gill also observed the change in the energy. I could feel a power struggle – good versus evil. I felt when this energy came in it was very heavy and very powerful but in a different way to the positive power of the first Spirit Being. This was Crowley! And he was invading the space but just momentarily as he was moved on again by the positive energy of the Spirit Team. Hence the feeling of good versus evil. The positivity quickly returned but not as powerful as before it was lighter and less personalised – as if the communication was being finished off by the Spirit Team as a whole. I felt this was a demonstration of how they would and could protect us but also showed how the strong energy that was with me initially had to withdraw to deal with other presences. I took this to be an example of how the energy from our Spirit Team can be diverted away from us by the presence of other entities. I also felt less concerned about Crowley now I had experienced him 'up close and personal' whilst at the same time experiencing the power of our own Spirit Team and knowing they were the greater. I then heard Jim's name mentioned – they are pleased with him and the work he does.

'Mairi, they want to thank you for all your support. Actually, they are mentioning each one of us in turn and there is an overwhelming sense of love. They are acknowledging each member of the Group and saying how valued each individual is. The individual qualities that each member brings to the Group are invaluable. The whole is greater than the sum of the individual parts. There is now a star above us and an angel. It's about re-birth renewal and they seem to be welcoming us back.'

On 6th December:

Gill commenting on Ann: 'Ann was sitting very still and Spirit were very close. The aura was very focused. It was as if they were trying to take her to a different level. You are beyond mental mediumship now. They want you to do more but you need to meet them half way. Just allow it to happen – in whatever form it takes – you just need to be in the moment. I know that's not in your personality but you need to try to stop pre-meditating and all this preparing for the platform stuff – just forget it and throw away the bit of paper – it's not needed, go back to spontaneity.'

So, 2007 was another eventful year. We had just as much phenomena but different from the year before. We had experienced the presence of evil but I feel this too was a lesson from Arthur as we realised our Spirit Team were more powerful but that their power was dissipated by a negative presence. All of the Group members were allowed to experience different physical phenomena in their own homes and they were all thanked and recognised by Spirit for all they do. But for now we had found a new place for our future meetings and so this fittingly was the last meeting in the Theosophical Society building. Creepy Crowley could have his room back.

Footnote: Spiritualists generally do not believe in evil or 'bad spirits'. There is a general tendency to believe that Spirit is all 'love and light' – this is a common mantra – and whilst operating in this environment they are unlikely to experience anything other than this. So their experience is true.

I have had the opportunity to speak with spiritual leaders, most in high office and some from many of the long-standing, traditional religions – they all believe that there are negative forces at play i.e. where there is light there is darkness. I have no desire to frighten people – this would be contrary to my mission – however it is logical that for every action there is an equal and opposite reaction, science tells us so. But a more appropriate analogy for me comes from the yin and yang philosophy of the I Ching. This philosophy is ancient, pre-Christian and states that the universe is made up of opposing elements - light and dark, sun and moon, male and female, good and evil. There are aspects of each element in the opposite element – they are interdependent. Where the yin is stronger the yang will be weaker and vice versa. This sums up my own thinking more accurately than most religions can and if applied to the situation I described earlier in this chapter concerning the presence of Crowley, would look something like this: He is definitely in the yin category which tends to be inward focused, dark and negative (he spent a lifetime developing this), whilst I and the Spirit Team were of the yang variety, outward facing, bright, light, positive energy. Arthur and I along with the Spirit Team held the strongest power over the negative Crowley and so he retreated – but with him went some of our yang energy expelled in this encounter. He on the other hand would have left some of his energy with us. We were left very aware of his presence, his power and his negativity – and therefore more knowledgeable and less scared in this arena - if a little depleted. Conversely I like to think that this interaction will have cast a little light into the darkness and this again is one of my aims. From my experience as a Paranormal Investigator I can list the criteria that create conducive conditions where negative paranormal events can manifest. And these tend to be around people who themselves are suffering some form of negativity in their lives. It can be very difficult for people to see their way out of this when they are scared and all around them the yin energy is dominant. It is our job – and I mean all of us – to shed some light where there is darkness and bring in some yang energy to help balance things just a little for those who are suffering – in whatever form. We are, after all all connected – again a philosophy from the I Ching but one which the Spiritualists would endorse – what we give out, we get back.

To finish and just before I get off my soapbox, there is an inspirational saying used by many life coaches and inspirational speakers that says, '*This is not the dress-rehearsal – this is the real thing*', the message being; do what you want to do, be what you want to be, enjoy yourself – you only live once. I would counter that by saying '*This IS the dress-rehearsal, the real thing is yet to come* – and how you perform in this life will dictate the role you are given in the main event'. I do not disagree with those inspirational speakers indeed I strongly agree that you should 'be all you can be' and not be discouraged by those in the 'yin'. However, if more people were aware of how their actions affect others but ultimately impact upon themselves, there would be fewer atrocities and hopefully the world would be a more peaceful place.

25 FROM WILDERNESS TO WONDERLAND

In 2008 and 2009 we entered what I called the wilderness years when things just were not functioning the way they had before. At the end of 2007 we left the Theosophical Society but in October of that year my very good friend Mayumi left too, emigrating to Canada. She was a sad loss to the Group but even more so to me. I've made mention earlier in this book of what a spiritual person Mayumi was. I've never met a person so intuitive, caring and with a humility that was obvious for all to see. Her spirituality shone from her. You will also notice from this book that there is not a lot of comment attributed to Mayumi as she didn't say very much, but her power in the Group was immense and so when she went she left a big gap in our Circle. We missed her.

At the beginning of 2008 the Group moved to the Edinburgh Association of Spiritualists building in Morrison Street, Edinburgh. This was a Spiritualist Church and I was acting Secretary there at that time and when a space became available in the curriculum on Thursday nights after another group cancelled their activities there I offered to move my Group in – so we had a new venue. It wasn't one that we had consulted Spirit about or dowsed for, it was simply that we knew now why we had to leave the Theosophical Society and this was the first available space, so we took it. The energies were good in the Church after all it had been used for spiritual activities so the Group settled down and we had no risk of the negative influences we had previously experienced with Crowley.

We also gained a new member of the Group. We had been looking for someone else to join us after Mayumi had moved away but we were always concerned about how the energy of a new person would impact on us and I was always of the opinion that it was better to have no one than have the wrong person. We also implemented an initiation period of 3 months which would be a trial period where we would sit with the new person and see how their energy felt. Equally they could assess us and decide if they wanted to stay on as part of the Group or not. It only required one of our original Group members to object or even just to feel uncomfortable in this changed energy for us to discontinue working with the new recruit and go back to the status quo. And so it was that Tricia joined the Group.

I had met Tricia a few years earlier when she used to sit in Gill's Class. Now Gill was recommending her to the Group – so we gave her a trial and then invited her to join us – and our Group was back to six people again. Tricia was a retired Social Worker and Counsellor. She was a very articulate and feisty person who had brought up her children almost single-handedly and had dealt with some of the worst cases of deprivation in her social care duties. She struggled sometimes with her spiritual work as we all do from time to time and now she was looking for somewhere safe and secure where she could develop and explore these gifts. She came to us.

As always we kept our activities confidential but after a few months of being in the Spiritualist Church their committee wanted us to share the space with another group which wanted to use the Church Hall on the same night as us, so we decided it was better that we move once again. Gordon knew of a place where he worked from time to time by hiring their therapy room to do his healing. This was a new age crystal shop in Edinburgh but with a therapy room to the back of the shop. Gordon asked if we could rent this therapy room on a Thursday evening after the shop closed, which was duly agreed. This place was not as conducive to our activities as the Spiritualist Church but we coped with it. We had it to ourselves it was quiet it was confidential and it was pretty cramped too – six of us squeezed into one wee therapy room but we made it work. I do remember one evening when we were ready to leave to go home after our session and when Gordon turned the key in the lock of the front door the barrel of the lock just turned in the door and didn't move the lock – it was broken and we were stuck inside. We ended up shouting through the letterbox at some passing stranger to help get us out. We passed the key through the letterbox to the man and hoped he would be able to open the door from the outside which he eventually did much to our relief.

After another number of months we moved back again to the Spiritualist Church. They missed us or missed our rental payments especially since the other group had stopped going too so now they were welcoming us back and this time they would respect our need for privacy. It was a much better space than the crystal shop and at least we didn't get locked in.

These were the wilderness years. We continued with our development which was mainly mental mediumship but it was interesting to discover during this time how the venues impact on the energy of a Group. We had experienced both positive and negative influences and it's not something that's very readily taken into consideration by most Groups or Circles but we were allowed to experience those differences and perhaps begin to understand why Spirit was trying to direct us to a certain venue. Throughout this time we continued to receive those prompts from Arthur and our Spirit Team to find this new venue where great things were promised. We were told this place had to be just for us. It would not be used for any other purpose. It would be quiet and confidential and a spiritual place where the energy could flourish and would be conducive to our further development - after all we had been promised more physical phenomena. But where would this new venue be – no one knew. Each week we would come up with various suggestions but each time for one reason or another those venues were rejected. We were becoming dejected.

And then just as Arthur Conan Doyle had revealed himself to me right at the beginning of the formation of our Group he began to give us little clues again – this time about the venue that Spirit had in mind for us. One week while we were sitting in the therapy room of the crystal shop Gill was giving feedback from her meditation and said 'I can see a building in Edinburgh's New Town. It's a town house and it connects to you, Ann?' At this point Gill was simply trying to give me a personal message from whoever was communicating with her and telling me what she had picked up during the period of silence.

'You must attend something in the New Town, Ann?'

'No' I said, I couldn't think of anywhere that I go to that would connect me to someone in the New Town. We dropped that line of questioning and Gill moved on to something else.

A few weeks later Gill said 'I see that building again – the townhouse but I now know that it's not the New Town at all it's the West End and it's a corner building?' She was looking at me again in the hope that I would recognise such a building and accept that I would know why she was referring to it in a message for me. But I didn't know anything about a building in the West End on a corner site. I didn't know anyone who lived or had lived in the West End nor did I have reason to go there for any purpose – it didn't make sense to me and I said so.

A further week elapsed and then Gill said 'I can see that building again and it definitely connects to you Ann as I can see you standing on the doorstep. It's as if you're walking into the building – you must go to something there?' she said hopeful of a positive answer.

'Ah, is it the College of Parapsychology?' Of course, this is where Gill used to hold her class. This is where we met and coincidentally this is where we both met Tricia – why hadn't I thought of it before?

'No', Gill said showing her frustration toward me 'I know the College – it's not that building.'

'Well I can't think of anywhere else Gill I'm sorry.' I could see Gill's annoyance. I could see that she was sure of the information that she had received and that she was determined to give it to me.

'Maybe it's for someone else, Gill' I said trying to pacify her.

'No I don't think so' she said as once again we moved on to other things.

Another few weeks elapsed before Gill reverted to her connection again 'I have that building again Ann – the one for you.' Then speaking with all the authority of an ex-police officer[44] she said 'And it's definitely for you because I see you standing with the keys in your hand.'

'I see it too, Ann,' says Tricia, 'and they're rolling out the red carpet for you.'

'And, there's a grand staircase', Mairi adds, 'It looks like a scene from Gone with the Wind.'

'Listen, if I am to be given a Town House in the West End and someone hands me the keys whether it's Rhett Butler or Clark Gable, I'll gladly accept them.' The Group laughed at me gently mocking them as it sounded ridiculous that I would have the keys of a building such as this. (To put that into perspective the sort of building they was referring to was in a posh part of Edinburgh with a price tag to match – somewhere around two million pounds).

So the Group once again moved on with their deliberations. At the same time I was now Vice President of the Spiritualist Church. I had originally just offered to help out as the previous president, an elderly man, struggled with the technology of a very old and antiquated computer and I had simply offered one day to help him type a letter – that was it, I was captured and reluctantly accepted the position of Acting Secretary just so I could type his letters for him. When he was replaced by a younger more active President I thought this was the perfect time to make my escape. I didn't really want any position of responsibility whatsoever. I had had my fill of that in my corporate life - I had ended up becoming Chief Operating Officer of a subsidiary company of National Australia Bank – one of the top ten companies in the world by assets size at that time. Whilst there's a gulf of differences between that and being the Secretary of a wee spooky church, I didn't want to do it. I was actually enjoying the fact that for once I had no responsibilities to shoulder and it was nice.

However what I was to learn about John the new President is that he is nothing if not persistent and although I did resign as Acting Secretary and left him to recruit his own team he phoned me several months later to say that he needed help and that he couldn't do this on his own – he wanted me to come back and be his Vice President. I also learned that he can be very persuasive. The Church was housed in a terraced tenement block near to Edinburgh's second railway station, Haymarket. It is not a very salubrious area at all and the church premises were on the top floor of a two-story building with shops on the bottom. The entry was just a doorway between the shops which opened into a communal stair shared with the pub to the right and the Chinese restaurant to the left. The church hall extended across the floor above these two establishments also taking in the Indian Restaurant which was next to the Chinese. As you might imagine the smells wafting up from these restaurants mingled with the smell of beer from the pub gave the church hall a strange aroma to say the least. As well as that the noise of beer barrels being moved around and the music from both Chinese and Indian restaurants was annoying at times. However since the church service took place on a Sunday morning for the most part those issues described did not really impact all that much. It was only really when there were events on in the evening that sometimes it could be a problem. All in all we rubbed along with our neighbours not too badly. But the real issue became the stair. We had an aging congregation and trying to climb a double flight of stairs to access the church hall was the real stumbling block – if you pardon the pun.

As well as that I remember one Sunday morning coming into the building to attend church and being greeted by John who said to me 'Where is everyone – the church is very empty'.

'They're all at Stansted', I said. 'Stansted' is the Arthur Findlay College, a world-renowned college for the study of psychic and spiritual development. It was bequeathed to the Spiritualist National Union (SNU), the parent body which regulates the Spiritualist Churches around the country. From here they run a series of training courses each week from various visiting mediums/tutors. These courses are residential; indeed it is one of the few places where you can go to undertake a more intensive week of study immersed in both the training and the energy that are needed for such things. The building is a large country mansion set in a few acres of farmland and woodland. It was previously the home of Arthur Findlay, a Scotsman and an entrepreneur who had a keen interest in Spiritualism who left his house to the SNU.

I was counting on my fingers all the members of our congregation whom I knew to be at Stansted that week attending a training course. I counted eight. As John nodded his head in despondent confirmation I had a flash of inspiration and said 'You know John we should be running our own courses here. We have the space (as I wafted my arm across this large church hall) and you have the contacts. And we are next to the railway station. We don't have to provide accommodation; students could choose their own and choose their own standard of accommodation – we are within walking distance of anywhere between The Hilton and a hostel'.

Suddenly my diatribe was over as soon as it had started and I could see that I had hit him with this sudden vision when he wasn't ready for it. 'Why would students want to come here Ann?'

'John, we are in Edinburgh. Scotland's capital city. It's a top visitor attraction – why wouldn't they want to come here.' I've always been entrepreneurial but I still don't know where this vision came from it wasn't something I particularly wanted to do other than possibly attending the courses in a more accessible location – my home town. Realising this had come out of the blue I stopped hassling him and took my seat in the congregation probably realising that this was a step too far.

I didn't give it another thought until a couple of months later but my idea had obviously percolated in John's head and now he called me saying 'You know that idea you had about us running our own training courses up here. I was thinking about that and I think we'd need to find a country house hotel somewhere as a venue where we could run these courses.' John had taken my idea and adapted it to his own version – a country house hotel. He was working on the same principle as Stansted, that is to say a country house with accommodation. My idea was that students would come to our Church in Edinburgh and choose their own accommodation. The standard of accommodation in Stansted at that time was very basic – it had hardly been updated since Arthur Findlay donated it. That's perhaps an exaggeration but there were no bathrooms en suite – the bathroom was at the end of the corridor and was shared by a number of bedrooms and each bedroom had a number of beds a bit like small dormitories so there were always queues for the toilets – though I have to say that it's a bit better than that now.

Meanwhile John asked me 'Why don't we take a day out and drive round a number of possible hotels and see if we can find one that would suit us?'

'Okay' I said and soon we were driving round some of the most scenic parts of Scotland visiting a number of luxurious country house hotels in the hope that by offering them a number of block bookings we could negotiate a deal. But they didn't really need our block bookings, they were perfectly able to fill their hotels without our help and so the prices they quoted were just not cost-effective for us. Ironically the best deal came from a hotel less than a mile from John's house.

So that idea fell by the wayside and was forgotten. But by the end of 2009 he was trying to persuade me to take up another position of responsibility. He had been re-appointed as Chair of the Spiritualists National Union Trust (SNU Trust). This was the financial body of the SNU. It was an independent charity but with the objective of looking after the money of the SNU and all its Churches. It operated a bit like a mutual building society by taking in its members' funds and collectively investing them on the stock market and elsewhere in order to make a return on the investment that would then be shared amongst the members in terms of interest. Conversely the SNU Trust could also make loans and provide mortgages to buy new churches and to carry out repairs to existing churches. John had sat on this Board of Trustees before but he had been asked to go back and take up his old position again as there had been a couple of resignations. It is difficult enough to get fit and proper people to sit on a Board of Directors as Trustees of a Charity, but if the selection pool is narrowed even further by the requirement that those people need to have financial experience and be a member of a Spiritualist Church or the SNU, you can imagine that the likely candidates will be thin on the ground. Of course I fitted these criteria perfectly and John knew it. Not only that but I was his Vice President so it would have been convenient and a support to him as the incoming new Chair to have his 'right hand man' by his side so to speak. The fact that his 'right hand man' was a woman was even better as the SNU Trust like most other organisations at the time were examining the ratio of men to women represented in their senior roles. Despite my protestations I was once again persuaded to take up a position of responsibility, this time as a Trustee of the SNU Trust. John promised me 'It's only four meetings a year - it's not onerous'.

The SNU Trust's head office was in Stansted too, located in the grounds of the Arthur Findlay College but in a separate building. When I flew down from Edinburgh to London Stansted with John for my first meeting I was aware that I was here as the first female who had sat on that Board in the last 20 years and as I glanced at the four elderly gentlemen sitting round the table there was a sense of déjà vu as I remembered my corporate days of walking into boardrooms filled with old buffers – some of them asleep – and those who were awake were wondering who this 'girl' was who had entered their domain and dared to tell them a thing or two. John was right though, the meetings were not onerous, mainly pretty boring and sometimes they'd get bogged down in too much detail. However horses for courses: this was not corporate life, this was the Third Sector, the Charity Sector, and what I had learnt from taking on the VP position in the Church was that one's approach had to be very different when working with volunteers.

Ironically the biggest issue we had to deal with was surprisingly a global one. Most of the western world had just suffered the biggest financial crash since the Great Depression. The banks were collapsing, starting with Lehman Brothers in the United States who collapsed on my birthday in September 2008 closely followed by Merrill Lynch, Goldman Sachs and Morgan Stanley. These were the big names in investment banking and mortgage lending and it was their exposure to sub-prime lending that caused their downfall. Sub-prime is banking-speak for 'worthless'. They were exposed to bundles of mortgages that sooner or later were going to default – it was sooner in this case and their downfall caused a ripple effect throughout Europe and beyond with governments trying to prop up their financial institutions and stock markets.

We on the SNU Trust could no longer rely on making a return on investments on the stock market. Whilst we had spread our portfolio and there was some investment in property which produced a rental income to the SNU Trust the bulk of our returns usually came from the stock market. We had a dilemma. How could we keep paying out interest to our members if we didn't receive any interest on our own investments? It was then that John revisited the idea of running training courses in Edinburgh but this time coming back to my original suggestion that the students find their own accommodation – we just needed to find a building that would be suitable for the training courses. 'What's wrong with the building we've got – it's got plenty of space?' I asked.

'I know but it's got to look the part' John said, 'and we could solve the Church's problem at the same time if we find something with a good ground floor room so there are no stairs to climb; then we could kill two birds with one stone and find a home for the Church too.'

I could see how that would work but I knew this would be a long process. We had firstly to find a building that was suitable and secondly find one that was affordable. However that second issue of affordability could be resolved by killing three birds with the one stone in that we could also help out the SNU Trust with their investment concerns by investing their money in a building. Recently their auditors had warned of the need for the charity to be able to prove that it was of public benefit – how was it do this when it was not public-facing. The Trust had other property investments which paid an income but none served the public; there was hardly any income to be had from the stock market now so property investment in a public service building was a reasonable option - especially now when the market was dead and prices had bottomed out; and Edinburgh is always a good property investment even in the downtime. We decided we would start property hunting.

It was really John who conducted our search. Although it had originally been my idea to run the training courses in Edinburgh, I hadn't intended to buy a building – this was his idea I was planning on using our existing building. But John had come up with the plan to utilise the SNU Trust monies by buying a property and as it was his initiative, I let him get on with it. Ironically, I was too busy in the property market myself because my husband and I had set up a small business renovating and refurbishing properties for the rental agents. Despite the fact there was a recession on we had more business than we could cope with thanks in part to the property crisis; people could no longer afford a deposit to buy their own home and this pushed up demand for rental properties and with it the need to have them refurbished.

Every now and again John would phone me and tell me that he'd found a property and would I accompany him to view it. We saw a lot of properties. John was always keen to buy – he was more enthusiastic than me – I was usually the one pointing out why one property or another would not be suitable either for the Church or for running Training Courses. We looked at a lot of old churches that were on the market as they were no longer viable, their congregations having grown older or died. But most were in the wrong location – we did not want to move our existing congregation too far away from their existing church. It was difficult finding properties that had ground floor rooms that would be big enough for our purpose- which is why we were looking at churches. I remember looking at an old church that had since been redesigned and refurbished and the large ground floor had been cleared of pews and the organ, pulpit etc and was now a large open-plan business space housing a number of desks. The gallery had been turned into a mezzanine floor which had been divided off into individual offices. John was very keen to buy this one – it was a 'turnkey property' i.e. ready just to move into - until I asked him if he had observed the area we had just walked through on our way into the building. 'No' he said looking at me quizzically. This was the red-light district and we had had to weave among a number of 'ladies of the night' on our way into this place.

On another occasion there were two office buildings in Queen Street for sale. Queen Street runs parallel to Princes Street, the main thoroughfare in Edinburgh, so this was an excellent location. It had originally been a row of terraced houses but these had long since been converted into shops and businesses. But, as is normal in Edinburgh, the biggest room, the old drawing room, the one most suitable for a Church, was often on the first floor. We had spent months looking for property and this was the only thing we had seen that was remotely possible – not ideal but possible. We were now heading towards the winter of 2010-2011 which turned out to be one of the worst winters ever, seeming perhaps to reflect the state of the economy. There was compacted snow on the ground for eight weeks from the start of December 2010 when the temperature never moved above freezing. But it was only mid-December when John phoned again – what was I doing on Sunday? He'd found another property to view. 'I'm going to my sister's on Sunday there's a family get together for my niece's birthday which I have to be at'. I was happy I had this excuse. It was December, a busy time of year with Christmas fast approaching and as well as that my family all seemed to conspire to have their birthdays this month too. I could do without another wild goose chase. Undaunted John picked me up from my house and we headed into town. I hadn't asked him about the property we were about to see so didn't know where we were going. It didn't matter. I wasn't really that interested in another fruitless visit and I was much more focused on getting to my niece's party. Eventually we stopped near the corner of a dignified street – Palmerston Place I saw it was.

I was slipping on the compacted snow as we approached a large corner house, and complaining under my breath at John for getting me out here in this weather. He opened the large front door and now I was at his back. I followed him in and that's when it hit me – this was the building we were to get – but for us, the Thursday Group! John was clearly focused on getting a venue that could be a home for the church and would also be suitable as a venue for training courses; I was beginning to realise that this was the building Spirit had been foretelling us, the Thursday Group, about all this time and here it was. They had said I'd know it when I saw it and they were right. People talk about walking into a house and getting the 'wow factor' and this is how it was for me, but in my case it was nothing to do with how the building looked - in fact it looked dreadful inside - but the energy within the building hit me like a wrecking ball whenever I stepped over the threshold and at that very moment I was 110% convinced that this was the building for us. This was meant to be and this is where we were meant to be.

My mind was racing. I started replaying in my head all of Gill's 'messages' to me that the others had added to in the Group meetings; yes, this was the West End, yes, this was a corner site and I remembered Mairi saying this is like a scene from 'Gone with the Wind'. Well even although we were still standing in the vestibule I could see a stair that Rhett Butler would have been proud of.

My mood had gone from being disgruntled at being dragged out in bad weather on a wild goose chase to being buoyed up and excited by the energy and by the fact that we'd finally found our place. I had to keep a smile from playing on my face. After all John knew nothing of my Group. And why should he? The two things (the Spiritualist church and our wee Group) had nothing to do with each other – until now. We had to buy this building.

The dirty terrazzo-tiled vestibule had two glass doors propped open by fire extinguishers. We walked through into the main stairwell and what a stair it was. It had a domed ceiling high above lighting the magnificent sweep. It was all rather the worse for wear but you could see it had been a grand building in its day. As we glanced round the open doors of the three ground floor rooms each one was worse than the last. There were damp patches on the walls, missing floor boards, electrical cabling dangling in mid-air and a spaghetti junction of electrical cabling on the floor intermingled with discarded paint pots and other rubbish.

'Right, let's go' said John, as he moved back towards the front door. I had to act quickly – he was leaving.

'This is it John this is the building for us.'

I can still see his face as he said to me in total disbelief:

'*This?*' You want to buy *this?*'

'Yes I do. This is it John. This is the building'.

'But look at the state of it Ann. Think how much it would cost to refurbish it? It'd cost a fortune.'

'It's not that bad John. I know it looks bad but most of this is superficial. If the structure of the building is okay most of this can be put right'. I was working hard to put a positive spin on something that I could see from his face filled him with horror. 'Let's go up the stairs and at least look at the rest of it'. I was hoping that the condition of the building might improve as we went higher – it didn't.

As we climbed the stone stairs to the first floor we had to dodge the ice on the steps where leaking water had frozen; had it not been so cold outside I think there would have been running water on the stairs as well as running down some of the walls. As we got to the first floor, as if to give me further confirmation, there was the red carpet, just as Spirit had foretold – *'they're rolling out the red carpet for you'*. It was old and nasty but it was there. I had never been so sure of something in my life.

On the first floor was the expected drawing room – a beautiful room with a deep cornice and an ante-room off of it. Most of the cornices were broken and as I looked at this sad destruction of what had been a beautiful building, I wondered why that should be – some of the damage looked deliberate. Then I worked it out. The previous owners must have partitioned these large rooms off to form smaller bedrooms and they had broken the cornices where the stud partition walls met the ceiling. These partitions had seemingly been broken down and most of the debris was lying strewn across the floor together with the electrical cabling for the sockets that had once been set into the partitions. This explained the cabling that was dangling from the ceiling with light switches attached to them dangling in mid-air.

'I've never bought anything like this before' said John. I could see the worry in John's face as he was torn between his eagerness to buy somewhere and the sight before him coupled with my enthusiasm for this wreck of a building. 'I've always bought 'turn-key properties.' I've never bought anything that you need to do up'. He sounded genuinely worried.

As we continued climbing the stairs to the next level and the condition of the property got steadily worse I continued reassuring him by explaining what needed to be done in each room. Some floorboards needing replacing and there would have to be some re-wiring, some plumbing, a lot of redecoration and refurbishment of walls and ceilings and lots of carpeting. 'But if the structure is okay John this could be done bit by bit – we could get the downstairs rooms done first. That's enough to be going on with and we can make our way up the stairs and do the other rooms as we have the money. It's not that bad', I lied.

'Well could you do it?' I wasn't ready for that one

'What – could I do it. How could I do it?'

'Well if you say it's not that bad. You do property refurbishment - could you do it?'

'I could do it but I'd lose my business. What would I say to all my clients – *'sorry I'm off refurbishing a six-storey town house for the next six months; I'll be back after that?'* – I wouldn't have any clients to go back to they would all have gone elsewhere by then. But I could manage the project and bring in tradesmen to do it. I know what's required so I'd be happy to do that'. I had hoped this was a compromise which would give him some comfort. I needed him to agree that we should buy it.

'Okay' he said reluctantly 'well let's see if it's structurally sound as you say – that's a starting point. We'll get it surveyed'.

Yeah, I thought. We had a way forward. I was delighted. I just knew everything was going to be all right. Especially when I spotted the plaque on the wall on my way out that told that this building had previously been a school – again, just as Spirit had told us. I couldn't wait to tell my Group on the Thursday. I was so excited I almost skipped out of the building even with the ice on the ground. I couldn't believe that after all this time I had found the building that Arthur and the Spirit Team had been telling us of. I got back into the car with John and he handed me the big bunch of keys that he had used to open the front door of the building and asked 'could you hand these back to the Agent for me. I said I'd get them back for tomorrow morning'.

'Yes no problem I can do that' but what I actually did was telephone the Agent the following morning and ask if I could keep the keys for a few more days. I told them that I wanted to bring in a couple of tradesmen to look at the building and help us determine how much work was required as this would help us make a decision as to whether we wanted to buy it or not. And that was true - I did want to do that in case I had bitten off more than I could chew, but I also just wanted to be back in the building on my own.

'Keep the keys for the week' the agent said 'bring them back next Monday'. Nothing was moving on the property market and certainly not on the commercial market so it wasn't as if he had a whole list of viewers lined up. It was in his interests to let me keep the keys.

I went back the following day and wandered round this huge building on my own. I was being careful not to fall through the floorboards or fall on the icy stone stairs as after all no one knew I was there. The sun was streaming through the large windows on the southern elevation yet the building was like walking into a deep freeze. I didn't care, I knew we had found our building.

On the Thursday I went to our Group meeting after again having visited the building that morning. I decided to say nothing act normally and wait and see if anyone got anything. I had asked Spirit to confirm to the Group that this was the right building. I had no doubt whatsoever but I didn't want the Group just to take my word for it. I hoped they would get some confirmation.

We sat in silence as usual and afterwards Gill said 'I'm seeing a set of keys. I think it's something to do with the building that we've to find where the Group can sit. I'm also seeing The Eye of Horus[45]!'

I remembered that I had the keys in my coat pocket. My coat was now on the back of my chair. This was good – it looked like I was getting some confirmation just as I had asked. But the Eye of Horus meant nothing to me.

Suddenly Gill shouts out 'Get the Ouija Board out. I feel something has happened'. I remained silent. The letters were set out round the table and the upturned glass put in place. Gill launches the first question:

'When are we going to find the place where we are to sit?'

The response: *'Found it'*.

The Group were aghast. 'Who's found it?' 'Where is it?' 'How do *we* find it?' They were firing questions out thick and fast around the circle.

'We've got to ask one question at a time' says Gill, 'Who's found it?' *'Ann'*.

My cover was blown. As they all looked at me waiting in anticipation for me to say something, I couldn't keep them in suspense any longer, I asked Spirit, 'Is it the building I visited today?' *'Yes'*.

Leading question - I needed more confirmation than that. Gill realising I wasn't about to divulge the information as easy as that. I think she understood I wanted Spirit to tell them.

Gill: 'Were the keys I saw in my meditation significant?' *'Yes'*.

'I've got the keys in my pocket' I said.

Gill: 'Is the Eye of Horus significant?' *'Yes'* it stated.

They looked at me again awaiting an answer. 'I don't know what the significance of that is – it doesn't fit'. I expected them to be disappointed by my response but undaunted Gill continued.

Gill: 'How is The Eye of Horus significant?' The glass spelt *'Keys'*

They looked at me again and I shook my head, 'I'm sorry this doesn't make sense to me'.

'Maybe it's a key? Like a clue to something? Like symbology', Mairi said but that didn't feel right to me. An Egyptian symbol – in Edinburgh – it didn't fit.

Gordon asked me 'Can you get the keys from your coat pocket?'

'Yes'. As I lifted out this big bunch of keys from my coat pocket there must have been around ten different keys on this bunch. Each key had the agent's labels tied on with string and there dangling among all the labels was a tiny little key-ring with a chain. At the end of the chain was a tiny symbol – The Eye of Horus. We had found our building – confirmed!

26 THE SIR ARTHUR CONAN DOYLE CENTRE

The building was eventually purchased in July 2011. I gave up my job (*again* – I was getting used to this) initially to manage the refurbishment programme together with my husband Iain and then to become Chair of the Charity which runs the building.

We were on a deadline to get the building refurbished and ready for an opening service of dedication which was to be conducted by the President of the SNU in October 2011. And as if to give me the final confirmation of what Arthur and our Spirit team had been working towards over the last five years, John the Church President said to me 'What do you think about giving the building a name?'

'I hadn't thought anything about it, John. *Should* the building have a name?'

'Oh yes a grand building like this deserves a name'.

'Okay' I said intrigued 'Did you have something in mind?'

'Now don't laugh, don't laugh' he said.

'Okay – tell me'.

'Well what do you think of ....'The Sir Arthur Conan Doyle Centre?'

I couldn't believe it. If ever I had any doubts they were removed in an instant by John's suggestion. I smiled as I thought that here was my guide, my inspiration, my master, Arthur Conan Doyle whom I had rejected time and time again until I had eventually accepted that it was he who was communicating, and now he had influenced someone else to confirm his presence and perhaps also to ensure he got his due reward in having the building he had found for us named in his memory. As the smile of that recognition played over my face John said 'Oh you're laughing at me. You don't like it'.

'John, I love it' I said.

The Sir Arthur Conan Doyle Centre was opened and dedicated on 23rd October 2011 – and then the fun really did begin!

ADDENDUM

Prior to going to print, as a courtesy, I sent excerpts of this book to those whose name appears in these chapters. (For those few whom I have been unable to contact, I have changed their names to pseudonyms.)

As part of this process, on 8th July 2019 I sent the last two chapters of this book to John Blackwood, as his name appears in both. This was the first time I had revealed to him the fact that Arthur Conan Doyle had been communicating with me and directing operations - and in particular directing me towards the building - which would become The Sir Arthur Conan Doyle Centre.

He was amazed that all this had been going on and he didn't know anything about it - I hadn't told him. But, he suggested that I include this addendum as he wanted to add his testimony. Here it is:

> "When I awoke that morning - the day I spoke to you about naming the building - the information had come to me in a dream the night before. I don't know where it came from but I knew with absolute certainty that the building *had* to be named 'The Sir Arthur Conan Doyle Centre', as well as that this information came with an urgency that I *had* to tell you (Ann) about it - as if somehow you'd know what it meant, or know why I had received it. Now that you have told me your story - it all fits into place and makes absolute sense."

John Blackwood, Past President, Edinburgh Assoc. of Spiritualists,
Past Chairman Spiritualists National Union Trust.

AFTERWORD

So what are we to make of this incredible journey taken by Arthur and me? Well some people will put all this down to coincidence or worse still delusion. Firstly, I now believe that coincidence is used as a tool by Spirit to make us sit up and take notice – there is more to this life than we are aware of. Secondly, the reason I have referred to my position in the corporate world was not to boast about these achievements but to demonstrate that I am not the sort of person who lives in an airy-fairy world of fantasy. I was a high-functioning senior manager when these premonitions took place. So the question remains – why choose me?

Well as Spirit told the Thursday Group, they wanted to choose members for the group whom people would relate to. They were going for the middle ground. My Group consisted of a Librarian, an ex-Policeman (now working in journalism), a Social Worker, a Psychiatric Nurse a Translator and me. Why me? Well I think they needed a workaholic – someone who had the determination to achieve their goals. And they had to do something very dramatic to get my attention and divert me from my career path in finance.

As you'll have read in the Foreword, these spontaneous paranormal experiences are surprisingly common, says Professor Chris Roe and it is normal for those affected to look for explanations. Is it just coincidence then that this led me to another Professor, Archie Roy whom I learnt so much from and set me on the path of Psychical Research that gave me the background knowledge to the paranormal, that I would later need in my journey?

Also from the front sheets of this book you'll find a quote from yet another Professor, Lance Butler, who graciously served as my Editor. He says, 'Many people have claimed to be in communication with Sir Arthur Conan Doyle since his death ….. there are none whose communications have resulted in the establishment of a large Centre in his name (in Edinburgh).'

This goal of establishing a Spiritual Centre was theirs (Spirit's) not mine. And to reach this goal was no mean feat – on their part. As I look back at it now I marvel at the pre-planning that went into this. Having chosen the people they wanted to make up the Group, Spirit then tested their resolve by devising challenges for each individual that were particularly contrary to their own beliefs and desires. For reasons of brevity and confidentiality to the others involved I have not illustrated all of these tests here but in my own case this involved use of the Ouija Board; the wearing of bracelets to signify our unity; and the need to find Blue Goldstone and a Caduceus.

If we look at the Ouija Board, again, I had been pre-prepared for this. Having been foisted into the world of Psychical Investigation, I had already come across the results of using the Ouija Board having been involved in numerous investigations as a member of the SSPR and also subsequently as a fellow investigator with Archie Lawrie, whom I've referred to earlier in this book.

In safe, experienced hands this method of communication can produce some remarkable results as we have seen but it must be controlled and for the uninitiated this does seem to be a forum that can open a path into our world for those whom I've described in Chapter Nine as 'lower level entities'.

This is not the forum to go into a long explanation of previous investigations but suffice to say that just as there is evolution in the physical world, there are entities in the paranormal world that are of a lower evolutionary level, often cannot be communicated with – as would be the case with Spirit – but have an energy and force nonetheless. *(For further reading on Psychical Investigations Archie Lawrie has a series of books entitled, A Psychic Investigators Casebook; referred to in Chapter 23. These can be purchased from Arthur Conan Doyle Centre.)* Thus I was already very wary of the Ouija Board when it was first mentioned in the Thursday Group, but I was prepared for what I might face – having encountered this before. So its introduction in this forum I believe was twofold, firstly to test my trust in Spirit to move beyond my fear and do what I had been instructed to do, but also to enhance my learning still further – you will notice in each intervention, it is me who shuts down communications via the Ouija Board when I realise it has been infiltrated. This, together with the episode where an entity claims to be my Granny, were designed to pique my awareness and acknowledgement that when dealing with the paranormal, one must exercise discernment and circumspect. Ultimately I learnt to trust my own judgement and that came from my own senses – when you can *feel* Spirit, there can be no substitute.

As for those bracelets, I thought that the idea of having bracelets to show that we were all members of the same gang, was particularly naff *(you'll notice that my Editor has politely edited out this word and replaced it with 'trivial' in Chapter Nine, however 'naff' sums up my feelings more accurately – if Princess Anne can use the term, so can I)*. The Collins Dictionary gives a definition of naff as *something which is unfashionable or unsophisticated and gives an example: naff = 'his and hers' matching outfits*. This example is a very accurate description of how I felt about the instruction to get matching bracelets – no matter what they were made of. But I accepted the task nonetheless. And, this task became more problematic as the direction from Spirit stated that the bracelets be made of the elusive Blue Goldstone. Had I been less conscientious in following the direction from Spirit, then I could have opted for any of the many Power Bracelets that the shops were full of, thereby making it easier for myself. As it was I ended up having to make the bracelets myself with loose stones and elastic.

Having done this, it is almost as if Spirit gives a reward for following their direction. Had I gone for the easy option and just bought any bracelet (or even ones that looked similar), then I would not have found out about the background and qualities of the stone (and the Caduceus) both of which were so relevant to our purpose.(The stone having been made from alchemy by Italian Monks using amongst other things, copper.) All of this information had already been received in the Group via mental mediumship but finding the stone meant the information was confirmed

And the Caduceus representing the messenger of the gods; guide of the dead and its use in astrology, alchemy and astronomy, not only provides further confirmation but demonstrates the intelligence of the Spirit World, or at least of those communicating with us.

I believe these tests and challenges from Spirit were necessary because they needed someone who would follow their lead with tenacity, overcome their own fear and therefore demonstrate their loyalty, commitment and willingness to act without question on the information received.

Equally I think Spirit recognised that in turn that person(me) would also require the loyalty and commitment of a group of willing individuals – the Thursday Group. And hence, each one of them also underwent their own challenges from Spirit.

One of the principles of Spiritualism is that we each have personal responsibility, indeed it was one of the things that attracted me most to Spiritualism, the fact that we must be responsible for our own actions.

Spiritualism will follow this up by saying that we all have freewill. And whilst I'm still a firm believer that we must all be responsible for our actions, I'm not so sure of the freewill aspect. What I've found is that when I listen to Spirit and follow their lead, things go well but when I exercise my freewill, or even just ignore my 'gut instinct' and do my own thing, then invariably I find I've made the wrong decision or sometimes I just go full circle and end up where I should have gone in the first place – I've just taken the long way round!

So no, I don't think we have freewill. I believe we're all here for a purpose – some are aware of that purpose and others are yet to find it. For me, I believe my purpose is one of communication. It is my job to work for Spirit and get their message across to the wider public. There is another world out there and it is an intelligent world where all is possible if you will just listen.

There are many atrocities going on in this world; there are wars in the name of religion, there are murders, rape and a decimation of the plant on which we live – to say nothing of the extremes in the distribution of wealth.

If people realised that we are all connected, that we are all part of the whole, then they would recognise that these acts are punishing themselves.

The Arthur Conan Doyle Centre is a spiritual centre for the benefit of the mind, body and spirit. It now enjoys an international reputation as a centre of excellence where those with an enquiring mind can come and receive quality, professional, training from some of the best proponents in the industry. We offer yoga, tai chi, pilates, spiritual development classes and of course creative writing classes – The Sir Arthur Conan Doyle Centre must offer creative writing - and equally following in Arthur's footsteps, we have a Spiritualist Church in the building. We extend a welcome to people of all religions and of none. In order to be as open and accessible to all, we aim to be a resource for the whole community and to attract as wide a range of the public as possible. To assist this aim, we are also home to the arts. We have artists who have studios in the building and we offer art exhibitions as well as music and musical evenings and events.

It is recognized that religion generally is in decline and we acknowledge that people can be put off from entering a Spiritualist Church (because of misconceptions of what happens inside) and so by offering more mainstream activities, we hope to normalise spiritual development and encourage people to explore their own spirituality and consciousness generally.

Another must for me in setting up The Centre was the need to have a Psychic Investigation Unit and this has been in situ since day one. It provides an active forum to conduct psychical investigations and to continue our research in this field. We also have an active lecture programme where we hear from the academics, scientists and university professors and lecturers who give talks each month on their specialist subjects.

All of this means that The Sir Arthur Conan Doyle Centre stands as testimony and a legacy to the great man himself but also provides a place for those like me who have encountered a spontaneous paranormal experience and need somewhere to go for help and understanding. And, as Professor Chris Roe says, these experiences are more common than we realise.

Finally, this grand building also helps portray its message to the wider world. To date, we have been host to some of the top Mediums internationally, as well as some film stars and TV personalities; we feature regularly in mainstream press; we have international students visiting, some from Universities in the US together with their Professors; and we have featured on BBC1 as well as Japanese TV. Suffice to say, Arthur's plan is working and I understand that this book also forms part of that plan. (You can help by passing the word to others to read it too – pass it on).

In writing this book I have come to realise that it is the first book of a trilogy and it documents the timeline up until the purchase of the building that was to become The Sir Arthur Conan Doyle Centre. The second book will detail what happened when The Centre opened and we took up residence.

And, if you think the content of this book is incredible, then there is much more to come after we moved into the building - Arthur and me - the building that he had been directing us towards for the previous five years.

Needless to say, he instructed me to tell you about it. I hope you enjoy it.

Ann Treherne,
Chair, The Sir Arthur Conan Doyle Centre

PHOTOS

The impressive Sir Arthur Conan Doyle Centre. And just as Arthur had foretold, a townhouse on a corner site in Edinburgh's West End.

Below: the entrance doorway to the building with the image of Arthur proudly featured. This image of the older Arthur (like the cover photo) is representative of how he appeared to me during the Group sittings.

ARTHUR AND ME

Above: an example of the condition of the building when it was purchased.

Below: an example of how it looks today. Here is our magnificent staircase, again, just as Arthur had said, Rhet Butler would be proud of it!

The Thursday Group pose with the table at The Theosophical Society. From left to right: Mayumi, Gordon, Mairi, me (Ann) and Gill. (Jim taking the photo.) Below: the rickety old table that gave us so much.

The Thursday Group again. From left to right: Mairi, Mayumi, Gordon, Gill (back to camera) and Jim (I'm taking the photo). Below: the brass-topped table, used to create the 'gong' sound which no-one heard!

The Thursday Group today. At a reunion with Mayumi in October, 2019.

From Left to right: Tricia, George, Jim, Gill, me (Ann) and Mayumi. (George joined the Group in 2013 and will feature in the next book).

TESTIMONIALS

'This book is a remarkable psycho-spiritual odyssey describing some striking physical phenomena involving a table moving around the room of its own accord and even levitating into the air. More evidential still of the active role of Spirit in our lives are the instances of the author's premonitions and clairvoyance, including the Dunblane massacre.

The reader accompanies Ann on her transformation from corporate executive to spiritual adventurer in the course of which she and her group are guided by none other than Sir Arthur Conan Doyle, himself a prominent spiritualist during his lifetime and with extensive connections to Edinburgh, where her centre now operates - itself the direct outcome of the whole Intriguing process described.'

David Lorimer
Programme Director Scientific and Medical Network

'I've known Ann for over 20 years, as a member of the Scottish Society for Psychical Research and as a fellow investigator, and I can vouch for her honesty and integrity. This book shows how Ann's courage in following mediumistic communications led to the foundation of the Sir Arthur Conan Doyle Centre - a beautiful building with its own remarkable phenomena.

I was personally involved in some of the experiences that Ann recounts and, as unbelievable as they are, they really happened. A book for the open-minded, written by a trusted experiencer.'

Nick Kyle
Past President, Scottish Society for Psychical Research

'This is a remarkable book about a remarkable man. I have a particular interest in it for two reasons:

Firstly, I have myself experienced what I believe to be psychic communications from Conan Doyle over a period of many years. These are described in detail in my own book, and suggest that the creator of Sherlock Holmes is still ready and willing to continue his mission of spreading the word about the reality of life after death. His methods of doing so seem as various and ingenious as his plots!

Secondly, I was invited by Ann to speak at the Arthur Conan Doyle Centre a few years ago, and while staying the night at the Centre I had an experience which I was quite unable to account for other than as a psychical phenomenon. This was totally unexpected as I knew nothing at the time about the results obtained by Ann's circle.

Anyone interested in exploring further the questions to which Conan Doyle devoted the latter part of his amazing life should read this intriguing and well-written book.'

Roger Straughan, Ph.D,
Author, 'A Study in Survival: Conan Doyle Solves the Final Problem' (O Books). Reader in Education at the University of Reading (retired).

I arrived in the UK in 1996, having been previously part of the Theosophical Society in Krotona, Ojai, California – the Head Quarters of the T.S.

When I first joined the T.S. in Edinburgh at 28 Great King Street, no-one used the room on the top floor, which is referred to in this book. I am aware however that McGregor Mathers, founder of The Hermetic Order of the Golden Dawn met there many years beforehand and Aleister Crowley must have been there too at that time as he was Mather's prodigy.

While I was in that room myself, I experienced some kind of energy of the negative sort affecting a particular area of the room. There was also a strange sensation from the floor where the energy seemed to manifest from.

There has been various attempts over the years, by a Bahai Master, Lama Rinpoche from Samye Ling Centre and various other spiritual masters, to close down these negative influences, therefore I am not surprised to hear that when a group such as Ann's sat to do spiritual work in that room, that they would encounter Aleister Crowley and some of the same energies I had experienced in that room myself.

Margot D Elliott
President, The Theosophical Society, Edinburgh

AND FROM THE THURSDAY GROUP

'My name is Mayumi Endo. I first met Ann when she was CEO of a subsidiary of National Australia Group and I had left my own career in banking having previously worked in The City of London and Tokyo, but after my move to Scotland was now working as an Interpreter/Translator for a subsidiary of Ricoh in Stirling. We sat in a development class together in 2002 and later Ann set-up a Home Circle to further her development and I was part of that too. When subsequent Circles didn't work out and Ann was about to give up she received communication from Spirit that she should set up her own private group and I encouraged her to do so. Later when she had invited all the group members to attend, I received communication from Spirit that this was going to be a Physical Group. When I shared this information with Ann, she too had received the same information. We decide to keep this information to ourselves and just wait to see what transpired in the Group and as you've read in this book, what transpired was utterly amazing.

When our Group started and Ann was asked by Spirit to record our meetings, I was the one who bought the tape-recorder and microphone and Ann would transcribe the recordings and send these out to each member of the Group immediately after each meeting. Therefore, I can testify to the accuracy of these records and this book is based on those records.

I left the Group in October 2007 when my husband and I emigrated to Canada but I continued to be in contact with Ann and the Group and indeed I have only recently (Oct 2019) returned to Scotland for a visit and for the first time, was able to enter the magnificent Sir Arthur Conan Doyle Centre. This is most certainly a powerful building and I was very aware of the energies present during my visit - but perhaps Ann may write about this in her next book!'

Mayumi Endo
Thursday Group Member

'My name is Mairi Anderson. I was a member of the Thursday Group from its inception, when Ann invited me to join - in late 2005 - although we had our first meeting as a Group in 2006. During this time I worked as a Librarian, at one of Edinburgh's Universities, I am now retired. We met every week and very early on in our proceedings Ann began recording our sessions. These taped recordings would then be transcibed and the typed transcripts circulated to all group members for approval. This book is based on those transcripts and therefore all that you read here, actually took place and was witnessed by myself and all those present.

I realise that some of what was recorded will be difficult for many to accept as much of what took place does not conform to what we understand of the laws of physics, but I can tell you that it did and I am happy to give testimony to this.'

Mairi Anderson
Thursday Group Member

'My name is Gill Muir, I started my career in the police as a serving officer. I have always been taught to find the evidence and that if it doesn't feel right it probably isn't, so I don't give my testimony lightly. Prior to meeting Ann I was working as an Administrative Assistant with a national publication and also a part-time Tutor of Evening Classes for mediumistic development. Mayumi was already a member of my Evening Class and asked if Ann could join the group, which she did. Ironically, Ann also helped me find a place to 'sit for Spirit' by inviting me to later join her group. The Thursday Group had just been sitting together for a few months then (in 2006) and I continue to be a member to the present day.

You will have read in this book about apports, tables levitating and physical manifestations, not least of Aleister Crowley. I witnessed them and have no hesitation in testifying to this.

Excitingly, much more has transpired since, so I hope Ann's next book will cover some of the 'fun' of The Sir Arthur Conan Doyle Centre.'

Gill Muir
Thursday Group Member

'My name is Tricia Gourlay, I'm a retired Statutory Social Worker. I joined the group after it had moved its meetings to the Church in Morrison Street, so I didn't witness some of the fantastic events that took place when it met in the Theosophical Society building. However, I have been fortunate enough to witness some amazing things in this group subsequently. Also, I was present when some of the information started to come through from our Spirit Team to direct us towards a building and the fact that this was made manifest was evidence enough for me of the intelligence of those in the Spirit World. It was fascinating to be able to witness all the 'clues' that had been 'down-loaded' from Spirit over the years to tell us of this building, that would later be so evident in The Sir Arthur Conan Doyle Centre.

I am still a member of the group today and I can vouch for the integrity of all those involved and of Ann herself. Her book gives just a taster of what was yet to come – let's hope we can persuade her to write her next book!'

Tricia Gourlay
Thursday Group Member

'My name is Jim Cleary and I am a retired Psychiatric Nurse. I first met Ann at a Weekend Workshop when we were paired up together for one of the exercises. I next heard from her several years later when completely out of the blue I received a telephone call from her. I remember her saying, 'You may not remember me...' or words to that effect, but I remembered her very well, she is an impressive lady and certainly not someone you would easily forget. I say this not only because of the many achievements in her life but also because of her honesty, integrity and her spirituality which was evident from our first meeting all those years ago. When she invited me to join her group I had no hesitation, I was delighted to be part of her group. She referred to me as the 'Elder Statesman', and invited me to be the facilitator of the Thursday Group - a role I accepted with honour.

I have been a member of the group since its inception until the present day. I have witnessed first-hand some of the strange and fascinating phenomena that our Spirit Team have allowed us to experience and have been impressed with Ann's diligence in dutifully recording everything in great detail - no mean feat in itself. Some of our experiences have been quite literally unbelievable - but believe it, for I was there and feel privileged to have had these experiences.

I witnessed the emergence of the elusive building, which became The Sir Arthur Conan Doyle Centre, and I am proud to say I am a Trustee and Director of that charity. This impressive building in Edinburgh's West End not only stands as a tribute to Arthur Conan Doyle, but also to Ann Treherne, who was brave enough to act on his lead. The rest of us simply followed.'

Jim Cleary
Thursday Group Member

'We met [Ann and I] at the Open Circle at Morrison Street Church. Irene Coull ran the Group. You and I were working in pairs in the Group when we were approached and invited to the Closed Circle. (Thought to be around 2002).

I had a variety of jobs throughout my working career. I was a Draftsman to trade and that took me away from my childhood love of healing... I then went into sales as a representative before going back to the drawing board and then on to working as a Social Services Manager before going full circle to become a Complimentary Therapist.

We [Ann and I] followed the same calling - we both left mainstream employment to answer Spirit.'

Gordon Soutar
Thursday Group Member (still)

My very good friend, Gordon, died on 24th March, 2013. This is an excerpt from a transcript he dictated to me in St Columba's Hospice, Kirklands House, Gogar, Edinburgh shortly before he died.

Ann Treherne
Author.

WITH THANKS

To my husband, Iain. The Sir Arthur Conan Doyle Centre was *my* vision, *my* dream, *my* mission and you not only accepted it and trusted in me but you adopted it as your own and gave it your all - thank you. I could not have done it without you.

To Prof. Lance Butler, for editing so gracefully and tactfully; for meeting my ridiculous timescales to get this book to print and for answering the call to action - you were there when I needed you - thank you.

To Shereen Elder, Centre Manager, for 'holding the fort' and diverting work away from me to allow me to focus on the completion of this book - thank you, you are an asset to The Sir Arthur Conan Doyle Centre.

To the wider team at The Sir Arthur Conan Doyle Centre, (both paid staff and volunteers), may I acknowledge your support of The Centre and all it stands for - the whole is greater than the sum of its parts - thank you.

Last but not least, to the Thursday Group. You believed in me and followed without question. Your undying commitment and loyalty are without bounds. For the trust, the camaraderie and the commitment to sit together over all these years right up until the present day - thank you all. And to those of the team in the Spirit World - to Arthur - I have tried to follow your lead, I have tried to answer your call - I hope I have proven myself worthy.

REFERENCES

[1] Hungerford is a town in England where on 19th August 1987 Michael Robert Ryan an unemployed antique dealer went on the rampage randomly killing people in the town who were going about their everyday business. This became known as the Hungerford Massacre

[2] Ferryman – a traditional reference to the person who transport the dead to the afterlife on his boat

[3] Aberfan was a small mining town in Wales where in 1966 a colliery spoil tip slid down the hillside as slurry following heavy rains engulfing part of the town and the village school, killing 116 children and 28 adults. This became known as the Aberfan disaster.

[4] DVLA – Driver and Vehicle Licensing Authority. The government body that holds records of all vehicles licensed to drive on our roads

[5] Mental Mediumship: This is the Mediumship most commonly seen on television and other public demonstrations of Mediumship. In a public demonstration it involves the Medium making contact with the Spirit World and giving short messages to members of the public to provide evidence of the Spirit Person communicating. This is the same process as a Private Sitting except the information has to be short and not too personal because of the public nature of the event. This is a mind to mind process like telepathy except that one of those minds is discarnate

[6] Scole Group and those experiments are featured in a book by Robin Foy in whose home the phenomena took place. 'Witnessing the Impossible' ISBN No: 978-0-9560651-0-0 published 2008.

[7] *The Scole Experiment: Scientific Evidence for Life After Death*, by Grant and Jane Solomon. Jane works together with Alan and Diane Bennett – members of the original Scole Group.

[8] Arthur Findlay College is a world-renowned centre owned by the Spiritualists National Union for psychic and spiritual development.

[9] Ectoplasm is a substance said to be formed of bodily fluids which is drawn from the body by Spirit to utilise as a material that can be manipulated to create the form of Spirit Communicators. It is often seen oozing from the mouth, nose and sometime ears in pictures from the Victoria era.

[10] Platform Mediumship is as described previously under 'Mental Mediumship' but is always a public demonstration, hence the Medium will be standing on some type of stage or platform.

[11] Fox Sisters: Said to be the birth of Modern Spiritualism which started by three sisters living with their parents in a log cabin in New York State heard knocks on the wall. They realised they could communicate with whoever was knocking and that they would receive an answer. This was the basis of what became the religion of Spiritualism.

[12] Swedenborg was a brilliant inventor and scientist who started seeing visions and believed he received divine intervention and felt he was a messenger of Jesus Christ. He wrote several theological works and became renowned in Christian circles.

[13] Table-tilting is where people place their fingers on a table and it starts to move without anyone exerting the pressure that would be required to move it under normal circumstances. This appears to defy the laws of physics. It is attributed to spirit energy. An alternative theory is that it is psychic or mental energy that moves the table, that is 'mind over matter'.

[14] Kinetic Energy is the energy of an object which is in motion. Like the velocity of a car, kinetic energy will continue moving the car forward even when the engine is no longer propelling it forward.

[15] Séance Room. A séance is an attempt to communicate with spirits. The word "séance" comes from the French word for "session", from the Old French seoir, "to sit". In French, the word's meaning is quite general: one may, for example, speak of "une séance de cinéma" (a movie session). Source: Wikipedia. From the Author – I am using the word 'séance' and séance room in the true sense of the word as detailed here. A more modern term is Circle.

[16] History of Spiritualism, Volume One, by Sir Arthur Conan Doyle, first published 1926. ISBN 0 85384 110 1. Volume Two ISBN 0 85384 112 8.

[17] Ouija Board is a board which displays all the letters of the alphabet together with the words 'yes' and 'no'. Traditionally participants would place their hands on a planchette (pointer), this was originally made of wood but more recently this was replaced by an upturned glass which would move across the board pointing at various letters which would spell out a communication from those in spirit. Sometimes called Spirit Board or Talking Board, this was originally a parlour game.

[18] Transcripts – Where the original transcripts are quoted throughout this book the text is indented and is in Times New Roman font. Transcripts are verbatim and responses from Spirit are in italics.

[19] Stansted refers to The Arthur Findlay College, in Stansted, England. A world-renowned centre for Spiritual and Psychic development.

[20] Mary Duffy was a well-known and excellent medium from Edinburgh. She was a tutor at Arthur Findlay College in Stansted and also in College of Parapsychology in Edinburgh. She and Gordon Higginson would have known each other and her name had come through the Ouija Board at the same time as his – on the first evening it was used.

[21] Rods – This refers to Spirit Rods which are reputed to be rods of energy built up by Spirit so that they can be used to move physical objects around a room.

[22] Mary Duffy was a local Medium from Edinburgh who was very talented and eventually became a Tutor at the world-famous Arthur Findlay College, in Stansted, England. Coincidentally she was the first medium I saw when I had that experience of a group 'sitting' with my fellow colleagues from the bank, when the chief cashier decided it would be a 'good night out'. (See Chapter 2).

[23] Oliver Lodge was a British Scientist – a physicist who held patents for radio and electromagnetism. He investigated Spiritualism and was President of The Society for Psychical Research. He attended séances and wrote to Arthur Conan Doyle telling him he had heard from his (deceased) son.

[24] Arthur Findlay was a Scottish Philanthropist, stock-broker and accountant. He founded The International Institute for Psychical Research and eventually left his home to the Spiritualist National Union, now THE most renowned Centre from spiritual development in the world – The Arthur Findlay College, Stansted.

[25] Reference to Arthur Conan Doyle being named after King Arthur – see 'Conan Doyle The Man who Created Sherlock Holmes, by Andrew Lycett, published 2007. ISBN: 978-0-7538-2428-3

[26] Crookes – refers to Sir William Crooks (1832-1919). A British scientist, physicist and chemist. Discovered thalium, invented radiometer, the spinthariscope and Crookes Tube. He announced to the newspapers that he would undertake a scientific investigation into Spiritualism. His own expectation was that this would uncover the fraud, deception, magic and necromancy. He investigated D.D. Hume (see page.......). His investigations led him to the conclusion that the phenomenon of physical mediumship was real and this 'psychic force' defied the logic of established scientific theory. His findings were published in the Quarterly Journal of Science in July 1871.

[27] Coldness or a sudden drop in temperature can be an indication of the presence of Spirit.

[28] Captain Birdseye. A reference to a character that appears in a TV advertisement for Birdseye Fish Fingers. The character is a fisherman with white hair and beard.

[29] Ectoplasm. (See page footnotes at Chapter 7)

[30] EVP. Electronic Voice Phenomenon. Used in ghost-hunting and parapsychology. It is allegedly the electronically recorded voices of spirit. This is often captured by using 'white noise' as a static background noise which allegedly can be manipulated by Spirit to make their voices heard. Some EVP is now captured on telephones, mobile phones and other electronic equipment.

[31] Green Man – a reference to the signal at a pedestrian crossing. The Green Man signals that the traffic has stopped and therefore it is safe to cross.

[32] Universal Consciousness - An ancient theory that the mind is universal and not part of the physical brain. Individuals 'download' information from the Universal Consciousness or the Universal Mind which is a central source of knowledge and information.

[33] Cushion Cover – I felt that this particular cushion cover or pillowcase would have been taken from one of the houses that had been broken into and used as a bag, probably containing their haul of jewellery and cash.

[34] Dictaphone. This was a hand-held recording device which I had previously used it for work but as the tapes for our usual tape-recorder were becoming harder to obtain we sometimes used my Dictaphone as a fallback solution.

[35] Rigor is when the body involuntarily starts shaking. It is a dangerous medical condition which often signals high fever or bacterial infection.

[36] Direct Voice is where Spirit communicates with all present in the room. The voice is heard from the ether and not via any other means of communication. In the past sometimes a Spirit Trumpet was used to amplify the sound of direct voice.

[37] Planchette is a little wooden board with casters on the bottom and a hole through which a pen or pencil is inserted. Someone then rests their hand on the board and holds the pen. The theory is that Spirit can move the planchette to produce communication in the form of written word. It was the precursor to the Ouija Board.

[38] The Bondagers by Ian MacDougall. ISBN: 1 86232 122 1 Published 2000.

[39] Rupert Sheldrake: PhD in Biochemistry from Cambridge University. A renowned Parapsychologist, Biologist and Author of several books and papers on related subjects, including *The Sense of being stared at*, (2003). Most famous for Morphic Resonance – a collective memory system.

[40] Bernard Carr: Prof of Mathematics and Astronomy, Queen Mary and Westfield College, University of London. Studied Cosmology under Stephen Hawking. Education Officer, Society for Psychical Research, London. Appeared in documentary film, 'The Trouble with Atheism',

[41] Tommy Cooper: British comic who wore a fez as part of his stage costume. A comedian/magician

[42] White Noise: The static noise that is heard by electrical equipment which is not properly attuned to the appropriate channel – like a radio that is not on the correct band-width. White noise is sometimes manipulated by Spirit entities to make their words heard.

[43] Distant Healing: The practice of Spiritual Healers making a connection with spirit in order to channel healing energy. Where the recipient is not present the energy is sent to them etherically – this is referred to as Distant Healing.

[44] Ex-Police Officer – Gill had been a Police Officer in the early part of her career before joining *The Times*, newspaper.

[45] Eye of Horus – Is an ancient Egyptian symbol said to bring peace, protection, health and rejuvenation. It is reputed to be a magic symbol.

Printed in Poland
by Amazon Fulfillment
Poland Sp. z o.o., Wrocław